SOCIAL PHILOSOPHY TODAY

International Law and Justice

Volume 23

Edited by
John R. Rowan

Social Philosophy Today is published by the Philosophy Documentation Center.

For information regarding subscriptions or back issues, please contact:

Philosophy Documentation Center
P.O. Box 7147
Charlottesville, VA 22906-7147
804-444-2419 (U.S. & Canada); 434-220-3300
Fax: 434-220-3301
E-mail: order@pdcnet.org
Web: www.pdcnet.org

ISBN 978-1-889680-51-4
ISSN 1543-4044

Recent issues of *Social Philosophy Today*:

Volume 22	Science, Technology, and Social Justice. ISBN 1-889680-49-1
Volume 21	Human Rights, Religion, and Democracy. ISBN 1-889680-43-5
Volume 20	War and Terrorism. ISBN 1-889680-40-0
Volume 19	Environmental Philosophy as Social Philosophy. ISBN 1-889680-35-4
Volume 18	Truth and Objectivity in Social Ethics. ISBN 1-889680-31-1
Volume 17	Communication, Conflict, and Reconciliation. ISBN 1-889680-30-3
Volume 16	Race, Social Identity, and Human Dignity. ISBN 1-889680-23-0

Social Philosophy Today is indexed in *Academic Search Premier*, *American Humanities Index*, *Bibliographie de la Philosophie*, *Current Abstracts*, *Index Philosophicus*, *Index to Social Sciences & Humanities Proceedings*, *International Bibliography of Periodical Literature* (*IBZ*), *International Bibliography of the Social Sciences*, *Philosopher's Index*, *Reference and Research Book News*, *Sociological Abstracts*, and *Worldwide Political Science Abstracts*. Electronic access to the full text of Social Philosophy Today is provided through POIESIS: Philosophy Online Serials.

Designed and produced by the Philosophy Documentation Center, Charlottesville, Virginia

Table of Contents

International Law and Justice

Volume 23

Table of Contents

Preface

The North American Society for Social Philosophy (NASSP) brings together philosophers, legal theorists, political scientists, and social scientists to discuss important contemporary social issues. This is accomplished through its international conferences, its contributions to the programs of other learned societies, and its publication program, including *The Journal of Social Philosophy* and the *Social Philosophy Today* series. All of the essays in this volume, number 23 of *Social Philosophy Today*, were selected by peer referees from among the best papers presented at the Twenty-third International social Philosophy Conference, held in July, 2006, at the University of Victoria in Victoria, British Columbia.

The editor would like to thank the many individuals whose efforts made this volume possible. In particular, Cindy Holder of the University of Victoria served as host of the conference, supervising the organizational aspects of all events and in general attending to an extraordinary number of details. The NASSP is extremely grateful for her service in this capacity. Appreciation is also expressed to Purdue University Calumet, which provided various resources that contributed to the completion of this volume. Additionally, the editor wishes to thank the individuals at the Philosophy Documentation Center for their hard work in publishing this and many previous volumes of *Social Philosophy Today*. Marty Klaif, Greg Swope, and Pam Swope have assisted the process in countless ways, and Director George Leaman has continued to provide guidance and helpful ideas and suggestions. George and his staff have played significant roles in helping the series to achieve its present level of quality.

John Rowan, Purdue University Calumet

Introduction

I. Global Justice and Human Rights

In the volume's opening selection, Will Kymlicka describes how international standards of minority rights have run into various problems. He cites two principal reasons for the increased attention to minority rights: a fear of the spread of ethnic violence after the collapse of Communism; and a hope for the possibility of a viable liberal-democratic form of multiculturalism. This has generated an unfortunate tension between a desire, on the one hand, to engage in ethnic politics in order to ensure that liberal democratic rights are distributed to all, and on the other hand fears about the destabilizing tendencies that can be generated by ethnic politics. A reasonable starting point is the question of how to identify and categorize the minorities who are the intended beneficiaries of minority rights.

To clarify the challenges, Kymlicka points to the distinction between generic and targeted minority rights, where the former apply to all ethnocultural minorities and the latter apply only to particular categories. He describes certain problems with the generic type, problems he suggests are inherent, claiming, "The commitment to identifying generic cultural rights limits the sorts of minority rights that can be recognized." Such problems have prompted more targeted attempts in Western Europe since the early 1990s. In Eastern Europe, however, there have been factors inhibiting the ability of national minorities there to attain territorial autonomy. One factor is the prospect of geopolitical stability, and another is the likelihood, as evidenced by recent history, that minorities acquiring autonomy are less likely to possess the value of respect for human rights. Indeed, one can observe the perverse effect of European organizations supporting minority groups which have used violence to secure territorial autonomy but opposing minority groups which have employed peaceful means of doing so. One way to protect vulnerable minorities would be going back to the generic approach and treating all ethnocultural groups as national minorities. Kymlicka, however, argues that the strategy of proposing additional targeted norms is preferable, though it may currently not be realistic in Eastern Europe.

Another strategy, employed by the United Nations, is to formulate rights that are specific to indigenous peoples, which one might note is not the same as "national minorities." The distinction is based on the UN viewing indigenous peoples as vulnerable but not (unlike the national minorities) a danger to national security.

However, this approach by the UN tends to posit a sharp distinction between the two groups which, according to Kymlicka, ought not exist in terms of allocation of international rights. The difference is morally unjustified, conceptually unstable, and politically it may be unsustainable. He concludes with some general ideas about how international minority rights might potentially be institutionalized more successfully.

Sharon Anderson-Gold discusses elements of Kymlica's arguments for cultural membership as a basis of minority rights at the international level. In the first part of her article, she discusses the history and evolving status of cultural rights. Some of the issues that have arisen concern, for example, the question of whether cultural rights are group or individual rights, the degree to which genuine group self-determination must be recognized by the groups (or the individuals therein) exercising their cultural rights, and the question of whether non-discrimination, as an implication of minority and civil rights, can allow for differential treatment of certain cultural groups based on the particular characteristics of those groups. Anderson-Gold notes that Kylmicka's liberal defense of minority rights derives from two interrelated assumptions: first, that individual freedom is tied to membership in one's cultural group; and second, that group-specific rights can promote equality between minority and majority groups.

In the second part, Anderson-Gold discusses conceptual connections among the ideas of group self-determination, democracy, and a right to cultural identity. The right to cultural identity, she claims, is a minority right, since it is likely to play a significant role in securing the resources the minority needs to sustain itself as a distinctive culture—something that would otherwise be rather difficult given that the majority culture tends to benefit disproportionately from state practices. This right to cultural identity should be understood as a form of group (cultural) self-determination, one that is within, rather than merely equivalent to, the broad right of political self-determination generally.

Alex Sager takes up the question of how liberal commitments apply to the question of immigration restriction. Kymlicka, Joseph Carens and others have occasionally argued that such restriction is justified on the basis of culture, since unchecked immigration into a nation would threaten societal culture, which residents have a right to protect. Sager contests this position. Against Kymlicka, Sager maintains that the sheer number of immigrants who would enter the United States would not itself generate the threat to U.S. societal (as opposed to general) culture alleged by Kymlicka; most immigrants would conform to the existing culture in the important ways, which is a principal motivation for immigrating in the first place. The specific worry about Hispanic (and primarily Mexican) immigration, posed by Samuel Huntington, is also misguided. Further, Sager argues that basic liberal democratic values, including toleration and free speech, not only allow groups with different views and even cultures to be admitted but require that they be admitted.

Arguments based on protection of general culture fare no better in justifying immigration restrictions than do the preceding arguments based on societal culture. Understood as "the set of beliefs, attitudes, practices, traditions, customs, behavior, ideas, values, food and artifacts of a human community," general culture is by nature dynamic and evolving, making it more difficult to defend a strict status quo justification for limiting immigration. There may exist certain objections based on the rate at which general culture is changing or on the nature of the change (since change will inevitably be better for some and worse for others). Nonetheless, as long as coercion is avoided and autonomy respected, then in accordance with liberal democratic principles, the threat to general culture cannot justify restriction. Furthermore, there exists the lingering problem that general culture, being general, is an extremely vague concept—the implication being that there is great difficulty in discerning the precise respects in which a potential immigrant possesses or lacks the elements of the culture.

Questions of global human rights are the subject of P. J. Lomelino's essay, in which she takes on the Universal Declaration model of human rights. That model is (inappropriately, according to Lomelino) aimed only at individual rights. She describes so-called first generation rights (aimed at preserving liberty) and second generation rights (concerned with social and economic goods, i.e., the provision of minimal resources). Her claim is that there is a third generation of rights, namely collective rights, which ought to be recognized. Understood principally as rights of minorities to protection against tyranny of the majority, collective rights are designed to protect what Jeremy Waldron calls "non-individualized goods."

Although various justifications for collective rights have been put forth by commentators, Lomelino uses the concept of relational beings as justification. In explaining relational beings, she relies on the Confucian idea that a principal component of human value is based on relationships with others, beginning with one's family and through time expanding outward without limit. Because rights are concerned with claims of value, and because value is often conceived and assessed in terms of one's relation to the larger whole, collective rights are necessary as a generation of human rights held by relational beings.

Before concluding with thoughts about how collective rights might be implemented, Lomelino addresses potential objections to her arguments. Included are the claims by Michael Ignatieff that all collective rights (1) ultimately serve to protect individual rights, and (2) would be trumped by individual rights in cases of conflict, which together are alleged to generate the conclusion that there is no need to incorporate collective rights into the Universal Declaration model. She also takes on Jack Donnelly's objection that the individual rights inherent in the U.D. model already protect collective group interests, making the third generation unnecessary, as well as the allegation that collective rights are not "human" rights properly understood.

Human rights are also a central issue in Edmund Byrne's scathing attack on the ethics of the international arms industry. Using standards of Corporate Social Responsibility (CSR), Byrne argues that the industry fails on several counts. First, there is obvious harm caused to the environment. Second, the industry fails in terms of social equity, a fact which is most obvious, according to Byrne, when the context of small arms is examined. He cites a study indicating that small arms account for an overwhelmingly large majority of human rights violations. Third, the industry (perhaps surprisingly) fails a profitability requirement, since it does not achieve "the desired result of risking capital to develop and market goods and/or services."

Byrne's most thorough discussion is reserved for his claim that the international arms industry cannot receive a pass on the basis of use of political power. Despite the three failings noted above, some have suggested that industry practices are justified on the basis of their importance to national defense along with their inextricable connection to the sovereign responsibilities of government. Byrne rejects this. Using the United States as a principal example, he goes through an historical account of defense spending from the beginning of the cold war through to the present days of enhanced worries over terrorism. During that time, there have been an artificially manufactured concerns (aided by power lobbies and corporate financial influence) over national security which have served to effectively keep the arms industry booming. The result has been the emergence of key arms manufacturers (such as Boeing) as entities whose power and influence rival that of many nation-states.

II. Cosmopolitanism and Liberalism

Jordy Rocheleau opens this section of the volume by addressing a conflict between these views of cosmopolitanism and liberalism that is alleged to obtain on the international level. There exists a traditional liberal view that legitimacy of international law requires the consent of the states that are subject to said law. This view is challenged by Allen Buchanan, who adopts a more cosmopolitan standpoint according to which legitimacy is a function not of consent but of substantive moral principles, namely human rights and their protection. His view, therefore, is essentially the claim that legitimacy of international law corresponds to the degree to which it protects human rights, leaving consent as neither necessary nor sufficient for such legitimacy.

Rocheleau agrees with this but stops short of concurring with Buchanan's additional point, which is that the consent requirement does not, instrumentally, promote the human rights protections which are the substantive standard for legitimacy. One side effect of denying illiberal states the opportunity to participate in norm formation is the risk of increased assaults on the rights of the least well off. In particular, Rocheleau worries that waiving the requirement of state consent would invite the most powerful nations in the world to engage in imperialism and impose their will on weaker nations in the name of the cosmopolitan good. In citing prudential concerns regarding the protection of populations even under authoritarian regimes, he rejects arguments for the claim that state consent will lead to increased incidence of human rights violations. The result, perhaps counterintuitively, is that the consent requirement even for illiberal states will serve to reduce conflict and foster stability. An environment of stability, in turn, serves to protect human rights. Institutionalizing a cosmopolitan rights system would undermine stability in important ways, including propensity for armed conflict, disincentives for obedience to the international standards, risks to international diplomacy and trade, and decreased progress in addressing contemporary challenges to human well-being.

Rocheleau concludes his defense of a combined liberal-cosmopolitan standard by addressing three objections, including the possible implication of his view that liberal nations may (somewhat paradoxically) be required to remain passive during extreme human rights violations perpetrated by illiberal states.

Cosmopolitanism is applied to the particular context of global public health in the second paper in this section, authored by Jan Sutherland and Elaine Gibson. The original International Health Regulations (IHR) of the World Health Organization had a distinctively non-interventionist tone, calling only for minimally required reporting of disease by nations; the emphasis was on voluntarism and consent of nations. By contrast, the IHR revisions, in effect since 2007, deemphasize state sovereignty in favor of preventing the international spread of disease.

While this is a more cosmopolitan approach, Sutherland and Gibson argue for a richer, more substantive brand of cosmopolitanism to be applied to global public health. For comparative purposes, they describe Anthony Appiah's version as too weak, as it allows significant partiality and fails to require assistance beyond one's "fair share." This is problematic, they claim, in that it fails a condition of bidirectionality; it imposes an obligation on poorer nations to inform wealthier nations of internal incidence of infectious disease without imposing substantive obligations on wealthier nations to aid those poorer nations in treatment and eradication. Any objection based on distance, they claim, fails to apply to this context, for epidemics are not confined to location but are by nature transitive, moving from place to place. What is needed, according to Sutherland and Gibson, is an elimination of the "us-them" dynamic in which these conversations are framed, for only then will a true cosmopolitanism of global public health be realized, one which recognizes the economic costs (such as trade restrictions) incurred by nations that fulfil their duties and report internal diseases.

Cosmopolitanism is paired with care ethics by Maurice Hamington, who uses Appiah as well as Jane Addams to argue that a complete cosmopolitanism cannot be founded on purely structural principles (such as rights and laws) but requires the trust and understanding that accompany interpersonal relationships. Care theory is ideal, he claims, for providing this additional component. He provides a sketch of the development of care theory during the latter part of the twentieth century, noting in particular the trend toward its application to social and political systems; this, in turn, makes care theory a promising contributor to contemporary ideas about cosmopolitanism.

Hamington discusses Addams and Appiah in turn. In focusing her efforts on populations including immigrants, elderly and the poor, Jane Addams demonstrated her commitment to what would later be called care theory. Meanwhile, her cosmopolitanism was manifest principally in her views of multiculturalism (most evident in big cities and for Addams in Chicago specifically) and of pacifism (since diversity, especially among immigrants, can help to prevent war). Meanwhile, Hamington finds in the writings of Appiah elements of care theory in the form of connection with others, specifically the meeting of particular others who would otherwise remain mere abstractions of humanity. This has, or according to Hamington at least should have, clear connections to the cosmopolitan project in terms of breaking down artificial boundaries which can frustrate support of formal structures of cosmopolitanism.

For Hamington, then, the works of both Addams and Appiah are instructive in that they warn against overcommitment to a rule-based, formulaic system of morality—a warning we would do well to heed in the quest for international cosmopolitan policies which provide substance and deeper meaning to traditional notions such as human rights.

In the subsequent entry in this chapter, Jon Mahoney discusses liberalism and its application to the issue of polygamy. The U.S. Supreme Court has determined that polygamy may not be protected on grounds of freedom of expression. While Mahoney does not necessarily disagree, he suggests there are other questions relevant to rights within liberal states that ought to be addressed. After discussing aspects of liberalism and its connection to polygamy, he proceeds to a critique of Marci Hamilton's arguments against allowing polygamy in a liberal society.

The first of these is the argument from public reason, according to which religion alone cannot be the basis for including a practice in society. In response, Mahoney argues that as long as the practice can in principle be supported by norms of public reason, then its being motivated solely by religious conviction is insufficient for disallowing it. Hamilton's second argument, referred to by Mahoney as the "argument from democracy," calls for a procedural test of legitimacy which includes the requirement of legislative enactment rather than judicial review as the origin. Combined with the further requirement that the practice serve the public good, the resultant view of democracy utilized by Hamilton is majoritarian, and this is the focus of Mahoney's criticism of the argument.

The third argument raised by Hamilton, the argument from exploitation, is found by Mahoney to be the most plausible. The idea is that the practice of polygamy is exploitative in that, minimally, it generates inequality by promoting the interests of men over those of women, and more strongly it reduces women (and children also) to the level of property. Either result is clearly inconsistent with the requirements of liberalism, and Mahoney concedes that current polygamist practices likely violate at least the minimal condition. However, traditional monogamist marriage is guilty of this as well and yet is usually defended as consistent with liberalism. The problem with polygamy is thus likely a function of external factors, according to Mahoney—factors that are culturally specific or historically contingent, for instance. As long as polygamy could potentially be practiced within the bounds of liberal constraints, we should not agree with Hamilton's call for rejecting it. Rather, the issue should remain an open one among liberals.

An issue with which liberalism is unable to adequately cope, according to Lisa Schwartzman, is women's adaptive preferences. Understood as desires which have been developed as a result of superior options being closed off, so that one adjusts her desires in order to match what she already has, adaptive preferences developed by women in a patriarchal social context present a problem for liberalism; in conforming to the existing background of gender inequality, women end up reinforcing their own oppression.

After reviewing the liberal emphasis on "choice" and the enhancements of Anita Superson, Schwartzman concludes that the liberal approach fails and that an alternative is necessary. One problem is that the liberal approach is not practical; it offers women no strategy for relinquishing adaptive preferences (the difficulty of which is an integral part of the problem), and further, it offers no alternative as a replacement once those desires are eradicated (which is also a significant challenge given the ongoing oppressive social context). A related problem is the inability of liberalism to facilitate the recognition of adaptive preferences in the first place—especially those in Western cultures, where frameworks of power and oppression are more opaque. A third problem is the liberal focus on the individual, which tends to obscure the influences of social groups and hierarchies on "individual" choice. To illustrate these points, Schwartzman considers the issue of family and career, in which the prevailing social norms often call for women to "choose" between these options. She also reviews the dubious nature of choice in the context of young women and their sexual desires.

Schwartzman concludes with some thoughts about elements that would need to be included in an alternative approach to liberalism—elements that would include emphasis on the effects of group membership on choice, and also, more radically, an overhaul of the existing social structure from which adaptive preferences are generated.

III. Terrorism and Torture

In her paper, Marilyn Friedman takes up an issue not often addressed in the literature, namely the question of female terrorists and how, if at all, gender makes a difference. Specifically, she asks whether the gender of a terrorist make a moral difference to understanding or justifying that person's acts of terrorism. In terms of effectiveness, the answer is that it does. Because women are statistically less likely to engage in terrorism, they tend to face fewer barriers and less scrutiny in their planning and execution of these acts. They also seem to receive more media coverage than their male counterparts.

Regarding the explanations for female terrorism that are commonly provided by commentators, these include situational factors (such as the grief over the loss of a loved one killed by the enemy) and individual characteristics (such as the possession of "masculine" attributes). Friedman notes that among these possible explanations is the absence of straightforward dedication to the terrorist cause, despite the fact that this is a frequently cited motivation underlying the actions of male terrorists. Reasons for downplaying this possibility seem to include a degree of commitment to an essential female nature which includes tendencies toward peace and nonviolence. Friedman suggests this consideration may be relevant but is not a complete explanation. Even terrorists, she claims, understand the presumptive wrongfulness of their killing; they just see their actions as justified in their particular circumstances. What needs to be recognized, Friedman argues, is that when women do engage in terrorism it should be taken seriously as testimony of their commitment to the cause in question—more seriously, in fact, than their male counterparts, since women (arguably) are imbued with a nature, a gender identity, that emphasizes peace and nonviolence.

The question of whether a terrorist (or anyone else) may ever be tortured is the topic of Bernard Prusak's paper, in which he focuses on the case of the ticking time bomb. If a terrorist were the only person aware of the location of a bomb set to go off in a densely populated community, would it be permissible to torture that terrorist in an effort to learn its location and diffuse it, thus saving millions of lives? Prusak's first point about this example is that it is extremely misleading in that it conveys the idea that torture can turn out to be permissible more often than is actually the case. The problem, he claims, is that it requires genuine knowledge that the terrorist is indeed aware of the bomb's location, and this condition of genuine knowledge is exceedingly difficult to meet.

However, this does not rule out the possibility that the condition, along with other requirements necessary for the permissibility of torture, could perhaps be met (unlikely though that is). The alternative of an absolute moral prohibition against torture is something Prusak finds too extreme. Again emphasizing the very limited applicability of this conclusion, however, he proceeds to caution against the extension of this (seemingly utilitarian) reasoning to the torturing of innocents in an attempt to prevent widespread harm; as torture is a cruel attack on the defenseless, it must be justified to its victims, and this is something that would be impossible when the victims have done no wrong. Other extensions on the warrant to engage in torture—including circumstances in which the terrorist knows (but is not revealing) information about hidden hostages, arms caches or future terrorist threats—cannot be justified either. Prusak claims that inherent in the potential allowance of torture in the ticking time bomb is the basis of self-defense. The allowance is based in part on the terrorist having created a situation in which someone must get hurt, the idea being that the terrorist is therefore a justified choice of the party to be hurt; the types of cases mentioned above, however, do not meet this self-defense requirement of necessary harm and thus do not allow for torture. Prusak's practical conclusion is that torture should be banned under international and U.S. law.

In a paper that parallels this discussion, Matthew Silliman and David Kenneth Johnson provide a hypothetical dialogue among three individuals, each of whom has certain views about the question of whether torture can be permissible. The character of Professor Erica Wolfe takes the position defended by Prusak in the previous article. Wolfe argues that even if torture were theoretically permissible in ticking time bomb cases, those cases are "hypothetical fantasies" which ought to have no bearing on law or policy. The problem, in line with Prusak's position, is epistemological; there is no way to ensure genuine knowledge or even a reasonable degree of knowledge about what the suspect himself knows; thus there is no way of "knowing" when the victim is telling the truth and, consequently, when to stop the torture. Meanwhile, the character of attorney Clarence Riggs argues for the moral acceptability (and in some cases even the moral duty) to engage in terrorism, such as in cases analogous to the ticking time bomb. More precisely, he claims that by making the practice legal under very clear and limited circumstances, it becomes transparent, allowing for those governmental authorities in charge to be accountable.

The third character is Aaron Langston, recently of the National Guard, whose position falls somewhere between the other two. In the dialogue, Langston raises the question of how the notion of coercion, which itself can be morally benign when dealing with interrogation in crisis situations, is ultimately related to the notion of torture, which in some ways seems qualitatively distinct from coercion yet in some ways seems to be a further extreme on the same qualitative continuum. In addition to frustration about his own view on the matter, Langston also indicates his confusion over the observation that the other two characters agree about the rarity of morally permissible cases of torture but disagree significantly about the practical recommendation stemming from this. Silliman and Johnson conclude the dialogue without providing the audience with a preferred solution.

IV. NASSP Book Award

In each volume of Social Philosophy Today, the final section is devoted to the award, sponsored by the North American Society for Social Philosophy, for the most outstanding book in social philosophy published during the previous year. The recipient of the award this year is Larry May, recognized for his book *Crimes Against Humanity: A Normative Account*. This section consists of remarks from three commentators, followed by a reply by May.

Marilyn Fischer opens the discussion by citing examples of where late twentieth-century history does not, in her view, align evenly with some of the claims in May's book. She asks May about the entities capable of holding sovereignty, citing Shell Oil and its involvement in Nigeria as a example of a potentially problematic example. She also presses May about the concept of a group in the context of the international harm principle. Cheryl Hughes also raises the issue of sovereignty as used by May, claiming that reliance on Hobbes and moral minimalism is inappropriate in the twenty-first century as a starting point for discussions of international crimes. Also problematic is the Hobbesian picture of the atomistic individual utilized by May. Other issues she raises as potential concerns are his call to downplay historical narrative and to replace in certain circumstances international criminal court proceedings with amnesties and pardons. Finally, Colin Mcleod rehearses three criticisms relevant to May's conception of international crime as it relates to the international harm principle. First, May's insistence that an international crime must be a harm to humanity itself is found by Macleod to be troublesome because of the grand nature of the victim ("humanity") and the corresponding difficulty in identifying its specific interests. Second, he questions the requirement that international crime be "group-based" harm. Finally, Macleod rejects the requirement that such harm be directed toward groups whose members did not voluntarily choose membership therein.

Part I:
Global Justice and Human Rights

Minority Rights and the New International Politics of Diversity

Will Kymlicka

Abstract: This paper address the challenges that have emerged in the attempt to codify and enforce international standards of minority rights. Without offering any magic solutions for overcoming all of these difficulties, my aim is to more clearly identify the challenges they raise and the pitfalls ahead of us if we ignore them. These include conceptual confusions, moral dilemmas, unintended consequences, legal inconsistencies and political manipulation. The paper concludes with some ideas about how international minority rights might be institutionalized more successfully.

I. Introduction

For a brief period from 1990 to 1995, a number of international organizations devoted extensive efforts to develop international norms of minority rights, both at the global and regional levels. To mention a few of the more prominent examples, the UN adopted a Declaration on the Rights of Persons Belonging to National or Ethnic, Religious and Linguistic Minorities in 1992, and formulated a Draft Declaration on the Rights of Indigenous Peoples in 1993. At the regional level, the Council of Europe adopted both a European Charter for Regional and Minority Languages in 1992 and a Framework Convention for the Protection of National Minorities in 1995, and the European Union declared in 1993 that respect for minority rights would be one of the criteria that candidate countries seeking to join the EU must respect.

This initial burst of enthusiasm for the project of formulating international norms of minority rights has largely run out of steam. There have been few significant advancements in the field since 1995, for reasons I will discuss later. But these various declarations, charters and conventions remain in force and have helped to redefine the ground rules for how states treat minorities. Moreover, a wide range of international working groups, advisory bodies and monitoring agencies has been established to publicize and oversee them. As a result, minorities today have unprecedented opportunities to draw upon international standards, and to use international fora, when pursuing their claims.

These developments offer the promise of protecting some of the most vulnerable groups in the modern world from serious injustices. Ethnic minorities have not fared well under the Westphalian system of sovereign "nation-states." Various policies of assimilation and exclusion have been directed at minorities in the name of constructing homogenous nation-states, and the international community has historically turned a blind eye to these injustices. Today, however, there is a growing commitment to remedy this situation, and it is increasingly accepted that the treatment of minorities is a matter of legitimate international concern and monitoring. At a minimum, these evolving norms set limits on the means that states can use to pursue their visions of national homogenization. But they also, implicitly at least, offer a competing vision of the state, one which views diversity as an enduring reality and defining feature of the polity, and which views tolerance as a core value.

However, efforts to codify and enforce international standards of minority rights have run into a veritable mine-field of conceptual confusions, moral dilemmas, unintended consequences, legal inconsistencies and political manipulation, and it's not clear that there is a road map for navigating around these obstacles. Faced with these obstructions, international efforts have sometimes come to a dead-stop, and sometimes been deflected off-course. My aim in this paper is not to offer magic solutions for overcoming all of these difficulties—some of them, I suspect, are unsolvable in the foreseeable future—but to more clearly identify the challenges they raise, and the pitfalls ahead of us if we ignore them.

II. Explaining the Internationalization of Minority Rights

The first task is to understand why the international community became involved in this field at all. After all, few if any international intergovernmental organizations (hereafter IOs) have an explicit mandate to address issues of ethnic diversity. Why then have so many decided to adopt standards and policies regarding the treatment of ethnocultural minorities?

This is not a simple question to answer given the diversity of IOs involved. For example, the reason why UNESCO has formulated a convention on cultural rights is different from the reason why the World Bank has a policy on safeguarding indigenous rights, which is different yet again from the reasons why the Organization for Security and Cooperation in Europe established the office of the "High Commissioner on National Minorities" to monitor state-minority relations. These are very different sorts of organizations, with very different mandates—some focus on culture and education, others on development, and others on peace and security. These differences in mandate affect how and why they become involved in the issue of state-minority relations.

However, if we step back from these details, we can see the recent international concern with minorities as resulting from the convergence of two factors: a fear of the spread of ethnic violence after the collapse of Communism, and a hope for the possibility of a viable liberal-democratic form of multiculturalism. Let me start with the fear. With the collapse of the Communist bloc, there was initially great optimism that liberal democracy would emerge around the world. Instead, what emerged in many post-communist countries was violent ethnic conflict, particularly in the Balkans and Caucasus. Overly-optimistic predictions about the rapid replacement of communism with liberal-democracy were supplanted with overly-pessimistic predictions about the replacement of communism with ethnic war. There were fears that violent ethnic conflict would spread from Yugoslavia to Central Europe (particularly Romania and Slovakia with their restive Hungarian minorities), and to the Baltics and Central Asia (with their sizeable Russian minorities), engulfing virtually the entire post-Communist world. The collapse of Somalia and Sudan, and the genocide in Rwanda, made clear that this problem was not limited to post-communist Europe, but affected much of the developing world. Writing in 1993, Daniel Moynihan, a former US Ambassador to the UN, captured the spirit of the times when he wrote, "nation states no longer seem inclined to go to war with one another, but ethnic groups fight all the time," leading to "ethnic pandemonium" (Moynihan 1993).

Such conflicts were not only a humanitarian catastrophe for the people within a country, but also had serious international repercussions, in the form of mass refugee flows and the destabilization of neighbouring states. Moreover, ethnic civil wars often create pockets of lawlessness which become havens for the smuggling of arms and drugs, or for terrorist groups. As a result, ethnic conflict came to be seen as a serious threat to international peace and security, and indeed as perhaps the main threat, as the danger of war between the superpowers receded. According to various IOs, these humanitarian and geo-political implications meant that issues regarding the treatment of minorities are "matters of legitimate international concern and consequently do not constitute exclusively an internal affair of the respective State."[1] There was a strong feeling that the international community needed to "do something" to help states manage this "ethnic pandemonium."

So the first factor underlying international initiatives in this field was a pessimistic, even apocalyptic, vision of ethnic politics as a threat to peace, democracy and development. The second factor, however, was the reverse—namely, the emergence within the Western democracies of new and seemingly benign forms of ethnic politics. The West had undergone its own "ethnic revival" starting in the 1960s, with a dramatic upsurge in ethnic political mobilization by a range of different groups. The 1960s witnessed the first serious mobilization by immigrant groups for multiculturalism policies, the birth of the contemporary indigenous rights movement, and the resurgence of minority nationalist politics, including the rise of secessionist parties in Scotland, Catalonia, Flanders, and Quebec.[2]

As in post-communist Europe, this Western ethnic revival was initially seen by many people as potentially destabilizing, and a threat to liberal democracy. And indeed some of its initial manifestations in the 1960s and 1970s were inspired by Marxist or anarchist ideologies that espoused the violent overthrow of the state.[3] By the early 1990s, however, there was a widespread (though not universal) sense of optimism that these fears were overstated, and that Western countries had found a way to contain ethnic political mobilization within the boundaries of peaceful liberal-democratic politics. In fact, many people argued that ethnic mobilization in the West was not just *constrained* by the rules of liberal democracy and human rights, but was in fact *inspired* by liberal values and human rights ideals. Ethnic politics in the West, on this view, was not a threat to democracy, but was itself a profoundly democratic phenomenon, as historically-disadvantaged groups rightly challenged their cultural stigmatization or invisibility in the pursuit of greater freedom and equality. The emergence and institutionalization of ethnic politics, like the rise of feminist and gay movements, was a manifestation and consolidation of a broader process of liberalization and democratization, not a threat to it.

This optimistic view of ethnic politics in the West was articulated in new theories of 'liberal multiculturalism' that first emerged in the late 1980s and early 1990s. According to liberal multiculturalists, the sorts of group-differentiated minority policies that had emerged in the West since the 1960s were worthy of our support, and indeed of celebration. This was true of the regional autonomy schemes and language rights adopted for substate national groups, of the multiculturalism policies adopted for immigrants, and of the land claims and self-government rights adopted for indigenous peoples. All were helping to build fairer and more inclusive democratic societies and should be seen as part and parcel of a free and democratic society.

Put another way, liberal multiculturalism in the West was seen as a process of "citizenization," in sociological jargon. Historically, ethnocultural and religious diversity has been characterized by a range of illiberal and undemocratic relations—including relations of conqueror and conquered; colonizer and colonized; settler and indigenous; racialized and unmarked; normalized and deviant; civilized and backward; ally and enemy; master and slave. The task for all liberal democracies has been to turn this catalogue of uncivil relations into relationships of liberal-democratic citizenship, both in terms of the vertical relationship between the members of minorities and the state, and the horizontal relationships amongst the members of different groups. In the past, it used to be assumed that the only or best way to engage in this process of "citizenization" was to impose a single undifferentiated model of citizenship on all individuals. But liberal multiculturalism starts from the assumption that this complex history inevitably and appropriately generates group-differentiated ethnopolitical claims. The key to citizenization is not to suppress these differential claims, but rather to filter and frame them through the language of human rights, civil liberties and democratic accountability. And this is what liberal multiculturalism seeks to do.

It was not obvious that strong forms of multiculturalism would prove to be an effective vehicle for consolidating relations of liberal-democratic citizenship in multiethnic states. Indeed, most commentators writing in the 1950s and 1960s would have rejected this idea, fearing that it would simply reproduce relations of enmity or hierarchy. But we now have 40 years of experience in the West with models of liberal multiculturalism, and there is a growing consensus that these models can indeed operate in this way.

So the early 1990s witnessed both a profound pessimism about ethnic politics in the post-communist and post-colonial world, and an equally profound optimism about ethnic politics in the West. The activities of the international community regarding state-minority relations have been profoundly shaped by both of these perspectives. The apocalyptic fear of spiraling ethnic conflict provided the impetus for the international community to get involved; the hopeful belief in a truly liberal and democratic form of multiculturalism provided the inspiring ideal and sense of moral direction. It is these two factors that help to explain the explosion of international efforts from 1990–1995, when virtually all of the major global and regional minority rights instruments were developed.

Both factors were necessary to generate the sorts of international initiatives that we have seen. Without the sense of urgent danger, IOs would not have overcome traditional state reluctance to sanction international intervention in state-minority relations. But without the belief in an ideal of multicultural justice, the fear of conflict could have easily led to very different kinds of international initiatives. After World War I, for example, fears of ethnic violence led many people to support either partition (to enable each ethnic group to form its own state, wherever possible) or population transfers (e.g., transferring ethnic Greeks from Turkey to Greece, and ethnic Turks from Greece to Turkey). After World War II, similar fears led to another bout of (what we now call) ethnic cleansing, as ethnic Germans were forcibly expelled from Czechoslovakia, Poland and other countries. And some people today continue to suggest that the international community should consider these options of partition or population transfer, at least as a last resort (Kaufmann 1998). In the early 1990s, however, the international community was profoundly committed to the view that it was feasible and desirable to build new forms of multicultural democracy. And so its response was to try to formulate norms of minority and indigenous rights that would help build liberal multiculturalism.

However, while both factors were essential, they stand in some tension with each other, and pull in different directions. Implicit in current international norms is a hopeful picture of a future where ethnic minorities and indigenous peoples are recognized as legitimate actors and equal partners in the governing of democratic societies. But this optimistic long-term desire to create more space for a democratic multicultural politics is mixed with powerful short-term fears that ethnic politics is too often a destabilizing force, particularly in countries that are not yet consolidated democracies. Ethnic mobilization is seen as potentially undermining democracy and development, and hence needs to be contained if not suppressed. In formulating international norms of minority rights, IOs have alternated between these two attitudes, as indeed is appropriate, since both perspectives identify aspects of contemporary ethnic politics. But the particular way in which these two perspectives have been combined is, I believe, unstable, generating a number of dilemmas that are limiting the ability of international law to promote justice for ethnocultural minorities.

The tension between long-term hopes and short-term fears arises at every step in the process of building an international framework of minority rights, but for the purposes of this paper, I will focus on the very first step in the process—namely, the question of how we identify and categorize the minorities who are the intended beneficiaries of minority rights. This provides a particularly clear example of the dilemmas facing the internationalization of minority rights.

III. Categorizing Minority Rights: Generic or Targeted?

In any attempt to formulate international norms of minority rights, the first step, and in many ways most fateful step, concerns the choice of categories: what kinds of minorities are we trying to protect? The sorts of rights that seem realistic and defensible will largely be determined by the prior question of which types of minorities we have in mind as the intended beneficiaries.

There are two general strategies for categorizing minority rights. One is to formulate what I will call "generic minority rights" that apply to all ethnocultural minorities; the other is to formulate "targeted minority rights" that apply to particular types of minorities, such as indigenous peoples, national minorities, immigrants, the Roma/gypsies, and so on.

The generic strategy is simpler, since it avoids the conceptual and political difficulties involved in developing a typology of minority groups, and so is the preferred approach of many IOs. A clear example of the generic minority rights strategy can be found in the United Nations, in Article 27 of the UN's International Covenant on Civil and Political Rights, which states that:

> In those States in which ethnic, religious or linguistic minorities exist, persons belonging to such minorities shall not be denied the right, in community with the other members of their group, to enjoy their own culture, to profess and practise their own religion, or to use their own language.

When first adopted in 1966, it was left deliberately unclear whether this Article was truly a generic minority rights provision intended to apply to all ethnocultural minorities. Various New World countries, for example, insisted that immigrant groups do not count as "ethnic, religious or linguistic minorities" and hence that the provision only applied to historic minorities in Old World countries created as a result of population transfers or the moving of international boundaries. Similarly, many African states insisted that the provision didn't apply to them either, since tribal groups in post-colonial states do not count as "ethnic, religious or linguistic minorities." In 1966, therefore, the range of groups covered by Article 27 was unclear.

But, over time, the Article has been interpreted by the UN's Human Rights Committee as applying to all ethnocultural minorities, on all continents, no matter how large or small, recent or historic, territorially concentrated or dispersed. Indeed, the Committee has recently declared that Article 27 applies even to visitors within a country.[4] Article 27, in other words, can be seen as a truly *universal* cultural right—a right that can be claimed by any individual, and carried with her as she moves around the world.

But just for this reason, it suffers from inevitable limitations. If we try to identify specific cultural rights that apply to all groups, no matter how large or small, new or old, concentrated or dispersed, it is difficult to think of many substantive examples. And indeed, for a long period of time, the Article 27 "right to enjoy one's culture" was understood primarily as a guarantee of negative rights of non-interference, rather than positive rights to assistance, funding, autonomy or official language status. In effect, it simply reaffirmed that members of minorities must be free to exercise their standard rights of freedom of speech, association, assembly, and conscience.

Understood in this way, the generic rights approach reflected in Article 27 was widely seen as insufficient to deal with the sorts of ethnic conflicts that had sprung up in the early 1990s in post-communist Europe. These conflicts typically involved various positive claims, such as the right to use a minority language in courts or local administration; the funding of minority schools, universities and media; the extent of local or regional autonomy; the guaranteeing of political representation for minorities; or the prohibition on settlement policies designed to swamp minority's traditional territories with settlers from the dominant group. Article 27 has nothing to say about such claims. It protects civil liberties relating to cultural expression, but it does not prohibit states from rescinding funding to minority-language schools and universities, abolishing local autonomy, gerrymandering electoral rules or constituency boundaries, or encouraging settlers to swamp minority homelands. None of these policies, which can be catastrophic for national minorities, and which often lead to violent conflict, violates the rights to cultural expression and association protected in Article 27.[5] If international standards are to be useful in resolving such conflicts, they have to address claims for positive minority rights.

The problem here is not simply the particular wording of Article 27; it is inherent in the very strategy of relying exclusively on generic minority rights. The commitment to identifying generic cultural rights limits the sorts of minority rights that can be recognized. In particular, it precludes claims that flow from facts of historic settlement or territorial concentration. Since Article 27 articulates a universal and portable cultural right that applies to all individuals, even migrants and visitors, it does not articulate rights that are tied to the fact that a group is living on (what it views as) its historic homeland. Yet it is precisely claims relating to residence on a historic homeland that are at stake in all of the violent ethnic conflicts in post-communist Europe—e.g., in Bosnia, Kosovo, Macedonia, Georgia, Chechnya, Ngorno-Karabakh. Indeed, homeland claims are at the heart of most violent ethnic conflicts in the West as well (e.g., the Basque Country, Cyprus, Corsica, Northern Ireland). In all of these cases, minorities claim the right to govern themselves in what they view as their historic homeland, including the right to use their language in public institutions within their traditional territory, and to have their language, history and culture celebrated in the public sphere (e.g., in the naming of streets, the choice of holidays and state symbols). None of these claims can plausibly be seen as universal or portable—they only apply to particular sorts of minorities with a particular sort of history and territory. In short, these are all cases of ethno*national* (or ethnonationalist) conflict, revolving around competing claims to nationhood and national territory. If international standards are to be useful in resolving these pressing conflicts, they need to address the specific types of claims and specific types of groups involved in these conflicts, and that requires shifting towards a scheme of *targeted* minority rights.

So the generic strategy is unable to fulfil the short-term goal of addressing the destabilizing ethnic conflicts that emerged in Eastern Europe and elsewhere in the 1990s. It also fails in the more long-term goal of promoting the ethos of liberal multiculturalism. Liberal multiculturalism in the West is not based on generic minority rights. Rather, it operates in a strongly targeted or group-differentiated way: immigrants, national minorities and indigenous peoples are all accorded different types of minority rights. In particular, legal distinctions are drawn between "old" minorities such as indigenous peoples and substate national minorities, whose presence on their traditional territory predates the formation of the state, and "new" minorities formed through immigration. Both old and new minorities are typically accorded some form of group-differentiated rights, but the multicultural accommodations accorded to immigrant groups differ from the territorial autonomy and official language rights accorded to substate national groups, which differ yet again from the land claims, self-government rights and customary law rights accorded to indigenous peoples.

Liberal political theory has not always been comfortable with the idea of group-differentiated minority rights, or with the idea that historic settlement and territorial concentration on a homeland generates legitimate political claims for old minorities. However, legal distinctions between old and new minorities are in fact found in every Western democracy. And I would argue that this is key to the success of liberal multiculturalism. Liberal multiculturalism has found a way of acknowledging claims based on history and territory for old minorities, while simultaneously acknowledging the equal legitimacy of the (very different) claims for accommodation by new minorities, and framing both within the larger framework of liberal-democratic constitutionalism and human rights. Insofar as Western democracies have indeed managed to successfully manage their ethnic revivals in a way that is guided and constrained by liberal-democratic values, it has not been by enshrining a generic right to enjoy one's culture, but rather through these group-differentiated patterns. A purely generic minority rights strategy obscures this aspect of liberal multiculturalism. Article 27 provides no insight into the organizing logic of liberal multiculturalism and no indication of the categories and concepts that structure state-minority relations within contemporary liberal democracies. Any attempt to diffuse liberal multiculturalism has to explain the necessity and legitimacy of such group-differentiated claims. And so here again, a more targeted approach is needed.

In short, the generic minority rights strategy fails in relation to both of the underlying impulses that motivated the development of international standards: it doesn't provide guidance for resolving the urgent problem of potentially violent and destabilizing ethnic conflict; and it doesn't articulate the underlying moral logic of liberal-democratic multiculturalism as a long-term goal. Both of these motivations require a more targeted approach.

As a result, most of the work that has been done since 1990 in developing international standards has involved targeted rather than generic minority rights. There are two main examples of such targeted minority rights regimes: European organizations have developed targeted rights for "national minorities;" and the UN has developed targeted rights for "indigenous peoples." I will discuss each of them in turn, and the dilemmas they face.

IV. Targeted Rights for National Minorities in Europe

The most elaborate scheme of targeted rights has developed in Europe, spearheaded by the Organization for Security and Cooperation in Europe (hereafter OSCE) and Council of Europe (hereafter CoE). Confronted with the threat of spiralling ethnic conflict in the Balkans and Caucuses in the early 1990s, these European organizations decided to adopt norms that were tailored to the specific types of groups that were involved in these conflicts, which they labelled as "national minorities." Whereas Article 27 lumps together "national, ethnic, religious and linguistic minorities" and accords them all the same generic minority rights, the European norms developed by the CoE and the OSCE refer exclusively to "national minorities" (e.g., the CoE's "Framework Convention for the Protection of National Minorities;" the OSCE's "High Commissioner on National Minorities").

What are national minorities? While there is no universally agreed-upon definition of the term, it has a long history in European diplomacy, where it has referred to historically-settled minorities, living on or near what they view as their national homeland. These are the sorts of groups involved in the violent and destabilizing ethnic conflicts that generated the call for European norms, and it was appropriate therefore to focus on them in the first instance when formulating targeted norms. Most European countries have explicitly stated that immigrant groups are not national minorities, and some have also excluded the Roma from the category of national minority, on the grounds that they are a non-territorial minority.[6] These exclusions are increasingly contested, for reasons I discuss below, with the result that the traditional understanding of national minority co-exists alongside newer and broader definitions of the term that are less tied to history and territory. But originally at least, European organizations were primarily targeting their efforts at historically-settled substate national minorities.

This commitment to developing targeted norms for national minorities was courageous. No other international body has attempted to formulate such norms. Several IOs have developed targeted rights for other types of minority groups. For example, the UN, ILO, and the OAS have all developed targeted norms regarding indigenous peoples, as I will discuss below. Some of these organizations have also formulated norms targeted at migrants.[7] However, no IO had previously attempted to formulate norms directed at national minorities.

This gap is puzzling. If one thinks about the types of state-minority relations with the greatest potential for large-scale harm, injustice and violence, one could argue that they typically involve national minorities. While both indigenous peoples and migrants are vulnerable groups in need of international protection, most of the violent and destabilizing ethnic conflict around the world involves conflicts between states and homeland ethnonationalist groups. This is true not just of Western and Eastern Europe, as we've seen, but also Asia, the Middle East and Africa (e.g., Pakistan; Sri Lanka; China; Indonesia; Turkey; Iraq; Iran; Israel; Sudan; Ethiopia; Nigeria). Developing international norms that address the issues raised by such ethnonational groups is a central task for the theory and practice of minority rights around the world.

The challenge facing European organizations, then, was to formulate targeted norms for national minorities that address the two underlying goals—i.e., to promote a distinctively liberal-democratic conception of multiculturalism as the long-term goal, while providing effective guidance for dealing with the immediate risks of destabilizing ethnic conflict.

What does the theory and practice of liberal multiculturalism suggest regarding the treatment of such groups? If we examine the main cases of substate national minorities in the West—such as the Scots and Welsh in the United Kingdom; the Catalans and Basques in Spain; the Flemish in Belgium; the Québécois in Canada; the Puerto Ricans in the United States; the Corsicans in France; the German minority in South Tyrol in Italy; the Swedes in Finland; and the French and Italian minorities in Switzerland—a clear pattern emerges. In all of these countries, substate national groups have been offered a significant degree of territorial autonomy (hereafter TA), usually through some form of federal or quasi-federal devolution of power, as well as some form of official language status.

These are obviously very strong forms of multiculturalism, involving a substantial restructuring of the state and redistribution of political power. As a result, the changes were initially very controversial in most Western democracies. And yet, today, the basic idea of TA for national minorities is widely accepted. It is inconceivable that Spain or Belgium, for example, could revert to a unitary and monolingual state. Indeed, no Western democracy that has adopted TA for its national minorities has reversed this decision. Moreover, this model is widely seen as successful. It has enabled countries to deal with a difficult and potentially explosive issue—namely, the existence of a substate group that perceives itself as a distinct people or nation with the right to govern its historic territory—in a way that is consistent with peace and democracy, firm respect for individual civil and political rights, and economic prosperity.

It is not surprising, therefore, that the initial impulse of European organizations was to promote this model in post-communist Europe, at least as a "best practice." The very first statement by a European organization on minority rights after the collapse of communism—the 1990 OSCE Copenhagen declaration—went out of its way to endorse TA:

> The participating States note the efforts undertaken to protect and create conditions for the promotion of the ethnic, cultural, linguistic and religious identity of certain national minorities by establishing, as one of the possible means to achieve these aims, appropriate local or autonomous administrations corresponding to the specific historical and territorial circumstances of such minorities and in accordance with the policies of the State concerned. (Article 35)

Similarly, the Parliamentary Assembly of the Council of Europe has passed numerous declarations on "Positive Experiences of autonomous regions as a source of inspiration for conflict resolution in Europe" (e.g., Recommendation 1609).

Some commentators felt that TA should be given an even firmer endorsement, not simply as a "best practice" or "source of inspiration" but as a legal right or norm. In 1993, the CoE's Parliamentary Assembly, for example, adopted a Recommendation stating that

> in the regions where they are a majority, the persons belonging to a national minority shall have the right to have at their disposal appropriate local or autonomous authorities or to have a special status, matching this specific historical and territorial

> situation and in accordance with the domestic legislation of the State. (Recommendation 1201; article 11)

Similar ideas were circulating at the UN. In 1994, for example, Liechtenstein submitted to the General Assembly a "Draft Convention on Self-Determination through Self-Administration," which recognized a right of internal autonomy for all "peoples," where peoples were explicitly defined to include substate national minorities.[8] Article 2 of this Draft Convention states:

> All peoples have the right of self-determination. Within the framework of that right, each State party to the present Convention shall respect the aspirations of all communities within its territory to an appropriate degree of self-administration and shall secure that degree of self-administration to them.

In short, there was much talk of an "emerging right to autonomy," both in Europe and the UN. Attempts to formulate such a norm go well beyond the meagre provisions of Article 27, but it would not be entirely unprecedented in international law. The UN's 1993 Draft Declaration on the Rights of Indigenous Peoples, for example, includes a right to "internal" self-determination (i.e, to significant levels of autonomy within a larger state), though not to "external" self-determination (i.e., to form an independent state). Many commentators felt that a similar principle of autonomy or internal self-determination should be extended to national minorities.

However, as it turns out, the Parliamentary Assembly's Recommendation 1201 reflects the high-water mark of support for TA within European organizations. Since then, there has been a marked movement away from it. The Framework Convention for the Protection of National Minorities (hereafter FCNM), adopted just two years after Recommendation 1201, decisively rejected the Parliamentary Assembly's advice, and avoided any reference to TA. Not only is TA not recognized as a "right," it is not even mentioned as a recommended practice. Nor does TA appear in any subsequent declaration of European organizations, such as the series of Recommendations on minority rights adopted by the OSCE from 1996 to 1999,[9] or the new draft constitution of the EU.[10] For all intents and purposes, ideas of autonomy and internal self-determination have disappeared from the debate about European standards on minority rights.

There are a number of reasons for this, but the most important is the disjunction between long-term ideals and short-term fears. However much TA is seen as a successful model in the consolidated Western democracies, and however much it is seen as a desirable long-term goal for other countries, it is seen as a dangerous and destabilizing principle to adopt in the immediate circumstances of democratic transition in post-communist Eastern Europe.

The reality is that some of the key factors that have enabled the successful adoption of TA in the West simply did not exist in post-communist countries in the 1990s. Let me mention two such factors: geo-political security, and human rights protections.

Geo-Political Security

Most post-communist states have one or more enemies on their borders who would like to destabilize the state. One familiar tactic for doing so is to recruit minorities within the state, and to encourage them to engage in destabilizing protest, even armed insurrection. In such a context of regional insecurity, national minorities are perceived as potential fifth-columnists or collaborators with neighbouring enemies, and autonomy for such minorities is perceived as a threat to national security. This perception is particularly strong when the national minority is related by language or ethnicity to the neighbouring country, and hence is presumed to be more loyal to its 'kin-state' across the border than to its own government. For example, ethnic Serbs living in Bosnia and Croatia are assumed to be more loyal to Serbia than to their own states; ethnic Hungarians living in Romania and Slovakia are presumed to be more loyal to Hungary than to their own states; ethnic Albanians living in Kosovo or Macedonia are presumed to be more loyal to Albania than to their own states; and so on. Under conditions of regional insecurity, granting autonomy to such potentially disloyal and irrendentist minorities is seen as weakening the state in relation to its neighbouring enemies, and indeed as putting the very existence of the state in question.

Western countries, by contrast, are surrounded by allies, not enemies, and are integrated into broader regional security alliances. As a result, no Western state today has an incentive to destabilize its neighbours, and hence no incentive to use discontented national minorities as a vehicle for weakening their neighbours. To be sure, there are examples of this in Western history prior to World War II. Germany, for example, had a long history of inciting ethnic German minorities in neighbouring countries as a way to weaken its rival states. But since World War II, and the emergence of NATO, the perception of homeland minorities as potential collaborators with neighbouring enemies has virtually disappeared from the West.[11]

As a result, in the West today relations between states and minorities are seen as precisely that—i.e., issues of domestic policy about how a state treats a particular part of its population. They are not seen as having repercussions for foreign policy or regional security. In most of the post-communist world, by contrast, state-minority relations are heavily "securitized" and perceived in the first instance as issues of national security policy rather than domestic policy. Under these conditions, there is little space for an open-minded debate about the merits of liberal multiculturalism.

Human Rights Protection

A second factor that distinguishes the West from post-communist Europe concerns the sequencing of minority rights in relation to broader issues of state consolidation, democratization and economic development. In the West, with the important exception of Spain, the restructuring of the state to accommodate national minorities occurred after the development of reasonably well-functioning state institutions, with well-established traditions of constitutional limitations on government, the rule of law, an independent judiciary, a professional bureaucracy and police, a democratic political culture, and a prosperous market economy. The existence of such well-rooted traditions of liberal constitutionalism was crucial to the sort of liberal multiculturalism that emerged in the West. As I noted earlier, liberal-democratic norms both inspire and constrain contemporary forms of ethnopolitics in the West, and this provides a sense of security to all citizens that emerging forms of multiculturalism will operate within well-defined parameters of democracy and human rights.

For example, insofar as national minorities have acquired autonomous governments, these governments have typically been subject to precisely the same constitutional requirements to respect human rights as the central government. In many cases, they are also subject to regional and international human rights monitoring, and more generally are integrated into a dense web of rights-protecting mechanisms (including constitutional courts, human rights commissions, ombudsmen, etc). People who live in the autonomous entities of Scotland, Catalonia or Quebec have access to some of the most advanced systems of human rights protection in the world.

This dual role of human rights—both as inspiration and constraint—has played a pivotal role in enabling the adoption and acceptance of TA. It legitimizes the claims of historically disadvantaged minorities, yet reassures members of the dominant group that no matter how debates over autonomy are resolved, their basic human rights will be protected. This in turn generates confidence in multiculturalism's potential contribution to "citizenization"—i.e., the replacement of earlier hierarchical relations with relations of democratic citizenship.

In the post-communist world, however, claims for self-government by homeland minorities are often occurring prior to the consolidation of well-functioning state institutions, and prior to the emergence of a democratic political culture. This dramatically increases the risks associated with adopting TA. There are fewer guarantees that minorities who receive autonomy will exercise their powers in a way that respects human rights, rather than creating islands of local tyranny, or establishing authoritarian regimes based on religious fundamentalism or ethnic intolerance. In particular, national minorities may attempt to attack the rights and property of "outsiders" residing (perhaps for generations) on the minority's traditional territory. In the absence of an effective human rights framework and political culture, such outsiders may be dispossessed of their property, fired from their jobs, stripped of their residency rights, even expelled or killed. Indeed, this is what happened in several cases in Eastern Europe where minorities seized territory and established their own autonomous governments: ethnic Georgians were pushed out of the Abkhazia region of Georgia when it declared autonomy/sovereignty; ethnic Croats were pushed out of the Serb-dominated region of Slavonia when it declared autonomy; ethnic Serbs were pushed out of Albanian-dominated Kosovo when it achieved autonomy; and so on. Neither side could rely on effective legal institutions and an impartial police to ensure that human rights were respected. Under such conditions, the operation of TA can literally be a matter of life and death.

These two factors explain much of the resistance to TA amongst state elites and dominant groups in post-communist Europe. Even if they were attracted to the principles of liberal multiculturalism as a long-term goal, they might still view it as too risky in their circumstances. In a condition of regional insecurity surrounded by neighbouring enemies, TA can be a threat to the security of the state. In the absence of democratic consolidation, TA can be a threat to the life and liberty of individual citizens who belong to the "wrong" group. Under these circumstances, the intended goal of liberal multiculturalism—namely, replacing uncivil relations of enmity and exclusion with relations of liberal-democratic citizenship—may be subverted. Institutions and policies designed to promote "citizenization" in multi-ethnic states may be captured by internal and external actors seeking to perpetuate and exacerbate relations of enmity and exclusion.

Given these obstacles, it is not surprising that efforts to codify a right to autonomy for national minorities have failed. Indeed, European organizations have not only backed away from formulating TA as a legal norm, they have also, in many cases, stopped recommending it as a best practice, and indeed are actively discouraging it.[12]

Having abandoned a right to autonomy, the minority rights norms that were ultimately adopted by European organizations are quite weak. Indeed, the CoE's FCNM and the OSCE's Recommendations are essentially updated versions of the UN's "right to enjoy one's culture" approach. They move beyond Article 27 by explicitly including certain modest positive rights, such as the right to spell one's surname in accordance with one's own language, and the right to submit documents to public authorities in a minority language. These changes are significant, but are essentially variations on the "right to enjoy one's culture."

As such, they do not articulate any principles for how liberal-democracies should deal with the distinctive characteristics and aspirations of national minorities—i.e., their sense of nationhood and claims to a national homeland. As we've seen, what such groups typically seek is not just the right as individuals to join with other individuals in enacting particular cultural practices, but the right as a national community to govern themselves on their homeland, and to use their self-government powers to express and celebrate their language, history and culture in public space and public institutions. Both the FCNM and the OSCE Recommendations are silent on how such claims should be addressed. They do not discuss how to resolve (often-competing) claims relating to territory and self-government, or how to assign official language status. They neither endorse the models of TA developed in the West, nor offer any alternative to these models. They simply sidestep the issue.

In the end, then, the long-term goal of promoting a liberal-democratic model of multiculturalism for national minorities was abandoned in response to the short-term exigencies of maintaining stability in the process of democratic transition in post-communist countries.

This retreat from a right to autonomy was understandable under the circumstances, and probably even inevitable. The result, however, suffers from some obvious shortcomings. The European framework of targeted national minority rights was intended to overcome the limitations of the original UN approach based on a generic right to enjoy one's culture. In the end, however, it largely replicates these limitations, and indeed exacerbates them.

As we saw earlier, the UN's generic minority rights strategy fails to meet either the short-term or long-term motivations for formulating international norms: it is ineffective in addressing the immediate problem of destabilizing ethnic conflict; and it does not clarify the underlying moral logic of liberal multiculturalism as a long-term goal. The same can be said of the European framework of national minority rights.

Existing European norms are ineffective because they do not address the immediate problem of destabilizing ethnic conflicts. Recall that the original point of developing these norms was to deal with violent ethnic conflicts in post-communist Europe, such as Kosovo, Bosnia, Croatia, Macedonia, Georgia, Azerbaijan, Moldova, and Chechnya. None of these conflicts revolved around the right of individuals to join with others to enjoy their culture. The violation of such rights was not the cause of violent conflict, and respect for such rights would not resolve the conflicts. The same is true about the other major cases where European organizations feared potential violence, such as the Hungarian minorities in Romania and Slovakia, or the Russian minorities in former Soviet republics.

In all of these cases, the issues in dispute are not covered by the FCNM or the OSCE Recommendations. These conflicts involve large, territorially-concentrated groups who have manifested the capacity and the aspiration to govern themselves and to administer their own public institutions in their own language, and who typically have possessed some form of self-government and official language status in the past. They have mobilized for territorial autonomy, official language status, minority-language universities, and consociational power-sharing. None of these groups is satisfied with the meagre rights guaranteed by the FCNM and OSCE Recommendations.[13]

To be fair, the ineffectiveness of current European norms in dealing with these pressing conflicts may be inevitable. The question of how to deal with destabilizing ethnonationalist conflicts may simply be too tough a nut to crack in terms of legal principles. Perhaps the only realistic approach to these conflicts is through ad hoc case-specific interventions, rather than through general legal norms. And indeed, this is what European organizations have ended up relying on in several cases, such as in Macedonia, Bosnia, Moldova, Georgia, Azerbaijan, and Kosovo. In each of these cases, Western organizations have pushed post-communist states to go far beyond the requirements of the FCNM. They have pushed states to accept either some form of TA (Moldova, Georgia, Azerbaijan, Kosovo) and/or some form of consociational power-sharing and official language status (Macedonia, Bosnia). However, precisely because these provisions are case-specific, and not based on pan-European standards, there is no consistency in approach across different countries. These country-specific interventions are not derived from any common set of standards. There are no clear criteria for explaining why European organizations endorse official language status for some groups but not others, or support TA in some countries but not others.

The result is not only the appearance of arbitrariness, but also the appearance of rewarding belligerence. Insofar as there is a common factor underlying the cases where European organizations have endorsed TA, it is the fact of violence. Where minorities have taken up violence in pursuit of autonomy, and have illegally seized territory, European organizations have supported TA in the name of resolving the conflict and re-establishing the rule of law. But where minorities have peacefully pursued TA through legal and democratic means, European organizations have opposed their claims, on the grounds that they go beyond the standards set out in the FCNM. This is a perverse effect, but it is the virtually inevitable consequence of the decision to abandon any attempt to formulate targeted norms that grapple with the distinctive claims of national minorities. The project of formulating targeted norms for national minorities was intended to offer a principled way of resolving ethnonationalist conflicts, as an alternative to the old-fashioned approach based on power-politics and threat potential. As the former goal has been abandoned, the latter has filled the void.

So current European norms are ineffective in addressing the short-term threat of destabilizing ethnonationalist conflict. They also fail to articulate the logic of liberal multiculturalism as a long-term goal. Unlike the UN's generic minority rights strategy, European norms are targeted, and in that sense reflect the group-differentiated structure of liberal multiculturalism. Unfortunately, these norms do not in fact capture the categories and principles of liberal multiculturalism. On the contrary, they are conceptually confusing and unstable.

Put simply, there is a mismatch between the targeted form of the rights and their generic content. Existing European norms target the category of national minorities, but then recognize only generic minority rights of the sort recognized in the UN's Article 27. Why should generic minority rights to enjoy one's culture only be guaranteed to one type of group? The initial goal was to identify principles for dealing with a particular type of homeland group characterized by its historic settlement and territorial concentration. But since the actual rights that were codified in the FCNM and OSCE Recommendations do not recognize any rights arising from historic settlement and territorial concentration, there is no obvious reason why they shouldn't apply to non-territorial groups like the Roma, or to immigrant groups, as well. Surely generic minority rights should be protected generically?

And indeed we see a movement within both the CoE and the OSCE to enable a wider range of groups to benefit from existing standards. The main strategy for broadening the class of eligible groups is to simply redefine the term "national minorities" so that it becomes an umbrella term for all ethnocultural groups, regardless of their historic presence in a state or degree of territorial concentration. The older understanding of national minorities as one type of group amongst others, distinct from indigenous peoples, the Roma, and immigrant groups, is being replaced with a much broader understanding of national minorities which encompasses these different types of ethnocultural groups.

For example, the Advisory Committee that monitors the FCNM has criticized Denmark's claim that indigenous peoples fall under a different category of international law than national minorities. It has also criticized claims by Albania that the Roma do not fall under the category of national minorities, and claims by Estonia that the ethnic Russian newcomers who entered the country during the period of Soviet occupation do not qualify as national minorities. More generally, it has encouraged all countries to apply an "inclusive" understanding of national minorities, one that does not require minorities to have a historic presence or traditional territory in the country, or even to be citizens of the country. In short, in the Committee's usage, the term national minorities is no longer one type of group amongst others in a taxonomy of minorities, but rather is becoming the umbrella term used to encompass all ethnocultural groups.[14] Most academic commentators and advocacy groups support this push to redefine the term.

If this inclusive re-definition of national minorities is adopted by European organizations, it would essentially complete the retreat from the original goal of developing targeted norms that address the distinctive issues raised by ethnonational minorities. At present, the FCNM is targeted in form but generic in the substance of its rights provisions. If the Advisory Committee is successful, the FCNM will become generic in both form and substance. The FCNM would no longer be an important experiment in developing targeted minority rights: it would revert to the original Article 27 approach that articulates generic cultural rights applicable to all minorities, new or old, large or small, dispersed or concentrated.

This debate about how to define national minorities for the purposes of the FCNM crystallises several profound dilemmas confronting the future development of international norms of minority rights. There are powerful arguments for abandoning the targeted character of the FCNM and shifting to a more generic minority rights strategy. But there are also costs associated with this shift, and how we evaluate these benefits and costs has implications not just for the FCNM, but also for the broader project of using international law as a tool to promote justice for minorities.

There are several arguments for treating all ethnocultural groups as national minorities under the FCNM. One is simple consistency: since the rights identified in the Convention are not grounded in facts of history or territory, it seems arbitrary to limit its scope to historic or territorial minorities. But there is a more important reason—namely, that many of the groups excluded by the original restrictive definition of national minorities are desperately in need of international protection, and have no other means of legal protection than the FCNM. Consider the Roma. From a humanitarian point of view, the Roma are, if anything, even more in need of international protection than traditional national minorities. They are often the most disadvantaged members of society, facing pervasive and entrenched forms of discrimination, harassment, and racial prejudice, often at the hands of state officials, as well as suffering from political marginalization, residential segregation, and poverty. Or consider the millions of post-war immigrants into Western Europe, particularly Muslims from North Africa, Turkey or South Asia. Like the Roma, they have often been subject to discrimination, harassment, and marginalization, and in many countries are severely disadvantaged in terms of income, education and employment. For many minority rights advocates, it is crucially important to find some way of ensuring international monitoring of their treatment, and the simplest option is to define them as national minorities for the purposes of the FCNM.

Given the pressing needs of these minority groups, it seems perverse to exclude them from the FCNM on the grounds that they aren't "national minorities" according to traditional usage or dictionary definition. The urgent need to extend international protection to these vulnerable groups helps explain why so many commentators and advocates take it as self-evident that Europe should adopt a more inclusive definition of national minority.

However, there is an alternative way of protecting these groups. Rather than turning the FCNM into a generic minority rights document that covers all groups, one could instead supplement the FCNM with additional targeted norms, formulated specifically for other types of groups that are currently unprotected. Indeed this has been proposed by various European organizations. For example, the CoE's Parliamentary Assembly recommended that a minority rights document be drafted that is targeted specifically for immigrants (Recommendation 1492). Similarly, the OSCE has discussed the proposal for a "Charter of Romani Rights," premised on the idea that the Roma are a "transnational minority" rather than a "national minority" (Klimova-Alexander 2005).

As these proposals show, one possible response to the fact that some vulnerable minorities are not covered by existing targeted norms is not to abandon the idea of targeted norms and shift to a generic strategy, but rather to fill the gaps by creating a "multi-targeted" framework of minority rights. Indeed, this is arguably a preferable approach. After all, it's far from clear that the Roma or immigrants would actually benefit that much from being covered by the FCNM. The FCNM was not drafted with their needs or circumstances in mind, and doesn't address any of their specific issues (such as residency rules or naturalization requirements for immigrants, or the issue of segregated schooling for the Roma). Extending the FCNM to these groups may actually make it less likely that effective international norms will be drafted to deal with their concerns—it pre-empts proposals to develop more effective targeted norms.

Moreover, insofar as our long-term goal is to promote the logic of liberal multiculturalism in a clear and consistent way, it is important to try to articulate its group-differentiated character, and that requires going beyond a purely generic minority rights strategy. This suggests that the best way to ensure that immigrants and the Roma are protected is not to turn the FCNM into a generic document that covers all forms of diversity, but rather to supplement the FCNM with other targeted minority rights instruments, tailored to meet the distinctive needs and aspirations of each type of group.

Unfortunately, this is probably not a realistic option in the European context. It is unlikely that EU states today would adopt a progressive declaration on the rights of immigrants, given that Europe is in the midst of a populist backlash against both immigrants and multiculturalism policies. Any new declaration on the legal status of immigrants is more likely to embody old-fashioned ideas of assimilation and exclusion than newer models of multicultural citizenship. There are also political difficulties confronting the proposal to draft a Roma Charter of Rights (Vermeersch 2005).

As a result, the only feasible way to extend international protection to the Roma or immigrants is through the back door—i.e., by fitting them under the pre-existing scheme of minority protection targeted at national minorities. Since it is unrealistic to expect any new minority rights provisions to be adopted in the foreseeable future, and since the only existing pan-European framework of minority rights targets national minorities, any group that wants to be protected has to qualify as a national minority. It is often said that for those who only possess a hammer, everything starts to look like a nail. Similarly, if the only tool of minority protection in Europe targets national minorities, then every minority starts to look like a national minority.

Under these circumstances, the decision to convert the FCNM into a generic minority rights document is understandable, and perhaps inevitable. It may be the only way to extend protection to vulnerable groups that would not otherwise be covered by international minority rights norms. But if this is indeed the path that Europe takes, we need to realize that it comes at a price. The first casualty is the original and courageous goal of developing minority rights norms that grapple with the distinctive claims of ethnonationalist groups. As I mentioned earlier, developing such norms would have been an enormous contribution to the theory and practice of minority rights, not just for Europe, but for the world generally, given the pervasiveness of ethnonationalist conflicts.

But it is not just traditional national minorities that will pay the price. As one of the first experiments in developing targeted norms, the FCNM could have served as a springboard for the development of other targeted norms in Europe, such as for the Roma or immigrants, and encouraged attempts to formulate targeted norms in other regions of the world. It could have established a precedent for the viability and legitimacy of the targeted strategy at the international level, and also thereby helped diffuse the group-differentiated logic of liberal multiculturalism more generally.

I do not know whether this sort of "multi-targeting" for national minorities, the Roma, and immigrants can be a realistic option for Europe in the future. To be viable, it would require a more systematic effort to coordinate the different proposals for developing targeting norms. At present, proposals for targeted norms have arisen in an ad hoc way, in different European bodies, at different times, often in response to particular crises. There has been no attempt to bring these different proposals together, and then step back and ask what it would mean to adopt a multi-targeted strategy, and how the different forms of targeting would work together as part of a larger framework of European standards. Perhaps the political circumstances have not been present for such an exercise.

But it is surprising how quickly advocates and experts in the European minority rights field have abandoned the project of developing targeted norms, whether for national minorities, Roma or immigrant minorities, and how quickly they have embraced the retreat to a more generic minority rights framework. Although this retreat is often justified in the name of greater "inclusiveness," the resulting norms are neither effective in resolving the pressing issues of destabilizing ethnic conflict, nor do they help in articulating the long-term logic of liberal multiculturalism.

As I've said, the decisions by European organizations about how to formulate and interpret the FCNM have been understandable, pragmatic, and perhaps even inevitable. But the result is that the bold experiment in developing targeted minority rights norms is on the brink of collapse. Indeed, we have come almost full circle in the European experiment in formulating minority rights. European efforts at establishing minority rights norms started from the assumption that the generic minority rights approach of Article 27 was too weak to address the sorts of issues underlying ethnopolitical conflict in post-communist Europe, in part because it only identified minority rights that are common to all groups, no matter how large or small, old or new, concentrated or dispersed. After a fascinating if flawed fifteen-year experiment in developing targeted minority rights, we seem to be returning to where we started.

V. Targeted Indigenous Rights at the UN

Let me shift to the second main attempt to formulate targeted rights—namely, the UN's efforts to develop a framework of rights specifically tailored to indigenous peoples. This is a more successful story, and provides some optimism that a targeted strategy can work. However, it is not without its own dilemmas.

While the UN's initial foray into the field of minority rights relied on the generic strategy, reflected in Article 27 of the ICCPR and the 1992 Minorities Declaration, the UN has recognized that this strategy cannot deal with the distinctive claims raised by certain types of groups, particularly those "old minorities" or "homeland minorities" whose demands and aspirations are rooted in facts of historic settlement and territorial concentration. And so the UN has also embarked on its own version of the targeted rights approach, alongside its ongoing generic rights strategy. The UN, however, has targeted a different category of homeland minority. Whereas European norms target national minorities, UN norms are targeted at indigenous peoples. This is an important difference, with profound implications for the role of international law, and we need to understand why these different targets have been chosen.

The first step is to clarify the terms. What precisely is the difference between national minorities and indigenous peoples? Like most labels used to categorize ethnocultural groups, these terms have contested definitions and unclear boundaries. There is a relatively clear and uncontroversial core to each category—what we might consider the paradigm examples of each type of group—and then a fuzzy periphery, where attempts to apply the term become increasingly contested.

If we focus on their respective core examples, the terms indigenous peoples and national minorities designate quite different types of homeland minorities. To oversimplify, the term "indigenous peoples" arose primarily in the context of New World settler states, and refers to the descendents of the original non-European inhabitants of lands colonized and settled by European powers. Most of the early work on indigenous issues at the UN, for example, focused on the `Indian' populations in Latin America. "National minorities," by contrast, is a term invented in Europe to refer to European groups that lost out in the rough and tumble process of European state formation, and whose homelands ended up being incorporated (in whole or in part) into larger states dominated by a neighbouring European people. National minorities were active players in the process by which the early-modern welter of empires, kingdoms and principalities in Europe was turned into the modern system of nation-states, but they either ended up without a state of their own (often called "stateless nations"), or ended up on the wrong side of the border, cut off from their co-ethnics in a neighbouring kin-state (often called "kin-state minorities").

These are the core cases for the two categories. A preliminary and crude way of distinguishing them is to say that national minorities have been incorporated into a larger state dominated by a neighbouring European people, whereas indigenous peoples have been colonized and settled by a distant colonial European power. But there are other ways of marking the distinction that supervene on this basic historical difference. It is widely accepted, for example, that the subjugation of indigenous peoples by European colonizers was a more brutal and disruptive process than the incorporation of national minorities by neighbouring societies, and that this has left indigenous peoples weaker and more vulnerable. It is also often assumed that there is a "civilizational" difference between indigenous peoples and national minorities. Whereas national minorities typically share the same modern (urbanized, industrialized) economic and socio-political structures as their neighbouring European peoples, indigenous peoples are often assumed to have retained pre-modern modes of economic production, engaged primarily in subsistence agriculture or a hunting/gathering lifestyle. And, as a result of large-scale colonizing settlement, it is also often assumed that indigenous peoples have been relegated to isolated and remote areas, unlike national minorities.

In their core cases, therefore, the two terms refer to different types of groups, rooted in fundamentally different historical processes, and differing in their contemporary characteristics, including their vulnerabilities, mode of production, and habitat. So understood, both terms have their origins in distinctively Western historical processes. National minorities are contenders but losers in the process of state formation within continental Europe itself; indigenous peoples are the victims of the construction of European settler states in the New World. As such, it's not clear whether either term can usefully be applied outside Europe and the New World. And indeed, as we will see below, various African and Asian countries have insisted that neither category applies to them.

However, if we focus on the contemporary characteristics that typify these two types of groups, we can find analogous types of groups in other contexts. For example, several groups in Asia or Africa share the cultural vulnerability, pre-modern economies, and remoteness of some indigenous peoples in the New World, even if they are not the subjects of a European settler state. Such groups include various "hill tribes," "forest peoples," and "pastoralists."

Similarly, we can find groups in many post-colonial states that are similar to European national minorities in being active players, but eventual losers, in the process of decolonization and post-colonial state formation. These would include groups like the Tamils in Sri Lanka, Tibetans in China, Kurds in Iraq, Acehnese in Indonesia, Oromos and Tigrayans in Ethiopia, or the Palestinians in Israel. Like national minorities in Europe, they may have hoped to form their own state in the process of decolonization, or at least to have secured a degree of autonomy. Indeed, some of them were promised autonomy to gain their cooperation in the decolonization struggle. Yet they ended up being subordinated to a more powerful group within a larger state, or divided between two or more post-colonial states.

So while the distinction between indigenous peoples and national minorities as two different kinds of homeland minorities has its origins in Europe and European settler states, there are plausible ways of extending its application to the larger world.

Having distinguished the two types of groups, we can now return to the question of why European organizations targeted national minorities while the UN targeted indigenous peoples. In the former case, the answer is that European organizations saw national minorities in post-communist Europe as posing a profound threat to international peace and security, with risks not only of intra-state violence, but also of spillover effects that could destabilize the entire region. It was on this basis that European organizations declared that the treatment of national minorities was a matter of legitimate international concern.

At the UN, we see a different rationale for developing targeted rights. There was no comparable fear that indigenous people form a threat to international peace and security. This is partly because indigenous peoples do not have nearby kin-states that might call upon them to serve as a fifth-column, and partly because they are seen as falling outside the main battle-lines of inter-state rivalries and regional geo-politics. In any event, they are often too small or remote to pose an effective challenge to state power. Just as it is part of the everyday image of national minorities that they are potential players or pawns in regional geo-politics, it is part of the everyday image of indigenous peoples that they are isolated from regional geo-politics.

The explanation for targeting indigenous peoples, therefore, was not geo-political security threats, but a humanitarian concern to protect a particularly vulnerable group. The initial expression of this humanitarian concern was paternalistic, based on the assumption that indigenous peoples were too "backward" to be able to deal with the challenges of the larger world. For example, the International Labour Organisation's Convention 107 on the "Protection and Integration of Indigenous and Tribal Populations," adopted in 1957, endorsed special measures for indigenous people, but only as temporary paternalistic protections for a vulnerable population that was seen as unable to cope with the rigours of modern life, until such time as they were ready to stand on their own as equal and undifferentiated national citizens. This was a humanitarian concern laced with cultural contempt. But the more multiculturalist models of indigenous rights that have emerged in the 1990s reject this paternalist approach, while still emphasizing the distinctive vulnerability of indigenous peoples to state-imposed projects of assimilation and development. The explanation for this distinct vulnerability is no longer located in the alleged deficiencies or idiosyncracies of indigenous cultures, but rather in the brutal way that European settler states have colonized and settled indigenous lands. The way that indigenous peoples have been dispossessed, resettled, and dispersed in the name of 'national development' became a major embarrassment not only to states, but also to the IOs that had been promoting these development projects.

These newer ideas of indigenous rights can be understood as an outgrowth of the post-war human rights struggle against ethnic and racial hierarchy, building upon earlier struggles for overseas decolonization and racial desegregation. The ideas advanced by the "Red Power" movement that arose in the US in the 1960s (and comparable indigenous movements in other New World countries) were modeled on these earlier struggles, drawing on the discourse of both decolonization and anti-racism. When the international community first endorsed the principle of decolonization, it only applied this principle to overseas colonies, not to the indigenous peoples colonized by European settler states in the New World. But from a moral perspective, this is clearly inconsistent. Indeed, given that indigenous peoples were subject not only to imperial conquest (as with colonies in Africa or Asia), but also to colonizing settlement, one could argue that they suffered an even greater injustice from colonialism than overseas colonies. In any event, once the international community had accepted principles of overseas decolonization and racial desegregation, it was difficult to deny the historic injustice of the colonization of indigenous peoples, or to deny the appropriateness of some form of (internal) decolonization.

International support for indigenous rights, therefore, reflects a mixture of motivations, drawing on powerful moral arguments about the injustice of colonization and racial discrimination, combined with lingering paternalistic ideas about the distinctive vulnerability of "backward" cultures. Whatever the precise mixture of reasons, it is clearly a different motivation from that which underpinned the targeting of national minorities in Europe. National minorities were targeted for reasons of geo-political security; indigenous peoples were targeted for moral and humanitarian reasons of historic injustice and protection of the vulnerable.

This, then, was the context in which UN embarked on the task of formulating targeted norms for indigenous peoples. The fact that UN norms of indigenous rights are based on humanitarian concerns rather than security fears has a number of implications. In particular, the absence (or at least relative mildness) of geo-political security issues has made it possible to develop norms that reflect the logic and best practices of liberal multiculturalism.[15] As we saw earlier, this proved impossible in the context of European national minorities. The very geo-political security fears that led European organizations to target national minorities have also inhibited these organizations from endorsing the models of liberal-democratic accommodation that have developed within the West. Indeed, these security fears have paralyzed European organizations from addressing any of the distinctive issues raised by national minorities. As a result, the evolving European norms are targeted in form but generic in content, and because of this inconsistency, the very project of developing targeted rights for national minorities is in danger of collapsing.

UN norms on indigenous rights, by contrast, clearly do address the specific needs of indigenous peoples, and in a way that is close to the best practices of liberal democracies. If we consider the main examples of indigenous peoples in the

Western democracies—i.e., the Indians and Inuit/Eskimos of the United States and Canada, the Maori in New Zealand, the Aborigines in Australia, the Greenlanders in Denmark and Sami in Scandinavia—we see a clear trend. In all of these countries, there has been a shift since the 1970s towards recognizing some form of indigenous self-government over (what remains of) their traditional territory. This is reflected in a wide range of land claims settlements and self-government agreements, and in some cases a degree of legal pluralism (e.g., recognizing customary law).

The emerging UN norms of indigenous rights endorse and extend this trend. At their most ambitious, these norms are very powerful indeed. Whereas the European norms on national minorities start from the Article 27 right to enjoy one's culture, the UN's norms on indigenous rights start from a modified version of the right to self-determination. The 1993 UN Draft Declaration on the Rights of Indigenous Peoples, for example, includes the following articles:

> Article 3: Indigenous peoples have the right of self-determination. By virtue of that right, they freely determine their political status and freely pursue their economic, social and cultural development.
>
> Article 26: Indigenous peoples have the right to own, develop, control and use the lands and territories . . . which they have traditionally owned or otherwise occupied or used. This includes the right to the full recognition of their laws, traditions and customs, land-tenure systems and institutions for the development and management of resources. . . .
>
> Article 31: Indigenous peoples, as a specific form of exercising their right to self-determination, have the right to autonomy or self-government in matters relating to their internal affairs. . . .
>
> Article 33: Indigenous peoples have the right to promote, develop and maintain their institutional structures and their distinctive juridical customs, traditions, procedures and practices, in accordance with internationally recognized human rights standards.

In short, the Draft Declaration recognizes indigenous rights over territory and resources, as well as rights to autonomous legal, political and cultural institutions. Although these articles are being proposed as minimum standards that all countries should meet, they represent a fairly well-developed articulation of the ethos of liberal multiculturalism as it has developed in the West in relation to indigenous peoples.

This Draft Declaration is still just a draft, but its core ideas have been picked up by various organs within the UN system, and similar ideas have been articulated by the ILO and in the draft declaration on indigenous rights of the OAS. So these ideas are circulating widely throughout IOs, and they have had demonstrable effects, especially in Latin America.

In this way, the UN's targeted norms for indigenous peoples can be seen as a genuine success. They address the distinctive needs of indigenous peoples in a way that European targeted norms for national minorities do not, and thereby provide evidence that the strategy of developing targeted norms is a legitimate and potentially effective one. Whereas European norms shy away from addressing issues of history, territory and autonomy, the UN's indigenous norms focus precisely on the distinctive issues raised by the fact that indigenous peoples define themselves in relation to their historic homelands, and express a strong desire to retain or regain political control over themselves, their institutions, and their territories. Indeed, virtually all of the international instruments relating to indigenous peoples reiterate the intention to respect and honour this connection between indigenous peoples and their historic territories. As a result, many commentators point to the emergence of international indigenous rights as one of the few truly successful examples of how international law can be used as a tool of "counter-hegemonic globalization," promoting justice for the disadvantaged (Falk 2000).

The fact that the targeted indigenous track is based on humanitarian motivations, not security issues, has made this progress possible. However, the UN's decision to shift from a security-inspired focus on national minorities to a humanitarian focus on indigenous peoples also has its drawbacks. One obvious limitation is that it leaves us with no global legal norms addressed to the distinctive issues raised by national minorities. Yet, as we've seen, it is precisely conflicts involving such ethnonational groups that pose the greatest threat to peace, security, human rights and development in much of the post-colonial world. It is the ethnopolitical struggles of groups like the Tamils, Kurds, Kashmiris, Palestinians, and Oromos that pose a potential threat to regional peace and stability, not the struggles of pastoralists or forest dwellers.

One potential response to this gap would be to supplement the existing UN norms on indigenous peoples with another set of targeted UN norms directed at national minorities. As I noted earlier, this sort of "multi-targeting" would reflect the logic of liberal multiculturalism, which involves a range of group-differentiated legal tracks, including distinctive tracks for national minorities and indigenous peoples.

Unfortunately, the prospects for developing global norms on national minorities are non-existent in the foreseeable future. The one attempt to formulate such norms at the global level—namely, the Draft Convention on Self-Determination through Self-Administration submitted by Liechtenstein to the UN General Assembly in 1994—was never seriously considered. And this shouldn't surprise us. The same factors that inhibited the development of meaningful national minority norms for post-communist Europe—in particular, fears about geo-political security and human rights protection—apply equally to most countries in Africa, Asia or the Middle East. Indeed, these fears are if anything even more pervasive in the post-colonial Third World than in post-communist Europe, and there are fewer institutional resources available for managing them.[16] If European organizations were unable to overcome these fears, despite their formidable economic, legal and military capacities, it is unrealistic to expect the UN to succeed in this task. And indeed it has never seriously tried.

So the current UN framework which adopts targeted norms for indigenous peoples but not for national minorities is unlikely to change. For some commentators, the absence of targeted protection for national minorities is a regrettable gap, but doesn't put into question the validity of the targeted indigenous norms. We should make progress where we can, and if current circumstances only allow for progress on the indigenous track, then we should move forward there, and not wait until we can move forward on all the possible targeted tracks simultaneously.

In my view, however, the matter is more complicated. The sharp distinction in legal status between indigenous peoples and national minorities is creating a number of paradoxes that may destabilize the indigenous track itself. A sustainable system of targeted indigenous rights may require a system of targeted norms for national minorities as well.

In order to understand the problem here, we need to recall how the category of indigenous peoples fits into the broader pattern of liberal multiculturalism. As I noted earlier, both indigenous peoples and national minorities are treated as "old" or "homeland" minorities in most Western democracies. There are important sociological and historical differences between the two types of homeland minorities, and these carry with them legal implications in most countries, but both types of groups are acknowledged to have legitimate interests with respect to the governance of their traditional territories and to the expression of their language and culture within its public institutions and public spaces. In this respect, they are distinguished from new minorities composed of immigrants, guest-workers and refugees. From the perspective of the theory and practice of liberal multiculturalism in the West, indigenous peoples and national minorities belong together as self-governing homeland minorities, in a different category from new minorities.

In the emerging international discourse, however, the important commonalities between indigenous peoples and national minorities have been obscured, and instead an artificial chasm has been created between them. There was, at first, an understandable moral justification for this trend. As we've seen, the subjugation of indigenous peoples by European colonizers was typically a more brutal and disruptive process than the subjugation of national minorities by neighbouring European societies, and this has left indigenous peoples more vulnerable, and hence in more urgent need of international protection. As a result, there was a plausible moral argument for giving priority to indigenous peoples over national minorities in the codification of rights to self-government in international law.

However, what began as a difference in relative urgency between the claims of indigenous peoples and national minorities has developed into an almost total rupture between the two at the level of international law. Across a wide range of international documents, indigenous peoples have been separated out from other homeland minorities, and claims to TA have been restricted to the former. National minorities, by contrast, are lumped together with new minorities and accorded only generic minority rights, ignoring their distinctive needs and aspirations relating to historic settlement and territorial concentration.

The distinction between indigenous peoples and other homeland minorities has thereby assumed a significance within international law that is absent in the theory and practice of liberal multiculturalism. This attempt to draw a sharp distinction between indigenous peoples and national minorities in international law raises a number of difficult questions. It creates (i) moral inconsistencies, (ii) conceptual confusion, and (iii) unstable political dynamics. Let me explain each of these points.

The sharp distinction in rights between the two types of groups is morally inconsistent, because whatever arguments exist for recognizing rights of self-government for indigenous peoples also apply to the claims of self-government for other vulnerable and historically-subordinated homeland groups. This is clear from the UN's own explanations for the targeted indigenous track. In a recent document, the Chair of the UN's Working Group on Minorities (Asbjorn Eide) and the Chair of the UN Working Group on Indigenous Populations (Erica-Irene Daes) were asked to explain their understanding of the distinction between "indigenous peoples" on the one hand, and "national, ethnic, religious and linguistic minorities" on the other (Eide and Daes 2000). In trying to explain why indigenous peoples are entitled to targeted rights beyond those available to all minorities under the generic Article 27, the two Chairs identified three key differences: (a) whereas minorities seek institutional integration, indigenous peoples seek to preserve a degree of institutional separateness; (b) whereas minorities seek individual rights, indigenous peoples seek collectively-exercised rights; (c) whereas minorities seek non-discrimination, indigenous peoples seek self-government. These are indeed relevant differences that the theory and practice of liberal multiculturalism attends to. But none of them serves to distinguish indigenous peoples from national minorities. On all three points national minorities fall on the same side of the ledger as indigenous peoples.

In an earlier document prepared for the Working Group on Indigenous Populations, Daes offered a somewhat different account (Daes 1996). She stated that the crucial distinguishing feature of indigenous peoples, compared to minorities in general, is that they have a strong attachment to a traditional territory which they view as their historic homeland. As she puts it, "attachment to a homeland is nonetheless definitive of the identity and integrity of the [indigenous] group, socially and culturally. This may suggest a very narrow but precise definition of 'indigenous,' sufficient to be applied to any situation where the problem is one of distinguishing an indigenous people [from] the larger class of minorities" (Daes 1996: para 39). But this criterion—"attachment to a homeland"—obviously picks out homeland minorities in general, including national minorities, not indigenous peoples in particular.

As these quotes show, discussions within the UN of the distinction between indigenous peoples and minorities often proceed as if national minorities simply don't exist. Consider Daes's concluding summary of the fundamental distinction between minorities and indigenous peoples:

> Bearing the conceptual problem [of distinguishing indigenous peoples from minorities] in mind, I should like to suggest that the ideal type of an 'indigenous people' is a group that is aboriginal (autochthonous) to the territory where it resides today and chooses to perpetuate a distinct cultural identity and distinct collective social and political organization within the territory. The ideal type of a 'minority' is a group that has experienced exclusion or discrimination by the State or its citizens because of its ethnic, national, racial, religious or linguistic characteristics or ancestry. From a purposive perspective, then, the ideal type of 'minority' focuses on the group's experience of discrimination because the intent of existing international standards has been to combat discrimination, against the group as a whole as well as its individual members, and to provide for them the opportunity to integrate themselves freely into national life to the degree they choose. Likewise, the ideal type of 'indigenous peoples' focuses on aboriginality, territoriality, and the desire to remain collectively distinct, all elements which are tied logically to the exercise of the right to internal self-determination, self-government, or autonomy. (Daes 2000: paras. 48–9)

This is a fine summary of the distinction between two ideal types of groups, but it provides no justification for distinguishing indigenous peoples from other homeland minorities. On all of Daes' criteria, national minorities and indigenous peoples fit into the same ideal type based on territory and autonomy, while new and dispersed minorities fall into the other.

In short, virtually all of the principles advanced within the UN for targeted indigenous rights also apply to national minorities, and the sharp gulf in legal status between the two groups lacks any clear moral justification. For realpolitik reasons, it may be impossible to extend international norms of self-government to national minorities. As we've seen, states are less willing to contemplate demands for self-government by groups that pose a credible threat to the state, and these groups tend to be national minorities rather than indigenous peoples. But we shouldn't dress up realpolitik in the language of moral principle, or ignore the moral inconsistencies it generates.

The sharp distinction in legal status between national minorities and indigenous peoples is not only morally problematic, it is also conceptually unstable. The very distinction between indigenous peoples and other homeland minorities is difficult to draw outside the original core cases of Europe and European settler states.

In the West, as we've seen, there is a relatively clear distinction to be drawn between European national minorities and New World indigenous peoples. Both are homeland groups, but the former have been incorporated into a larger state dominated by a neighbouring people, whereas the latter have been colonized and settled by a distant colonial power. It is less clear how we can draw this distinction in Africa, Asia or the Middle East, or whether the categories even make sense.

In one familiar sense, no groups in Africa, Asia or the Middle East fit the traditional profile of indigenous peoples. All homeland minorities in these regions have been incorporated into larger states dominated by neighbouring groups, rather than being incorporated into settler states dominated by European settlers.[17] In that sense, they are all closer to the profile of European national minorities than to New World indigenous peoples. And, for this reason, several Asian and African countries insist that none of their minorities should be designated as indigenous peoples.

In another sense, however, we could say that all homeland groups in these regions (including the dominant majority group) are "indigenous." During the era of colonial rule, all historically-settled groups, majority and minority alike, were designated as "natives" or "indigenous" in relation to the colonial rulers.[18] In this sense, all homeland groups in post-colonial states (including the dominant group) are equally "indigenous." And indeed the governments of several Asian and African countries declare that *all* their groups, majority and minority, should be considered "indigenous."

These two approaches yield diametrically opposed results, but whether we say that all groups are indigenous or that no groups are indigenous, the upshot in either case is to undermine the possibility of using the category of indigenous peoples as a basis for targeted norms within postcolonial states. For this reason, some commentators have argued that international norms of indigenous rights should not be applied in Africa and Asia. However, this would leave some of the most vulnerable homeland minorities in the world without any meaningful form of international protection. If targeted indigenous norms do not apply in Asia or Africa, that leaves only the (very weak) generic minority rights under Article 27, and these provide no protection for homeland-related interests.

In order to extend the protections of international law, therefore, the UN has attempted to re-conceptualize the category of indigenous peoples so that it covers at least some homeland minorities in post-colonial states. On this view, we shouldn't focus on whether homeland minorities are dominated by settlers from a distant colonial power or by neighbouring peoples. What matters is simply the facts of domination and vulnerability, and finding appropriate means to remedy them.[19] If homeland groups suffer from domination and vulnerability, we should use the indigenous track to protect them, even if their oppressors are their historic neighbours and not long-distance colonizing settlers. Hence various IOs have encouraged groups in Africa and Asia to identify themselves as indigenous peoples in order to gain greater international protection.

This push to extend the category of indigenous peoples beyond its core case in the New World is a logical, perhaps inevitable, result of the humanitarian motivation that led to the targeting of indigenous peoples in the first place. Insofar as the motivation for targeted rights was the distinctive vulnerability of indigenous peoples in New World settler states, it was natural to expand the category to include groups elsewhere in the world that share similar vulnerabilities, even if they were not subject to settler colonialism.

The difficult question however is how to identify *which* homeland groups in Africa, Asia or the Middle East should be designated as indigenous peoples under international law, and on what basis. Once we start down the road of applying the category of indigenous peoples beyond the core case of New World settler states, there is no obvious stopping point. Indeed, there are significant disagreements within IOs about how widely to apply the category of "indigenous peoples" to homeland minorities in post-colonial states. Some would limit it to isolated peoples, such as "hill tribes" or "forest peoples" in southeast Asia, or to pastoralists in Africa. Others would limit it to groups that fall outside the market economy—i.e., to those groups living as hunter-gatherers or subsistence cultivators, but not involved in either trade or the labour market. (This seems to be one of the World Bank's criteria, invoked to deny indigenous status to the Berbers in Algeria).

These narrow definitions are inconsistent with the way the term is used in the New World. In Latin America, for example, the term indigenous peoples applies not only to isolated forest peoples in the Amazon, such as the Yanomami, but also to peasants in the highlands who have been in intensive contact and trade with the larger settler society for five hundred years, such as the Maya or Aymaras. Similarly many indigenous peoples in North America have been involved in settled agriculture or the labour market for generations. To limit the category of indigenous peoples to groups that are geographically isolated or outside the market economy would exclude some of the largest and most influential indigenous groups in the New World.

And so other commentators would extend the category of indigenous peoples in post-colonial states much more widely to encompass all historically-subordinated homeland minorities that suffer from some combination of political exclusion, poverty or cultural vulnerability. On this view, the label "indigenous peoples" is virtually synonymous with "homeland minority." The difference between the narrower and broader conceptions of indigenous peoples is potentially enormous—estimates of the number of people who would qualify as "indigenous peoples" in Indonesia range from 2 percent to 60 percent of the population, depending on whether a narrower or broader definition is used (Evers 1995).

There is a vast literature on how to apply the category of indigenous peoples in Africa and Asia, and on the relative merits of broader and narrow definitions (e.g., Kingsbury 1998). This is a matter on ongoing debate within various IOs, each of which has adopted different definitions, to the consternation of commentators who wish that a single definition would be adopted across the international community. The more serious problem, however, is that all of these proposed approaches, whether narrow or broad, invoke criteria that clearly are a matter of degree. Homeland minorities in post-colonial states fall on a continuum in terms of their cultural vulnerability, geographical isolation, level of integration into the market, and political exclusion. We can, if we like, set a threshold somewhere along this continuum in order to determine which of these groups are called "indigenous peoples" and which are "national minorities," but any such threshold is likely to appear arbitrary and incapable of bearing the weight that international law currently requires of it. International law treats the distinction between indigenous peoples and national minorities as a categorical one, with enormous implications for their legal rights. In the post-colonial world, however, any attempt to distinguish indigenous peoples from national minorities on the basis of their relative levels of vulnerability or exclusion can only track differences of degree, not the difference in kind implied by international law.[20]

The attempt to preserve such a sharp distinction is not only morally and conceptually unstable, it may also be politically unsustainable. The problem here is not simply that the category of indigenous peoples has grey areas and fuzzy boundaries, with the potential for being over- or under-inclusive. That is true of all targeted categories, and there are well-established techniques of democratic deliberation and legal interpretation for dealing with such boundary disputes. The problem, rather, is that too much depends on which side of the line groups fall, and as a result, there is intense political pressure to change where the line is drawn, in ways that are politically unsustainable.

As should be clear by now, the current UN framework provides no incentive for any homeland minority to identify itself as a "national minority," since this category provides no rights that are not available to any other ethnocultural group. Instead, all homeland minorities have an overwhelming incentive to (re)-define themselves as "indigenous peoples." If they come to the international community under the heading of "national minority," they get nothing other than generic Article 27 rights; if they come instead as "indigenous peoples," they have the promise of rights to land, control over natural resources, political self-government, language rights, and legal pluralism.

Not surprisingly, an increasing number of homeland groups in Africa, Asia and the Middle East are adopting the label of indigenous peoples. An interesting case is the Arab-speaking minority in the Ahwaz region of Iran, whose homeland has been subject to state policies of Persianization, including the suppression of Arab language rights, renaming towns and villages to erase evidence of their Arab history, and settlement policies that attempt to swamp the Ahwaz with Persian settlers. In the past, Ahwaz leaders have gone to the UN Working Group on Minorities to complain that their rights as a national minority in relation to their traditional territory are not respected. But since the UN does not recognize national minorities as having any distinctive rights in relation to their areas of historic settlement or territorial concentration, the Ahwaz have run into a dead end. And so they have re-labeled themselves from a national minority to an indigenous people, and have attended the UN Working Group on Indigenous Populations instead. Similarly, various homeland minorities in Africa that once attended the Working Group on Minorities have now started re-branding themselves as indigenous peoples and attending the Working Group on Indigenous Populations, primarily in order to gain protection for their land rights (Lennox 2006: 18).

This is just the tip of the iceberg. Any number of minorities are now debating whether to adopt the label of indigenous peoples, including the Crimean Tatars, the Roma, and Afro-Latin Americans. Even the Kurds—the textbook example of a stateless national minority—are debating whether to redefine themselves as an indigenous people. So too with the Palestinians in Israel, the Abkhaz in Georgia, Chechens in Russia, and the Tibetans in China.

In all of these cases, national minorities are responding to the fact that generic minority rights are "regarded as fatally weak" (Barsh 1994: 81), and as "completely inadequate . . . to their needs" (Aukerman 2000: 1030), since generic rights do not protect any claims based on historic settlement or territorial attachments. Given international law as it stands, recognition as an indigenous people is the only route to secure protection for these interests. Perhaps, in time, the Scots and Basques will also claim this status. After all, what homeland minority wouldn't want the rights currently being formulated for indigenous peoples?

The net effect of such shifts in self-identification would be the total collapse of the international system of indigenous rights. As we've seen, the UN and other IOs have repeatedly rejected attempts to codify rights of self-government for powerful substate national groups, in part because of their geo-political security implications. They are not going to allow such groups to gain rights of self-government through the back-door by redefining themselves as indigenous peoples. Yet there is little within the current UN indigenous rights track that prevents such a shift from taking place.

If more and more homeland groups adopt the indigenous label, the likely result is that IOs will retreat from the targeted indigenous rights track. The first signs of a retreat are already visible. There are a number of ways this could take place. The most obvious is that member-states may bring negotiations on the UN and OAS Draft Declarations to a halt. Or they may gut these declarations of their substantive content—e.g., by removing rights to land or self-government, and limiting their focus to generic cultural rights. Or they may narrow the scope of application of these declarations—e.g., by limiting them to "remote" groups who do not participate in the wage economy, such as forest-dwellers. Whatever the technique, the result would be to undermine the major progress that has occurred to date in the indigenous track.

This suggests that the long-term future of the UN's targeted indigenous track is not yet clear. This track is often cited as the clearest success story in developing international minority rights, and rightly so. But it is in danger of becoming a victim of its success. The achievements of the targeted indigenous track in the New World, particularly in empowering indigenous peoples in Latin America, is encouraging the UN to extend the category in ways that are morally inconsistent, conceptually unstable, and politically unsustainable.

It is not obvious how we can overcome this instability. As we've seen, the dilemma has arisen as a combined result of two decisions about how to develop targeted norms at the global level. First, a decision was made to create a sharp gulf in legal status between indigenous peoples and national minorities, highlighting the former as a beneficiary of strong targeted rights, while ascribing only generic minority rights to the latter. In principle, one could imagine an alternative approach in which the UN would adopt a strategy of dual-targeting (or multi-targeting), developing separate legal tracks for both indigenous peoples and national minorities. But as we've seen, the attempt to develop targeted norms for national minorities in Europe failed, and the prospects for success at the global level are even worse. As a result, the decision to create a legal firewall between the two types of groups was clearly a pragmatic decision, even if it introduced an element of moral inconsistency into the UN framework.

The second decision was to extend the category of indigenous peoples beyond its original context of New World settler states to Asia, Africa, and the Middle East. Here again, one could imagine an alternate approach in which the UN would acknowledge that the category of indigenous peoples is essentially rooted in the history of Europe and European settler states, and would therefore attempt to develop a different framework of targeted categories for minorities in other regions. But we have no proposals for what these alternate categories might be, and regional organizations in Asia, Africa, and the Middle East have shown little interest in developing their own region-specific forms of targeted rights. The only realistic way to extend targeted international protection to minorities in post-colonial states, therefore, was to broaden the category of indigenous peoples. Since the only available tool of international protection was targeted at indigenous peoples, it was pragmatic to redefine minorities in need of protection as indigenous peoples.

The combined result of these two pragmatic decisions, however, is instability. The second decision to globalize the category of indigenous peoples makes it increasingly difficult—morally, conceptually and politically—to sustain the legal firewall between indigenous peoples and other homeland minorities required by the first decision. Globalizing the category of indigenous peoples, therefore, yields short-term pragmatic benefits but also raises long-term risks. Perhaps the benefits outweigh the risks. But it is surprising how quickly and almost unanimously activists and their academic advisors have accepted that this is the right way to proceed.[21]

Perhaps this is indeed the best strategy. But if so, we should be conscious of the risks involved, and we should start to think creatively about how we will deal with the instabilities that will inevitably arise.

In my view, the long-term success of the indigenous track will depend on developing a more coherent account of the relationship between indigenous peoples and other homeland minorities. The international community has systematically avoided addressing this question to date, but it cannot be postponed forever. The firewall strategy was important to get the indigenous track off the ground, but it cannot provide a stable long-term foundation.

VI. Future Directions

Motivated by a fear of escalating ethnic conflict, and inspired by a hope for a liberal-democratic form of multiculturalism, the international community has embarked on wide-ranging efforts to codify new standards for the treatment of ethnocultural minorities. While these developments offer the promise of greater justice for minorities, the results to date have been uneven at best, and have run into a series of moral dilemmas and instabilities.

What then is to be done? One option is to abandon the project of formulating international norms of minority rights, and to turn back the clock to the era before 1990, when state-minority relations were not a priority issue for the international community. After all, the initial impulse to formulate international norms of minority rights was arguably based on a mistaken prediction about the likelihood of escalating ethnic conflict. And the attempt to formulate these rights has led to an impasse. So why not give up on the whole idea of formulating international norms of minority rights?

In my view, this would be undesirable. The international community has a legitimate, and indeed essential, role to play in assisting both states and minorities. Minorities around the world are demanding greater respect and recognition, and there is no reason to expect that such demands will diminish in the foreseeable future. Contemporary struggles for multiculturalism emerged out of earlier human rights struggles against ethnic and racial hierarchies, and appeal to some of the most powerful moral ideals of the modern world. Minorities are unlikely to back away from such claims simply because states and IOs find them awkward to deal with. And yet many post-communist and post-colonial states have difficulty responding to these claims, which threaten not only their traditional self-understandings as unitary and homogenous nation-states, but also pose potential threats to security, human rights and development. Even within Western states, liberal multiculturalism has proven vulnerable to backlash and retreat. State-minority relations are continually in danger of reverting to older patterns of illiberal and undemocratic relations—including relations of conqueror and conquered; colonizer and colonized;

racialized and unmarked; normalized and deviant; orthodox and heretic; civilized and backward; ally and enemy. If we are to break out of these patterns, and replace them with relations of democratic citizenship, the international community must be an active participant. IOs have a responsibility both to protect vulnerable minorities from serious injustice, and to enable states to meet these obligations of justice. To abandon this task would be a betrayal of the founding ideals of the international community.

In any event, a full-scale retreat from minority rights is unrealistic. The commitment to minority rights, while relatively recent, is now deeply institutionalized. There are multiple Working Groups, Advisory Committees, Independent Experts, and Monitoring Bodies operating at various levels of the international community (regional and global), and within different functional domains (e.g., peace and security; human rights; development and the environment). Minority rights are here to stay, in one form or another.

The alternative, therefore, is to rethink the goals and means underlying the project of internationalizing minority rights, in order to develop a more coherent and stable approach. How would we go about this? There are no magic solutions. Any concerted effort to internationalize minority rights will face unavoidable dilemmas. However there may be ways of alleviating some of the tensions.

The first task is to address head-on the issue of categories. IOs have repeatedly struggled with the issue of targeted minority rights for specific categories of groups, such as national minorities and indigenous peoples. These struggles suggest a number of important lessons. The first is that some degree of targeting is inevitable. As we've seen, the initial preference of IOs is for a purely generic minority rights approach that does not require putting ethnocultural groups into different categories for the purposes of international law. But in both the European and global contexts, a generic approach has proven insufficient. It is part of the very nature of ethnic conflict, and part of the very logic of liberal multiculturalism, that it raises group-differentiated issues, often related to the role of history and territory. This suggests that some degree of targeting is essential if international norms are to play a constructive role.

Yet we are very far from having a coherent or systematic account of the kinds of targeting that are desirable or sustainable. One thing we can safely say is that targeting only works if there is consistency between the form and content of targeted norms—i.e., if the distinctive set of rights being accorded to a particular type of group matches the distinctive needs or circumstances of that group. In the European context, a mismatch between form and content has emerged. European norms are formally targeted at national minorities but are generic in their substantive content, and the result is instability.

But even where there is a good match between targeted form and targeted content, as in the case of the UN's indigenous rights track, the result may still be unstable if this targeting exists in isolation from a more general understanding of the role and function of targeted rights. To date, targeted norms have emerged in an ad hoc fashion, and are often presented as unique exceptions to the rule of generic minority rights. But this sort of ad hoc "mono-targeting"—isolating one particular type of group for distinctive legal rights, while according all other groups only generic minority rights—is unlikely to be stable. If we start down the road of targeted norms, we need to do it in a more self-conscious and systematic fashion. It may be that the only way to develop a sustainable set of targeted norms for indigenous peoples is to make it part of a broader strategy of "multi-targeting," operating in conjunction with separate targeted norms for national minorities or other homeland groups, for immigrant groups, or for other types of groups with unique histories and needs, such as the Roma or Afro-Latinos. Otherwise, any set of mono-targeted norms will face intense pressure to redefine the category in ways that are unsustainable, as we are seeing in both Europe and the UN.

There have been few if any attempts to step back and ask what such a multi-targeted system of minority rights would look like. It is not clear what mix of categories could serve as the basis for a sustainable global system of multi-targeted minority rights. The intellectual task is complicated by the fact that many of the categories currently in use, such as indigenous peoples or national minorities, are "rooted in a particular time and space" (Lennox 2006: 4), and may not in fact be globally applicable. They work well in some regions, but not in others. We have only begun to think about the challenge of formulating a global scheme of multi-targeted norms.

A related condition for the success of any system of targeted minority rights is that we find a way of integrating short-term security concerns with long-term goals of justice. The harsh reality is that social and political factors that enabled the (uneven) adoption of liberal multiculturalism in the West are not present in much of the world. It is important therefore to distinguish what is feasible in the short-term from what is desirable in the long-term. The efforts of IOs to date have failed in this task, veering between naïve optimism and paralyzing pessimism. Initial attempts by European organizations to formulate a right to autonomy for national minorities articulated the logic of liberal multiculturalism as it has developed in the West, but were clearly unrealistic and potentially dangerous in the immediate context of post-communist transition. The norms ultimately adopted by these organizations, by contrast, are highly sensitive to the immediate risks of ethnic conflict, but have abandoned any attempt to clarify or promote the logic of liberal-democratic multicultural justice.

Is there some way to integrate, or sequence, these concerns? One option is to draw upon ideas of "progressive implementation" that have arisen in the broader human rights field in relation to social rights. It has long been recognized that some of the social rights listed in the International Covenant on Economic, Social and Cultural Rights cannot immediately be implemented by poorer countries (e.g., access to free university education). So it is common to distinguish those social rights that should be immediately and universally applied from those that we seek to achieve over time as the facilitating conditions are put in place. We can similarly imagine a theory of the progressive implementation of liberal multiculturalism, with different minority rights provisions kicking in as the underlying conditions are established.[22]

Unfortunately, we do not yet have a theory of the proper sequencing of liberal multiculturalism. Indeed, we don't have the empirical basis needed to construct such a theory. We simply don't know which preconditions are needed to enable the successful operation of different aspects of liberal multiculturalism.

For example, it is widely assumed that some level of democratic consolidation should be in place before countries experiment with models of TA. But that is not clear. Consider the Spanish case. After the death of Franco, there was widespread agreement that the state needed to be both democratized and federalized. But there was intense debate about the proper sequencing of these two tasks. Many democratic reformers argued that priority should be given to democratic consolidation, and only after that was secure should federalization take place. Many academics at the time agreed with this view. In the end, however, the decision was made to democratize and federalize simultaneously. And virtually every commentator today believes that this was the right choice, and that democratic consolidation would not have taken place if federalization had not occurred at the same time.

Spain may be an exception, and the presence of the EU and NATO played an important role in ensuring this successful double transition. But some IOs are clearly hoping that a similar story will unfold in other countries, from Sudan to Iraq, where both the democratization and pluralization of the state are being undertaken simultaneously rather than sequentially. We know that democratic consolidation assists in the successful operation of liberal multiculturalism, and that the latter is likely to be unstable without the former. That much is clear. But it doesn't follow that democratic consolidation should *precede* the adoption of liberal multiculturalist policies. Indeed, the former may not be possible without the latter, in at least some cases. We simply don't know enough about the sequencing here to make generalizations at a global scale about how to engage in the progressive implementation of minority rights.

In any event, any attempt to formulate a sequencing strategy presupposes that we agree on the long-term goal. But IOs offer conflicting messages about whether TA for homeland minorities is or isn't a long-term goal. Western examples of self-government for national minorities and indigenous peoples are widely cited by IOs as best practices, and are applauded for the way they have enhanced the effective participation of minorities. On this view, TA is a valid long-term goal, even if it is not feasible in the short-term under conditions of insecurity. Yet, at the same time,

IOs have not only discouraged various minorities from claiming autonomy, but often stigmatized such claims as "radical" and condoned state constitutions that make the idea of autonomy unconstitutional even in the long run. On this view, TA may be needed as a temporary concession to belligerent minorities in post-conflict situations, but shouldn't be seen as a long-term goal. This mixed message reflects an underlying ambivalence about the ideals of liberal multiculturalism and its group-differentiated logic. There is obviously no prospect for developing a sequencing strategy so long as such profound disagreement remains, not only about the short-term means, but also about the long-term goals.

These two broad challenges of categories and sequencing are difficult and unresolved, to say the least. Given the relatively rudimentary level of the public debate and social scientific evidence on these issues, it seems unlikely that either of these challenges will be resolved in the foreseeable future. And indeed, I am not particularly optimistic about the likelihood of a breakthrough on either score. We may need to accept that this is as good as it gets.

If so, there are certainly grounds for supporting the current framework, and for welcoming its development over the past fifteen years. The best can be the enemy of the good, and the current framework has done some good in highlighting the plight of many minorities around the world, and in helping to legitimize minorities as political actors. It has helped make space at the table—both domestically and internationally—for ethnic minorities to peacefully and democratically voice their concerns and aspirations, while simultaneously encouraging these minorities to formulate their claims within the framework of human rights norms.

These are all significant accomplishments. My concern, however, is that the status quo is not only imperfect, but unstable. The multiple inconsistencies and ambiguities in the current framework are under pressure, and we will either have to level up or level down. Unless we can think of intellectually compelling and politically viable ways of strengthening existing norms, the likely outcome will be a retreat from the more progressive aspects of the current system. Indeed there is already evidence that this is taking place. And if so, the long-term prognosis for the peaceful global diffusion of liberal multiculturalism is poor indeed.

Will Kymlicka, Queens University, Kingston, Ontario

Notes

1. OSCE, Geneva Report, Chapter II, para. 3 (1991).

2. All of these movements were inspired by the desegregation movement of African-Americans. For the links between the African-American struggle and subsequent movements for minority rights in the West, see Kymlicka 2007: chap. 3.

3. E.g., the more radical wings of the "Black Power" movement, or the use of terrorist tactics by minority nationalist groups, such as the FLQ in Quebec or ETA in Spain.

4. Human Rights Committee, General Comment No. 23, "Rights of Minorities (Article 27)," adopted 8 April 1994, para 5.1 and 5.2.

5. In recent years, the Human Rights Committee has interpreted Article 27 to potentially require certain positive measures, particularly in relation to indigenous peoples. But these modest expansions in the scope of Article 27 do not address the positive claims underlying the conflicts in post-communist Europe.

6. These limitations are often listed in the reservations that countries have filed when ratifying the Convention (see http://www.coe.int/T/E/human_rights/minorities/).

7. E.g., the UN's Convention on the Protection of the Rights of All Migrant Workers, 1990, or the 1977 European Convention on the Legal Status of Migrant Workers.

8. For the draft resolution submitted to the General Assembly, see UN A/C.3/48/L.17. The Draft Convention is reprinted in Danspeckgruber 2002.

9. Hague Recommendations on Education Rights of National Minorities (1996); Oslo Recommendations on Linguistic Rights of National Minorities (1998); Lund Recommendations on Effective Participation of National Minorities (1999).

10. For the various failed efforts to strengthen the recognition of "stateless nations" in the European Constitution, see McCormick 2004.

11. This perception still exists in relation to some immigrant groups, particularly Muslim groups after 9/11. But it no longer applies to historic homeland groups.

12. For example, the Hungarian minorities in Romania and Slovakia have been subject to international pressure to abandon claims for autonomy.

13. The fact that national minorities in post-communist countries are not satisfied with the rights provided under existing European norms is sometimes taken as evidence of the illiberalism of their political culture, or the radicalism of their leadership. But no sizeable politically mobilized national minority in the West would be satisfied either. National minorities in Catalonia, Flanders, Quebec, Bern, South Tyrol, Aland Islands or Puerto Rico would also be unsatisfied with minority elementary schools but not mother-tongue universities, or bilingual street signs but not official language status, or local administration but not regional autonomy.

14. As Wheatley puts it, the Committee has "rejected the idea that there can be a strict taxonomy of the ethno-cultural groups recognized in international legal instruments" (Wheatley 2005: 10).

15. Security issues are not entirely absent. Since indigenous peoples often inhabit border areas, their land claims and self-government rights are sometimes seen as raising security issues even if they are not suspected of collaborating with neighbouring states.

16. For example, most regions of the world lack anything equivalent to the European Court of Human Rights or NATO to offer either human rights or geo-political security assurances.

17. Some commentators argue that Israel should be included as a European settler state, and hence that Palestinians fit the traditional definition of an indigenous people (e.g., Jamal 2005).

18. This label was not extended to groups brought by the colonizers, such as the Indian labourers whom the British took with them throughout the Empire. They were (and in some cases are still) viewed as "foreigners" or "immigrants", not "indigenous" (e.g., in Fiji).

19. According to Daes, attempts to distinguish long-distance settler colonialism from incorporation into states dominated by neighbouring societies rest on an "unjustified distinction" (Daes 1996: para. 63). Similarly, the African Commission's Working Group on Indigenous Populations/Communities stated that "Domination and colonisation has not exclusively been practised by white settlers and colonialists. In Africa, dominant groups have also after independence suppressed maginalized groups, and it is this sort of present-day internal suppression within African states that the contemporary African indigenous movement seeks to address" (Report of the African Commission's Working Group on Indigenous Populations/Communities, 2005, 92).

20. See the frank admission of the Chair of the UN's Working Group on Minorities: "The usefulness of a clear-cut distinction between minorities and indigenous peoples is debatable The distinction is probably much less useful for standard-setting concerning groups accommodation in Asia and Africa." (Eide 2000: para. 25).

21. The main exception is the 1999 report by Miguel Alfonso Martinez, the UN's Special Rapporteur on the rights of indigenous peoples. He insisted that the category of indigenous poeples should be limited to New World settler states, and that the situation of homeland minorities in Africa and Asia was conceptually and morally different from the plight of indigenous peoples under settler colonialism. Within the UN, however, this was a lone voice.

22. This was implicit in Liechtenstein's Draft Convention on Self-Determination through Self-Administration, which involved a sequence of rights: minorities start with Article 27-type rights to enjoy their culture, then move on to non-territorial forms of autonomy, and then to territorial autonomy, but only if they meet benchmarks of democracy and human rights along the way.

References

Aukerman, Miriam. 2000. "Definitions and Justifications: Minority and Indigenous Rights in a Central/East European Context," *Human Rights Quarterly* 22: 1011–150.

Barsh, Russel Lawrence. 1994. "Indigenous Peoples in the 1990s: From Object to Subject of International Law?," *Harvard Human Rights Journal* 7: 33–86.

Daes, Erica-Irene. 1996. "Working Paper on the Concept of 'Indigenous people'", prepared for the UN Working Group on Indigenous Populations (UN Doc. E/CN.4/Sub.2/AC.4/1996/2).

Danspeckgruber, Wolfgang (ed). 2002. *The Self-Determination of Peoples: Community, Nation, and State in an Interdependent World* (Lynne Reinner).

Eide, Asbjorn, and Erika-Irene Daes. 2000. "Working Paper on the Relationship and Distinction between the rights of persons belonging to minorities and those of indigenous peoples," prepared for the UN Sub-Commission on Promotion and Protection of Human Rights (UN Doc. E/CN.4/Sub.2/2000/10).

Evers, Pieter. 1995. "Preliminary Policy and Legal Questions about Recognizing Traditional Land in Indonesia," *Ekonesia* 3: 1–24.

Falk, Richard. 2000. *Human Rights Horizons: The Pursuit of Justice in a Globalizing World* (Routledge).

Jamal, Amal. 2005. "On the Morality of Arab Collective Rights in Israel," *Adalah Newsletter* 12 (April 2005) (www.adalah.org).

Kaufmann, Chaim. 1998. "When All Else Fails: Ethnic Population Transfers and Partitions in the Twentieth Century," *International Security* 23/2: 120–56.

Kingsbury, Benedict. 1998. "'Indigenous Peoples' in International Law: a Constructivist Approach to the Controversy," *American Journal of International Law* 92/3: 414–57.

Klimová-Alexander, Ilona. 2005. *The Romani Voice in World Politics: The United Nations and Non-State Actors* (Ashgate).

Kymlicka, Will. 2007. *Multicultural Odysseys: Navigating the New International Politics of Diversity* (Oxford University Press, forthcoming).

Lennox, Corinne. 2006. "The Changing International Protection Regimes for Minorities and Indigenous Peoples: Experiences from Latin America and Africa" (presented to Annual Conference of International Studies Association, San Diego, March 2006).

McCormick, Neil. 2004. "The European Constitutional Convention and the Stateless Nations," *International Relations* 18/3: 331–44

Moynihan, Daniel. 1993. *Pandaemonium: Ethnicity in International Affairs* (Oxford University Press).

Vermeersch, Peter. 2005. "Marginality, Advocacy and the Ambiguities of Multiculturalism: Notes on Romani Activism in Central Europe," *Identities* 12: 451–78.

Wheatley, Steven. 2005. *Democracy, Minorities and International Law* (Cambridge University Press).

Human Rights, Cultural Identity, and Democracy: The Case for Multicultural Citizenship

SHARON ANDERSON-GOLD

Abstract: This paper traces the evolution of the international concept of a human right to culture from a general and individual right of participation in the public life of a state (1966, Article 27 of the IC of Civil and Political Rights), to a group right to a cultural identity (1992 Declaration on the rights of persons belonging to national or ethnic, religious or linguistic minorities). I argue that the original generic formulation of the human right to culture reflected the nineteenth-century ideal of one-nation, one culture which had proved inadequate from the beginning even in Europe and wrecked havoc upon newly evolving nations in previously colonized territories. International Human Rights doctrine has had to evolve in response to the conflicts that have erupted within multi-ethnic states. In this paper I will consider and defend the argument of William Kymlicka that culture is a necessary context for the exercise of meaningful choices and therefore, within limits, deserves protection within liberal regimes. I argue that providing political support for cultural identities in the form of group rights need not imply a right of secession and can support a robust conception of multicultural citizenship. I analyze the philosophical significance of cultural identity for human dignity and democratic participation in multicultural contexts and conclude that group rights are neither "collectivist" nor "individualist" but a necessary and significant byproduct of the fundamental human right to free association.

I. Introduction

While human rights have become an accepted element of the international political landscape, the theoretical grounding of these rights is still a work in progress. Questions such as whether human rights are grounded in the needs of individuals or the interests of groups, whether they are essentially civil and political or social and economic, and whether they derive from the obligations of states or the inherent dignity of persons have been hotly debated. The dominant view of human rights has been individualistic in orientation, deriving from the needs of individuals for protections against the power of the state. In his classic work, *Universal Human Rights in Theory and Practice*, Jack Donnelly argues that the dominant view reflects the experience of the rise of the modern state in the west and presupposes the breakdown of the power of groups below the level of the state to provide adequate protection for the vital interests of individual persons.[1] Thus while the individualist view of human rights may have originated in the west, Donnelly argues that its universality is guaranteed by the global dominance of states in international affairs. Given this view of the state as the main provider of essential goods and protections, the drafters of the *Universal Declaration of Human Rights* focused initially on civil and political rights because these rights spell out the ways in which individuals participate in the shaping of state power so as to benefit from these provisions and protections. Civil and political rights properly guaranteed, some drafters argued, should lead to the satisfaction of the individual's social and economic needs. Others, particularly those from socialist countries, argued that human rights should directly guarantee social and economic goods and this division led to the splitting of the more comprehensive list into two *Covenants*, the *Covenant on Civil and Political Rights* and the *Covenant on Social, Economic and Cultural Rights*.

This paper analyzes the history and status of cultural rights, specifically the right to a cultural identity. Cultural rights are something of an anomaly in the universe of human rights as currently constructed because they do not fit neatly into the individualist framework within which human rights were originally conceived. I shall argue that because cultural rights require the recognition of the special role of groups in generating cultural identities, cultural rights imply protection of group identities that in certain circumstances must be provided with legal scope and content if cultural rights are to be meaningfully implemented. The first part of this paper will consider the changing history and evolving status of cultural rights as human rights. As initially formulated in the *Declaration of Human Rights*, cultural rights presupposed a unified cultural community. Subsequent attempts to articulate specific protections for religious, linguistic and other forms of cultural identity led to the increasing recognition that subgroups within the state have unique cultural identities which they have a right to preserve, culminating in the *1992 Declaration on the Rights of Persons Belonging to National or Ethnic, Religious or Linguistic Minorities*. With the recognition of the cultural rights of minorities, political theory must give up the assumption of a unified cultural community and therewith the identification of the state with a specific cultural identity. The second part of this paper will consider the relationships among the idea of a right to a cultural identity, democracy and group self-determination. Although cultural rights may at first appear to be anomalous from the individualist perspective, I shall argue that they are compatible with the liberal value of individual autonomy and are natural extensions of the view that human rights are protections from the oppressive powers of the state even as exercised by democratic majorities.

II. Brief History of the Idea of a Human Right to Culture

During the discussion preceding the adoption of the *UN Charter*, several Latin American states proposed the inclusion of cultural rights within the *Charter*. This discussion was part of the larger debate concerning the social character of human rights. However, the idea of social rights had several controversial consequences that led to their eventual separation from civil and political rights. Even as ideals to be promoted, social rights entail a more active role for the state as provider than Anglo-American participants found desirable, and the admission that some rights are inherently social appeared to require a stronger recognition of the role of groups in securing human rights than the prevailing individualist ideology of rights admitted.

Although the notion of cultural rights was not introduced into the *Charter*, cultural rights were mentioned in passing in the *Declaration on Human Rights* and tacked onto the title of the second *Covenant*. But even within the context of social rights, cultural rights have been viewed as a kind of poor cousin.[2] Until the 1990s when cultural rights were reborn as rights belonging to national minorities, cultural rights had not been given the type of attention and sustained analysis necessary to provide them with adequate scope and legal content. This I would argue is because, even more than social or economic rights, cultural rights challenge the view that the state is the sole provider of essential human goods and implies the existence of groups below the level of the state that contribute to a life of human dignity. When cultural rights were first mentioned in the *Declaration* they were given a generic formulation that was either too vague to commit the state to any recognition of group rights or that suggested culture was the product of a *collective national identity* that all citizens, despite their differences, had a "right" to participate in. The idea that the state is and should be co-extensive with a collective national identity has been under challenge in political theory[3] as a dangerous corollary of a "politics of identity." In light of the potentially destabilizing effects of this identification of the state with a majority culture, the concept of cultural rights requires both more specification and a more comprehensive theoretical justification.

The *Declaration on Human Rights* in Article 27 formulates 'the right to cultural participation' in broad terms: "Everyone has the right freely to participate in the cultural life of the community, to enjoy the arts and to share in scientific advancement and its benefits." This passive formulation of a general right to participation appears to assume a pre-existing unified cultural community created by an active cultural elite. Its precise legal content was left unclear. It is interesting to note that in the *International Covenant on Economic, Social and Cultural Rights* (1966), which was intended to provide further specification for the rights mentioned in the *Declaration*, Article 15 drops the reference to "the cultural life of the community" as a singular entity. Instead it states that: "The State Parties to the present Covenant recognize the right of everyone: (a) to take part in cultural life;" and this is followed by the usual general references to the enjoyment of the benefits of the arts and sciences. The language of this *Covenant* is looser because at the time Article 15 was drafted, concern was raised over the possibility of using the reference to "the community" restrictively *to exclude* any right of minorities to participate in their own independent cultural life.[4] In this respect Article 27 of the *International Covenant on Civil and Political Rights* is more specific and articulates the rights of "persons belonging to minorities to enjoy their own culture." However, in keeping with the individualistic theory of human rights underlying this document, the right to enjoy "one's own culture" is carefully constructed as the right of *persons* who belong to minorities—not as the right of groups as such to existence. The relationship between the rights of persons to participate in a minority culture and the existence of groups committed to the continuation of such cultures was not directly addressed and has had to be construed indirectly from decisions made by the *Human Rights Committee* on specific cases.

In commenting on complaints submitted to the *Human Rights Committee* under the *ICCPR's Optional Protocol*, the *Committee* has made it clear that the right of persons to enjoy their own culture is not the equivalent of the right of groups to national self-determination which has traditionally been interpreted to belong only to states. Nonetheless, in reviewing the case of *Kitok v. Sweden* (brought by an indigenous people), the *Committee* had to recognize that enjoyment of a particular culture may consist of a way of life that can only be protected if some form of group right to local control of territory and resources is granted.[5] Thus, while trying to carefully distinguish the right to "enjoy one's own culture" from full fledged political self-determination, the *Committee* had to come to terms with some form of group self-determination.

That this reference to minority culture appears in the *ICCPR* and not in the *ICESCR* is evidence that cultural rights have been predominately conceived as *extensions* of the exercise of other individually based rights, particularly civil and political rights. The connection of minority rights to civil rights entails the concept of non-discrimination, which is considered an essential component of what it means to be a "citizen" of a state. However, the concept of non-discrimination, traditionally interpreted to mean "equal treatment," fits uneasily with the notion of a right to a distinct cultural life insofar as members of distinct cultural groups must treat one another differently in order to perpetuate their group or cultural identity. If there is a right to enjoy a cultural identity, then in some respects persons must have a right to have that identity affirmed through differential treatment or what Will Kymlicka has called "differentiated citizenship."[6] This leads to another conceptual puzzle. Can there be discrimination in accordance with, rather than in opposition to, a "human right"?

In 1964 the *Convention on the Elimination of All Forms of Racial Discrimination* received wide ratification. The language of this Convention recognizes the possible positive application of discrimination, which by permitting differential treatment can in some circumstances lead to the greater realization of human rights. It states that special measures undertaken for the purpose of securing the advancement of racial/ethnic groups if such are necessary for the enjoyment or exercise of human rights "shall not be deemed racial discrimination."[7] In other words, the equal realization of human rights does not mean that everyone must be treated in the same manner. In some contexts the state may be obligated to undertake affirmative actions to secure the "advancement" of vulnerable groups. In providing support for vulnerable groups the state presupposes the existence of "cognizable" groups with distinctive identities. While "advancement" has assimilative connotations, there is an inchoate assumption that advancement, while desirable, ought not to be at the very expense of the identity of the group. UNESCO's *Declaration on Race and Racial Predjudice* (1978) sums this assumption up in Article 1: "All individuals and groups have the right to be different, to consider themselves as different and to be regarded as such."[8] Thus, the overall direction of declarations on minority rights has been to combine opportunities for advancement with preservation of cultural identities. The right to a cultural identity has also been indirectly supported by means of its relation to other general rights, such as the right to exercise one's own religion and the right to education in conjunction with the right to the use and preservation of one's native language. The 1960 *Convention Against Discrimination in Education* affirms the right of national minorities to their own educational activities, the maintenance of private schools, and the use or teaching of their own language. Article 29 of the *International Convention of the Rights of the Child* recognizes this conjunction of education and cultural identity when it provides that the education of the child shall be directed to "development of respect for the child's parents, his or her own cultural identity, language and values."[9]

This growing concern for specific measures to protect distinct cultural identities as a precondition for the implementation of cultural rights came to a head in the 1990s, partly in recognition of the role that cultural identity was playing in fueling conflicts in Eastern Europe. Measures for the protection of the cultural identity of minorities became explicitly formulated in a number of human rights instruments adopted by the Council of Europe and the Organization of Security and Co-operation in Europe. The *Concluding Document* of the OSCE (1990) enumerates a long list of specific rights, requires state parties to create conditions for their protection, and recommends various forms of local administration and autonomy for their implementation. The concept of cultural rights that was emerging in the 1990s, fueled by the problem of national minorities, was beginning to articulate the role of groups in securing cultural rights and the need for the recognition of some form of group self-determination. This movement toward the explicit recognition of the role of group self-determination in cultural rights culminated in the adoption by the General Assembly in 1992 of the *Declaration on the Rights of Persons Belonging to National or Ethnic, Religious or*

Linguistic Minorities which specifically obligates states to protect the existence and identity of minorities, broadly conceived, within their respective territories. The obligation to protect both the *identity and existence* of minorities goes beyond the usual focus on the personal rights of individuals. The *Declaration* also engages the state in duties of active assistance. Of particular relevance to the issue of self-determination, this *Declaration* affirms the right of persons belonging to minorities to participate effectively in decisions "concerning the minorities to which they belong."[10]

In the course of fifty-plus years of legal commentary on cultural rights, many distinct political events have influenced the evolution of this concept. Can this complex political accommodation of individual and group rights into a single legal framework be provided with a coherent philosophical basis? Perhaps no one has done more to argue for the compatibility of certain types of group or collective rights with liberal individual values and democratic principles than Will Kymlicka. In *Liberalism, Community and Culture*, Kymlicka argues that cultural membership should be viewed as a primary good because it is membership in a cultural community that provides a context for choice. The range of choices available to individuals is never open-ended but is rather determined by cultural histories and narratives. Choices become meaningful to individuals because they are embedded in such cultural contexts and in this way become aspects of personal "self-esteem." Kymlicka concludes that "membership in a cultural community may be a relevant criterion for distributing the benefits and burdens which are the concern of a liberal theory of justice" particularly "because the members of minority cultural communities may face particular kinds of disadvantages with respect to the good of cultural membership."[11] Since unjust disadvantages in the distribution of primary goods such as cultural identity require rectification, a liberal theory of justice may require the defense of minority rights. The liberal defense of "minority rights" then derives from two interrelated assumptions: first, that individual freedom is tied to membership in one's cultural group; and second, that group-specific rights can promote equality between minority and majority groups.[12]

III. Cultural Identity, Democracy, and Group Self-Determination

If individual freedom is tied to cultural groups, and if group-specific rights are necessary to promote equality between groups, then human rights will have a group dimension. The underlying question then is in what sense there is and ought to be a distinct human right to the identity of cultural groups. Are "group rights" an important addition to the human rights arsenal or an unnecessary proliferation? Jack Donnelly has argued that a cultural identity is not a good or a status that can be provided by the state and that while it can be attacked by the state, cultural identity can be adequately protected by already existing civil, political and cultural rights of individuals.[13] This argument assumes that if each individual were able to exercise his/her civil and political rights without either active interference or support on the part of others, cultural identities would be secured. Are cultural rights such that they can be exercised in this individual manner or are such rights better conceived as collective rights exercised in community with others? Just how community is to be understood here is important in that a cultural or ethnic group cannot be defined as a simple aggregate of individuals with overlapping interests. Cultural groups are historically constituted; they precede and "enculturate" members. Nor is a cultural group constituted simply by the attitudes and choices of its members. Part of the test of the existence of a cultural group includes the recognition of the distinctive characteristics of its members by non-members. Were there no cultural "other," culture could never appear as the constructed characteristic that it is.

The drafters of the various conventions touching upon the cultural rights of minorities have been rightly reluctant to define "minority" in terms of strict categories that could be used by the state in a restrictive fashion. The most widely cited definition comes from the 1979 report to the *Sub Commission on Prevention of Discrimination and Protection of Minorities* which stresses "a sense of solidarity, directed towards preserving their culture, traditions, religion, or language."[14] A sense of solidarity suggests a dynamic concern with the existence of the group whose distinctive characteristics are to be preserved. Drafters have also been rightly reluctant to settle the question as to whether minority rights such as that of cultural identity are vested primarily in individuals or groups. To vest a right primarily in a group may require procedures to identify who authoritatively speaks for a group. This may be difficult to do in a group where authority is widely distributed and/or may be wrongfully claimed and abused. Investing the group right in persons allows for greater procedural flexibility as any number of individuals can then bring suit on behalf of the group's interests. If the existence of cultural groups is necessary to the appropriation of cultural identity and if cultural identity is a significant element of personal autonomy and well being, then despite the procedural individualism implicit in human rights, cultural groups would appear to have a right to existence as a corollary of the right to cultural identity. Cultural identity entails the availability of and access to cultural goods, such as language, religion, rituals and artifacts that are produced in conjunction with particularly situated others. Because cultural identity cannot be exercised except in social context, concern for the protection of cultural identity has an irreducible group dimension.[15]

The right to a cultural identity then has emerged as a consequence of concern for the ability of minorities to preserve their distinctive characteristics as cultural groups. While the right to participate in cultural life was originally formulated as a universal human right, a right to a cultural identity conceived as a minority right is a special right belonging to groups numerically smaller than the majority. Does this mean that majorities do not have a right to a cultural identity? This would appear to be an absurd result since if each individual person has a human right to a cultural identity then the group right would not appear to be a consequence of "size." However strange, the conclusion that majorities have no legal right against the state for cultural protection historically derives from the deconstruction of the initial identification of the state with a unified people invested with a unique "right to self-determination" to develop their social, political and cultural life. Because the "right to self-determination" in international documents had originally been interpreted as a right to *political self-determination*, it has historically been regarded as a unique group-right which precludes the recognition of subgroups with any equally strong claims to self-determination or existence. Individual human rights then, including the right to culture, are theoretically enacted within this unique group-context. This positing of a unified culture, as we have seen in reviewing the evolution of the concept of cultural life, does not capture the requirements for the realization of a human right to cultural identity. The problem clearly stems from assuming that political self-determination must include *a unique cultural determination* and, therefore, that no grounds for other forms of group self-determination are present. This theoretical proposition denies the political reality that most states are multicultural[16] and that cultural identities influence the way in which citizens access and exercise their rights. Given this reality, political theory faces the challenge of articulating a criterion of national unity that does not depend upon the identification of the state with a specific cultural identity.[17]

Cultural groups, I have argued, are the basis for individual cultural identity. While this is no less true for the majority because majorities have historically been able to sustain their culture without special legal protections, or, as some might argue, because majorities benefit from the state's use of the majority culture as a source of national symbols, the concept of a legal "right" to a cultural identity has emerged as a minority right. Minority rights then are legal protections against majorities that tend to monopolize the power and resources of the state thereby making the reproduction of other practices difficult. In many cases minority rights allow for greater participation in the national culture by delimiting independent spaces for minority expression. In the normal course of majority rule, without legal protections, minority cultures are not likely to be able to "compete" for the resources needed to support their respective communities. But this is quite in keeping with the theory that human rights are protections against the potentially oppressive power of the state even as exercised by democratic majorities.

This brings us to the question of the relationship between human rights and democracy. According to Beetham in *Democracy and Human Rights*, democracy as a set of political institutions should not be thought of as the momentary expression of popular opinion. Rather, he maintains that democracy is the set of conditions that make popular control of government possible over time. Human rights are among those conditions that are necessary to the long term control of government. Cultural rights in particular are important in order to give definition to the concept of a "people." He argues that basic questions having to do with the construction of the political nation and the relation between the communities within it are not to be decided by majority vote, but only through dialogue and consensus. According to Beetham, legitimate majority rule can only come into play "once there is agreement about who constitutes the people among whom majorities are to count as binding, and within what limits."[18] Historically, majority rule has been justified by the principle of reciprocity, which assumes that those who lose on a given issue will have a chance to become part of a winning majority on other issues. However, this procedure becomes morally problematic in the context of multicultural and multinational states where party competition determining who constitutes the "people" and who is privileged within it often coincides with lines of cultural division. Where the minority is a permanent one, the principle of democratic reciprocity has no application. Under such conditions formal declarations of equality and non-discrimination do little to ensure recognition of or respect for minorities because without a guaranteed share in public office and political power, social, economic and cultural goods are not likely to be equitably distributed and preserved. It is not necessary to assume malicious intent to predict that the numeric power of majorities will tend to be used to protect their own interests if there are not procedures designed to ensure sharing in broadly based political, economic and social powers. It is in this spirit that "gerrymandering," used to create districts within which group interests are concentrated, has been historically used in the United States.

Liberal democratic theory based on individualist assumptions has had difficulty with the notion of permanent minorities and group identities.[19] The very notion of consent derived from contract theory has been treated in individualistic terms. As Vernon van Dyke argues in defense of the recognition of group rights, if a social contract were ever deliberately made, it would likely have been a contract among groups differing as to religion, language and culture, rather than among individuals.[20] Those making the contract would not have been speaking for themselves but for the interests of their communities. Such a contract would have reflected an awareness of heterogeneity rather than an assumption of homogeneity. It can be argued that the constitutional separation of church and state in the U.S. federal constitution resulted from the historical fact that many states had distinct religious identities and wished to secure themselves from future religious oppression.

In his search for theories of the state which acknowledge group rights, Van Dyke cites Lord Acton as favoring multinational states: "the coexistence of several nations under the same State is a test, as well as the best security of its freedom A State which is incompetent to satisfy different races condemns itself; a State which labors to neutralize, to absorb, or to expel them, destroys its own vitality."[21] He also notes in this context the "consocciationalism" of Arend Lijphart, who defines democracy in terms of such standards as the "concurrent majority" rule, the proportionality standard and local autonomy.[22]

If there is a right to cultural identity it must be some form of group self-determination below the level of political self-determination. The idea of self-determination achieved its greatest prominence when Woodrow Wilson championed it at the close of WWI. He championed it in part on behalf of nations that found themselves within the Austro-Hungarian Empire and in part on behalf of national minorities living in border regions. Though concerned primarily with Europe, Wilson gave the term a broad meaning and the world endorsed his stand. If well-constituted nations within multinational states have a right of self-determination along with minorities living in border regions, why don't more dispersed minorities living elsewhere? Because the right of self-determination of peoples as articulated in the UN Charter is perceived as affirming political self-determination and prohibiting interference with the internal affairs of constituted states, it is also seen as prohibiting secession. However, not only is the affirmation of cultural self-determination not an endorsement of a right of political secession, it can be an antidote to the types of frustrations and tensions that have led to secession and therefore as a principle which can stabilize and strengthen a multicultural state. While dispersed minorities who have immigrated voluntarily have a different set of claims than "national minorities" who have been incorporated by conquest or federation, the right to a cultural identity remains important as a basis from which immigrant minorities draw upon the cultural capital needed to participate in the larger multi-ethnic community. Modifications of existing institutional and educational structures may be needed to facilitate the inclusion of distinct ethnic groups into the mainstream society.

The right to cultural self-determination should be interpreted as included within the right to political self-determination and not as a conceptual contrary. Cultural self-determination is generally best achieved within a well-constituted state by means tailored to local needs and by appropriate representation in decisions directly affecting the continued viability of the cultural group. This is especially important in terms of the protection of indigenous groups whose identity is more clearly tied to control of their territory and to decisions that are made by the collective than is the case with many other cultural minorities.

IV. Conclusions

States are under obligations to respect human rights including the right of minorities to preserve their cultural identities. Are other groups and individuals also under such an obligation? Increasingly the answer is yes. International law binds nations, groups and individuals to its norms. If there is a right to a cultural identity and to self-determination with respect to one's cultural identity and development, then those aspiring to cultural self-determination must respect similar aspirations on the part of others and states must assure adequate representation in political processes to ensure that each group has the resources to promote cultural self-determination and development. As an international human right, the right to cultural self-determination may never be used as a means to deny any recognized human right to others (including personal rights to participate in group decision-making or to change one's affiliations)[23] and this entails that cultural development must in turn be compatible with basic human rights and cultural cooperation within a context of multiculturalism. As Kymlicka has so eloquently articulated it in *Multicultural Citizenship*, cultural rights are important as protections against external oppression and to equalize power between groups. They should not be conceived as licenses to coerce individuals within the cultural group.[24]

Without the recognition and observance of cultural rights, human dignity and human development may not be guaranteed, nor may other human rights be fully implemented. Without the recognition of cultural rights, and particularly the right to cultural identity as a citizen right, diversity cannot be respected and democratic societies may not function properly.

Sharon Anderson-Gold, Rensselaer Polytechnic Institute

Notes

1. Jack Donnelly, *Universal Human Rights in Theory and Practice* (Ithaca: Cornell University Press, 1989) 68–75.
2. Janusz Symonides, "Cultural Rights," *Human Rights: Concepts and Standards*, ed. Janusz Symonides (Dartmouth: Ashgate, 2000), chap. 5.
3. Paul Gilbert, *New Terrors, New Wars*, (Edinburgh: Edinburgh University Press, 2003), 62.
4. Janusz Symonides, "Cultural Rights," 183.
5. *Report of the Human Rights Committee*, 43rd Session, case no. 197/1985.
6. Will Kymlicka, *Multicultural Citizenship*, (Oxford: Clarendon Press, 1995), 174–6.
7. Vernon Van Dyke, *Human Rights, Ethnicity, and Discrimination*, (Westport: Greenwood Press, 1985), 84.
8. Janusz Symonides, "Cultural Rights," 189.
9. Ibid., 189.
10. Ibid., 205.
11. Will Kymlicka, *Liberalism, Community and Culture*, (Oxford: Clarendon Press, 1989), 162.
12. Will Kymlicka, *Multicultural Citizenship*, 52.
13. Jack Donnelly, *Universal Human Rights in Theory and Practice*, 158–9.

14. Hurst Hannum, "The Rights of Persons Belonging to Minorities" in *Human Rights: Concepts and Standards*, ed. Janusz Symonides (Dartmouth: Ashgate, 2000), 287.

15. While group rights are vested in individuals and groups do not exist independently of individuals, the objective of a group right is not simply to reproduce individual rights. The objective or aim of a group right, exercised by individuals, is the preservation of a group identity through the preservation of its cultural significations. The attempt to reduce this issue to ontology is a red herring.

16. In his 1972 article in *World Politics*, Walker Connor reports that only 12 (9.1 percent) of the world's states can be considered ethnically homogeneous. Another twenty-five states (18.9 percent) contain an ethnic group that accounts for 90 percent of the population. But in 31 states the largest ethnic group represents only 50–74 percent, and in thirty-nine cases (which is 30 percent of the world's total), the largest group is not even half. In fifty-three states which is 40 percent of the world's total the population is divided into more than five significant groups. Citation from Vernon Van Dyke, *Human Rights, Ethnicity, and Discrimination*, 199–200.

17. Paul Gilbert, *New Terrors, New Wars*, Gilbert argues that many contemporary conflicts stem from a "politics of identity" that seeks to create antagonistic identities to undermine and challenge existing states and the international order that sustains them. He argues that states are better served by rejecting any identification of their sovereignity with such identities.

18. David Beetham, *Democracy and Human Rights* (Oxford: Blackwell, 2000), 113.

19. Kymlicka in *Multicultural Citizenship* argues that this was not always so and derives from the historic failures and abuses of the system set up by the League of Nations to protect national minorities existing within established states.

20. Recognition of religious differences played a key role in the constitutional separation of Church and State in the U.S. Constitution. While racial differences were not clearly constitutionally articulated the legal status of non white persons indicated that they were not considered active participants in the constitutional contract.

21. Vernon Van Dyke, *Human Rights, Ethnicity, and Discrimination*, 202.

22. Ibid., 203–4.

23. This compatibility requirement that cultural rights not conflict with human rights, while clearly in the spirit of the liberal tradition, does not mean that the structures within the culture that provide participation be exactly those adopted by the major cultural communities and dominant political societies. How to define compatibility is of course a complex issue best left up to the collective wisdom of the international community.

24. Will Kymlicka, *Multicultural Citizenship*, 35–44.

Culture and Immigration: A Case for Exclusion?

Alex Sager

Abstract: A number of prominent political philosophers, including Will Kymlicka and Joseph Carens, have suggested that one reason for limiting immigration is to protect culture, particularly what Kymlicka calls "societal culture": "a territorially-concentrated culture, centered on a shared language which is used in a wide range of societal institutions, in both public and private life (schools, media, law, economy, government, etc.)." I situate this claim in the context of liberal nation-building and suggest that the arguments for the protection of culture are often vague, confused or tend to conflict with liberal commitments. When clear, they gain their plausibility from other concerns (e.g., self-defense), not cultural protection. Finally, given plausible empirical assumptions, the dangers to societal culture are considerably exaggerated and provide little reason for preventing immigration. I then briefly consider the case of general culture and whether there are some grounds to limit immigration to protect it, using the example of Iceland and aboriginal cultures to situate my arguments. Once again, I conclude that the appeal to culture to limit immigration is weak and philosophers searching for arguments against open borders should turn elsewhere.

I. Introduction

I want to question a claim about the admission of potential immigrants that one often hears in the media, as well as from public figures and political philosophers.[1] The claim is that immigration policy ought to protect culture. It is not always clear what this means (should we restrict the number of immigrants admitted, select immigrants using criteria supposedly picking out cultural similarity, encourage and perhaps demand assimilation, etc.?), but the right to protect culture from certain types of change is often considered a straightforward ground for limiting immigration.

In fact, one of the most prominent defenders of (relatively) open borders, Joseph Carens, appears to accept the right to protect culture. Carens suggests that there is a preliminary case for exclusion "for the sake of preserving a cultural tradition and a way of life."[2] He is particularly concerned with relatively homogenous states—he uses Japan[3] and aboriginal groups as examples. Will Kymlicka makes a similar claim, arguing that "some limits on immigration can be justified if we recognize that liberal states exist, not only to protect standard rights and opportunities of individuals, but also to protect people's cultural membership."[4]

I want to assess this purported right. I situate immigration policy in a larger nation-building project and attempt to determine if it is compatible with widely held liberal principles. I conclude that the right to protect culture is weak grounds for limiting immigrant admissions and often reflects other motivations. Philosophers looking to justify sovereign control over borders should examine other, more plausible arguments.[5]

II. Culture, Nation-Building, and Immigration Policy

Immigration policy, from the perspective of the nation-state, is a tool for nation building.[6] Nation building, for my purposes, is the political attempt to shape national identity through policy, the construction of institutions and the use of public discourse (among other things). States typically view immigration policy as falling under their right to self-determination and use it to pursue economic, social, and cultural goals. They recruit immigrants to fill jobs and provide services, combat declining demographics, and reinforce national self-conceptions.[7] This is often explicit, with heated debates on the economic and cultural impact of immigration.[8]

Nation building, with respect to immigration, employs two main tactics. The first involves admission policy. States decide who gets in and on what basis. They set the ground rules for permanent residence (if any) and requirements for citizenship. These are done with clear goals in mind. Most explicitly, Israel's law of return (along with considerable obstacles for non-Jews wanting to immigrate) constructs a Jewish state. But even Canada's point system, which doesn't openly involve an ethnic component, has a clear goal in mind, namely the attraction of educated professionals who speak English and/or French. It is commonly believed that these people will be more likely to integrate and contribute to the economy.

The second tactic aims at shaping people who have already arrived. Besides having to adapt to a coercive legal regime, new immigrants usually must learn or perfect the official language, send their children to schools with standardized curricula, absorb a barrage of public media and symbols, and so on. This is true in states that have significant multicultural policies. Minority cultures, for the most part, are expected to pursue their goals within the larger, national setting.

Much has been said about how a state can treat minority groups who already have residence and I won't add to the debate here. Though these two issues are closely connected—migration leads to the formation of ethnic groups—I want to separate them. Unless we accept a particularly radical form of moral cosmopolitanism, there are differences between how we must treat people who are already members of our community and how we must treat strangers. So the question becomes, can we use our purported right to protect our culture to deny potential immigrants?

Once we understand immigration policy in the context of nation building, this becomes a question about what methods a liberal state can employ for nationalist ends. Historically, nation states have used a variety of methods, sometimes coercive (e.g., forced assimilation), sometimes persuasive to build national identity (e.g., providing free language classes). As Kymlicka and others have rightly emphasized, no state can remain entirely neutral. Liberalism, itself, is a substantial doctrine that conflicts with other views. Public education necessarily favors certain languages and histories. Certain public symbols will take prominence. It is hard to see how to avoid this, even if it were desirable. Some nation building is necessary.

How, then, should we view the right to protect culture within the context of nation building? If nation building is to be consistent with a liberal state, it must respect basic, liberal principles. These include the principle of autonomy, guaranteeing that every citizen can choose her own reasonable conception of the good. It also includes a commitment to moral equality and tolerance. Liberal states also uphold basic rights and freedoms, including freedom of conscience, speech, free movement within the state, the rule of law and democratic institutions. Finally, most liberals take pluralism to be basic to contemporary states: reasonable people disagree about substantial moral and ethical issues.[9] We need to determine if an immigration policy aimed at excluding people on cultural grounds can respect these principles, rights and freedoms.

III. The Right to Protect Culture

Before proceeding, we need to become clear on the meaning of culture. For our purposes, there are two ways of understanding culture, general and societal. Anthropologists differ on how to define what I am calling general culture, their definitions including reference to traditions, customs, behavior, ideas, values and artifacts, sometimes systematic, sometimes not. Societal—sometimes called public or political—culture is somewhat more straightforward. Following Kymlicka, we can define a societal culture as:

> a territorially-concentrated culture, centered on a shared language which is used in a wide range of societal institutions, in both public and private life (schools, media, law, economy, government, etc.). I call it a societal culture to emphasize that it involves a common language and social institutions, rather than common religious beliefs, family customs, or personal lifestyles. Societal cultures within a modern liberal democracy are inevitably pluralistic, containing Christians as well as Muslims, Jews, and atheists; heterosexuals as well as gays; urban professionals as well as rural farmers; conservatives as well as socialists.[10]

Political philosophers are more likely to defend the right to protect societal rather than general culture. There are a number of reasons for this. First, they recognize that cultures change, that they are products of past and present interaction between cultures. Every culture is multicultural in important ways, something that is particularly evident in the present era of cultural globalization.[11] Often, internal differences within cultures, at least in large states, vary more than differences between cultures. This raises the difficult question: *exactly what is being protected?* Second, given historical racism in the immigration policy of countries like Canada, Australia and the United States against Asians, blacks and other groups, liberal philosophers are aware that sometimes the desire to protect "culture" is simply a publicly acceptable way of referring to race. Third, liberals recognize moral equality among all human beings and accept that we shouldn't be penalized for involuntarily acquired disadvantages. But significant parts of our culture are acquired involuntarily, so discriminating on grounds of "cultural similarity" appears dubious. Liberals are more comfortable simply limiting the number of new arrivals, rather than making qualitative discriminations.

Leaving aside general culture for the moment, does immigration threaten societal culture, particularly the language of the majority and social institutions? This argument is often raised against the possibility of open borders. For example, Kymlicka writes, "Open borders would also make it more likely that people's own national community would be overrun by settlers from other cultures, and that they would be unable to ensure their survival as a distinct national culture."[12] The idea is that if borders were open, it would trigger mass migration from poorer, unstable regions to more prosperous areas. If this migration were sufficiently massive, it could strain institutions until they break. If it were sufficiently homogeneous, it could change the language of majority.

Let's consider this argument, which is quantitative: it's not the culture of individual immigrants, it's their sheer number that threaten societal culture. Mass migrations, when not imperialistic or belligerent, involve considerable burdens, particularly with refugee flows. But it's hard to argue that even huge refugee flows generally threaten the societal culture.[13] Nationalists might argue that states aren't obligated to provide for large groups of refugees (and, indeed, there is a strong case for more international cooperation, given that the majority of the burden rests on poorer bordering states like Pakistan, Iran, Chad, Uganda, Kenya, etc.). But considerable burdens, even large enough to be reasonably rejected, don't amount to the claim that the societal culture is being threatened.[14]

Surely, one might argue, there exists a point where this breaks down. For example, if migrants outnumbered the original population over a short period of time, it's hard to see how they could be integrated. There would be housing shortages, administrative backlogs and perhaps unemployment (though it's doubtful that immigrants would continue coming once they learn the job market is saturated).

We might be particularly concerned if our social institutions provide a generous social security net. It is commonly believed that open borders and a welfare state can't coexist. In countries where health care is already strained, schools lack teachers and pensions are endangered, aren't more people the last thing we need?[15]

What is notable about this argument is that it rests on an empirical claim: massive immigration will undermine these institutions. This is not obvious. There is a considerable danger of using immigrants as scapegoats for all of society's ills. Irresponsible media evoke hoards of greedy migrants eager to receive welfare and destroy already fragile public institutions.[16] In some areas, for example public education, they may initially consume more resources, but this is likely to be temporary. Most immigrants want to work, pay taxes, learn the official language and be good citizens. Once again, immigrants may, at least initially, be a burden. Perhaps we're not obligated to assume this burden, but we shouldn't pretend that this is a real threat to our societal culture.

Perhaps there is a point where massive immigration would simply overwhelm any hope of an orderly society. Once again, what's notable is this isn't really an argument for protecting one's societal culture, in terms of language and institutions. If migration truly causes chaos—and it has been shown that even mass displacement due to natural disasters or ethnic cleansing can be managed with sufficient resources and care—then what's really at stake is a Hobbesian right to self-defense. But if we make the plausible assumptions that most migrants want work, a better life for their family and increased security, and that their attitudes toward the host society are mostly favorable, it's doubtful that this will result.[17]

It is sometimes argued that the case of Mexican immigration to the U.S. is different in kind. While I am skeptical about a genuine threat to U.S. societal or general culture from Mexican immigration, recent debates make it worth discussing. Perhaps one difference is that Texas, California, Nevada and Utah, along with parts of Colorado, Arizona, New Mexico and Wyoming, belonged to Mexico prior to the Treaty of Guadalupe Hidalgo (1848, following the Mexican-American war). Much has been made about the Mexican "reconquest" of the Southwest. Samuel Huntington has argued this cultural claim most bluntly in his Foreign Policy article "The Hispanic Challenge" from his book *Who We Are?* He writes, "Mexican immigration looms as a unique and disturbing challenge to our cultural integrity, our national identity, and potentially to our future as a country."[18]

According to Huntington, Mexican immigration threatens to transform the U.S. from "an Anglo-Protestant culture" to a Hispanic-Catholic culture, since Mexicans are not willing to assimilate. This raises a number of questions, among them whether the U.S. is truly an Anglo-Protestant culture (and what this means).[19] Furthermore, Huntington's claim that the U.S. has an Anglo-Protestant culture isn't so much an empirical observation as a normative description. He writes, "Key elements of that culture include the English language; Christianity; religious commitment; English concepts of the rule of law, including the responsibility of rulers and the rights of individuals; and dissenting Protestant values of individualism, the work ethic, and the belief that humans have the ability and the duty to try to create a heaven on earth, a 'city on a hill.'"[20]

Despite the large number of Spanish speakers in the U.S., it is doubtful that the continued, often undocumented migration of Mexicans and other Hispanics to the United States undermines the societal culture. It is unclear why Huntington thinks Mexicans don't believe in rule of law or individual rights, reject Christianity (indeed, many *Protestant* churches offer mass in Spanish!) or the work ethic, and aren't pursuing some variation on the "American Dream." Unlike the case of Quebec in Canada, Scotland in the United Kingdom or the Basque in Spain, there is no serious Hispanic secession movement. Few Hispanic immigrants want the Southwest to become part of Mexico—they come to work in the U.S., not reclaim it for Mexico. Furthermore, the 2000 U.S. Census brief reported that out of the 28,101,052 people who spoke Spanish at home, 14,349,796 spoke English very well and another 5,819,408 spoke English well (72 percent in total). Only 2,801,448 didn't speak English at all (about 1 percent). Admittedly, there are some cities and regions with a very high concentration of Spanish speakers (New Mexico has around 43 percent, while California, Texas and Arizona have around 30 percent), but it's not clear how this poses a realistic threat to the U.S. societal culture.[21] As with other immigrant groups, most second-generation Spanish speakers are fluent in English, even if they continue to speak Spanish at home. English remains the dominant language in the U.S. Whatever one makes of the current controversy around the US-Mexico border, the claim that Hispanics threaten US cultural identity is mostly hysteria.

Hispanic immigration in the United States doesn't pose major threats to U.S. culture, but there is an issue that I have so far avoided, which is the case of minority nations. As nationalists are aware, one common means of eliminating minority nations has been to encourage mass immigration, swamping the minority and taking over their institutions. Chinese migration to Tibet is a pertinent contemporary example of this. However, if migrants come with the goal of overrunning the original population, replacing their institutions and marginalizing them, it would be odd to claim that the issue is the right to protect one's societal culture. Rather, it is the right to defend against aggression.

Maybe I'm being unfair to minority nationalists and there are grounds for protecting their societal culture, even from peaceful migrants. After all, one of the main pillars of Kymlicka's societal culture is language. Let's imagine an imaginary case where a relatively homogenous minority culture with one language (let's say they speak Esperanto) exists within a larger state. Until recently, there has been little migration, due to the fact that the region is isolated and relatively barren. Huge oil reserves trigger a massive migration of people from the majority culture, people who speak a different language (Klingonese). Long time residents find that when they go to the supermarket, they can't understand many of their fellow shoppers. The Klingons request services in Klingonese, form Klingon enclaves and soon there are areas where it is difficult to find fluent Esperanto speakers.

There may be considerable ill will towards the Klingons. Right-wing politicians will probably make speeches on how these people come to our land and refuse to learn Esperanto. Journalists will point out the strains on the school system unequipped to teach Esperanto as a second language, as well as the demands the Klingons have for schools in their native language. They'll note that the health care system doesn't have the resources to attend to people who can't communicate in Esperanto. There will probably be references to the strange customs of the Klingons and perhaps the suggestion that Klingon culture embraces fundamentally different values (though this will probably be exaggerated).

Now, does this necessarily undermine *societal* culture if the language of the original population is still used in government? Keep in mind that the Klingons share a good deal of the societal culture or are willing to adapt to it, since they support the main institutions. Any campaigns for privileges are undertaken democratically. Klingon leaders acknowledge the need to learn Esperanto, though they also want to preserve their own language and customs. Maybe somewhere down the line Klingonese will become a second official language, due to the large Klingon population. But if the major institutions are effectively bilingual, has the societal culture really been threatened? Remember, according to Kymlicka, a societal culture is "a territorially-concentrated culture, centered on a shared language which is used in a wide range of societal institutions, in both public and private life."

To return to a real world example, consider the case of Anglophones in Montreal, who have access to government services in English, neighborhoods where one really doesn't need to know French and a major English newspaper. Despite the large number of Francophones and Allophones, they're perfectly capable of accessing their societal culture. Nationalists are fond of pointing out that violent attempts to assimilate minority groups have largely failed. People are extremely unlikely to give up their culture, societal or otherwise. If they have official, institutional support, it would seem that they would be even stronger, something which reflects the status of English in the U.S. (even in Florida and California) and Quebec.

It is also important to keep in mind that admission policy is combined with integration policy. Take the U.S. case. As has happened with other immigrant groups that formerly "threatened" the U.S. societal culture[22] (e.g., the Germans, Scandinavians, Irish, Italians, Chinese, etc.), the children of migrants learn English and integrate into mainstream institutions. Immigration policy—especially in developed states with a history of migration—actively promotes a certain societal culture. *States coercively enforce their societal culture.* I am not suggesting this is necessarily problematic (or unproblematic, for that matter), but any sensible and just migration policy will implement efforts to integrate people, to provide language classes, cultural and social orientation. Immigrants are expected to adapt to the main social institutions—we require them to obey the law and send their children to recognized schools. We also encourage them to learn the language and exclude them if they don't (e.g., not speaking the native language severely restricts employment opportunities and may pose a barrier to receiving citizenship). Few immigrants protest this, though they often encounter obstacles, whether it's the challenge of learning a language while working full-time or systematic discrimination in the labor market.[23]

I think there is an argument here for granting the Esperanto speakers (and similar minority nations) control over its integration policy. Of course, the Esperanto speakers will also have to accommodate the Klingons—integration is a two-way street. But the claim that they can exclude Klingons to protect their societal culture—mainly their language—isn't very plausible. Maybe there are other grounds for exclusion, but it's an exaggeration to claim that societal culture is actually endangered.

So far I have discussed migrants who may not share exactly the same society culture, particularly language, but aren't opposed to it. What about people who have radically different values? Consider the case of what I call *democratic extremists*. Democratic extremists oppose liberal values—perhaps they are what Rawls calls *decent hierarchical peoples* in the *Law of Peoples*. Perhaps they don't believe men and women are equal and demand that religion plays a central role in the state. We can imagine them arguing that certain liberal values, such as freedom of conscience and speech, reflect Westernized, imperial values. Despite these views, they agree to respect the state's laws and use democratic means to achieve desired changes. Can we exclude democratic extremists, given that they directly and deliberately challenge our societal culture?

Is this permissible, on liberal grounds? If they're a small group, it's doubtful these democratic extremists pose a significant challenge to liberal societal cultures. Groups like the Mennonites, Amish, Hutterites and Mormon fundamentalists exist in largely closed communities in larger liberal states. Whatever we think about these groups, they certainly don't challenge the states' liberal character. To make the case more challenging, let's assume that democratic extremists, as I'm defining them, don't want to segregate themselves: they want to convince the rest of us that they're right. For our purposes, let's assume that they come in sufficient numbers that they have a realistic chance in doing so.

The first thing to note is that liberal principles ironically support the admittance of democratic extremists. First, liberals need to tolerate rival points of view, as long as their advocates respect the rights of others. Second, freedom of conscience and speech protect democratic extremists. Third, liberals leave open how we exercise our autonomy. It is perfectly consistent for liberals to adopt a traditional lifestyle (assuming they haven't been indoctrinated or otherwise coerced—something admittedly difficult to determine), if they so choose. This leads to a rather paradoxical result: if we try to exclude democratic extremists on liberal grounds, we're arguably making an illiberal decision.

Leaving this aside, democratic extremists are committed to at least *part* of our societal culture, respect for democratic institutions and rule of law. We might hope that democratic extremists would come to see the advantages of liberalism, particularly its advocacy of freedom and toleration. Maybe they would agree to something like a Rawlsian overlapping consensus: many of them would remain traditional, with religion playing a strong role in their lives, since a liberal political system allows for this. After all, people with highly conservative religious views are hardly uncommon in liberal states, but they certainly don't threaten the liberal societal culture. There are lively debates in liberal states about a woman's right to abortion,[24] gay rights and/or marriage, and the role of religion in the public sphere. It isn't clear why the majority should be allowed to exclude people with a different point of view. It disrespects their own minority groups.

Furthermore, if we decide not to admit democratic extremists, I wonder if we're not conceding too much to authoritarian views. One might hope that liberal values aren't simply our idiosyncratic preference, something that cannot be rationally defended. Perhaps the democratic extremists might convert some people, but it is at least as likely that we would convert them (especially over a generation or two). Take the example of Muslim communities in North America and Europe. Certainly there are some individuals who may fit the label of democratic extremists, wanting to reproduce their culture within the large state. The vast majority, however, consider their religious and personal commitments to be perfectly compatible with liberalism. Beyond that, many integrate into the mainstream societal culture. Perhaps societal cultures and liberalism aren't as fragile as sometimes suggested.

Let's reverse the case, with a large group of liberals immigrating to an authoritarian societal culture. Typically, authoritarian governments monopolize the media, limit free speech and crush opposition political parties. Here there is a real threat to the societal culture and the state needs violence and oppression to maintain the status quo. It's not so clear that the same holds when democratic extremists enter liberal states. Part of the advantage is that liberal states enjoy real and perceived legitimacy, with the vast majority willing to work within the system for change. This alone supports the continued existence of the societal culture.

So far I have argued that the right to protect societal culture has considerably less force than often thought. In fact, given a reasonable integration policy and empirical assumptions about the motives of immigrants, it's not clear that our need to protect societal culture provides any grounds for exclusion. Next, I will briefly examine whether the right to protect general culture is any stronger.

IV. General Culture

As mentioned above, we can define general culture as the set of beliefs, attitudes, practices, traditions, customs, behavior, ideas, values, food and artifacts of a human community. Unfortunately, as Bhikhu Parekh writes, "When used *sans phrase* culture encompasses more or less the whole of human life."[25] At the same time, an attempt to find a narrower definition is artificial. The desire to protect general culture generally involves an amorphous notion, where specific details take disproportionate significance. Actual cultures are dynamic, evolving, porous phenomena, characterized by interaction, not isolation.

We need to figure out exactly why we might think that migrants threaten general culture. Migrants certainly have some effect on the majority culture, but it's not obvious that this is more significant than international media, technological and economic change and natural cultural evolution. Nations like Quebec and Japan have changed enormously over the last 50 or 60 years, but very little of this change can be responsibly attributed to immigration.[26] Furthermore, we criticize states that censor foreign media and few, if any, liberals believe that we can prevent our citizens access to the rest of the world in order to preserve our culture.

Still, two options present themselves: We might object to the *rate* of cultural change or the *type* of cultural change. First, we might worry that our culture is changing too rapidly and that people are unable to adapt to the changes. Second, we might believe that the culture is changing for the worse, because some cultures are better *for some people* than others.

As I mentioned above, liberals might be initially worried about an attempt to protect general culture. What is immediately worrying about the desire to protect culture is that it is often thinly disguised racism (and classism).[27] "Culture," in what is sometimes referred to as democratic racism, has become a synonym for race.[28] Historically, "countries of immigration" like Canada, Australia and the United States forcefully excluded Asian and black migrants, using "culture" as one of the grounds for exclusion.[29] Until the 1960s, U.S., Canadian and Australian immigration policies were explicitly Eurocentric, aimed at attracting white, European immigrants.

A liberal state cannot endorse racist principles, because—among other things—it violates liberal equality. But isn't it possible to use culture in a non-racist way? After all, we don't think it's racist to celebrate cultures, including minority cultures. Can't a liberal state say, "We're not claiming other cultures are inferior. In fact, we recognize that they're perfectly wonderful for the people who share them. We simply want to maintain *our* culture. This involves limiting immigration and perhaps selecting people with particularly close historical and linguistic ties." There are plenty of examples of immigration policy favoring people from ex-colonies, as well as giving priority to people considered to share ethnicity. Maybe these could be used as a model.

I suppose we could test whether the policy is racist. For example, if Brits admitted Jamaicans over Germans and the French admitted Algerians over Australians citing linguistic and historical ties, we might suspect that this reflects culture, not race. Even so, this shows how dubious this project is. What exactly is it that defines cultural similarities? Language? Are the Quebecois, then, culturally closer to people from the Côte d'Ivoire than to Anglophone Canadians? This is unlikely, though they may be *in some respects*. The term culture is problematically vague. Of course vagueness isn't always an objection—plenty of concepts are vague, but perfectly useful. But we generally know how to employ vague but useful concepts (e.g., there are few cases where we are unsure whether something is a heap or a crowd). This isn't the case with culture.

I think the relevant test is this: can we make our policy acceptable to someone from outside our culture who wants admission? Iceland is an interesting case, with its low population, around 300,000, with about 20,000 born outside of the country. It's not homogenous and actually has a significant percentage of foreign born population (about 7 percent compared to around 18 percent in a country of immigration such as Canada). Still, we can assume there is more cultural homogeneity than a country like Australia. Now imagine we say something like, "Icelanders should accept people from Denmark because we share similar cultures, but not Chinese or Afghanis due to their differences."

The potential Chinese immigrant might question this argument. She realizes that Iceland won't admit her because of her *culture* and not on other grounds. She tries to determine exactly what it is about her culture that's different and is told that she doesn't speak the language. Really wanting to live in Iceland, she learns Icelandic. Next, she's told that they have different customs. Determined to adapt, she studies the culture, learns its history, its etiquette and does her best to adopt it.[30] The Icelanders applaud her effort, but there is still something different about her—her accent is strong, her manners are just a little off, something about her remains Chinese. You need, they tell her, to be born in Iceland (or arrive at an early age) to fully belong.

At this point, our potential Chinese immigrant may grow frustrated. "Am I really threatening your culture?" she asks. "What evidence do you have that if I enter, you will really lose your language, have to change your customs, be cut off from your history? Even if many Chinese immigrate, we're not coming to colonize you. We realize that Iceland will change and that your culture probably won't remain the same, but we're prepared to learn your language, respect your traditions, abide by your laws and send our children to your schools.[31] Be honest: You Icelanders today don't simply survive by fishing; they engage in computer programming, biotechnology and eco-tourism. You listen to music in English and watch American and Chinese movies. Are you resisting cultural change or do you simply not like Chinese? We are Chinese, not from Denmark, but this is simply an accident of birth. How can you keep us out, regardless of our efforts, just because of where we're born?"

I think the Icelanders would be hard pressed to respond. I don't think they can show that Chinese immigration will necessarily change their access to their culture that much. They will be able to continue with their language and private activities as before, perhaps in an enriched form given the additional options the Chinese influx provides. The more reflective members will realize that culture is not simply something that a given group possesses. It's also a product of others' attributions—our culture is defined, in part, by what others think of us. They will worry that maybe their policy unintentionally reflects their prejudices. As well, Icelanders are liberals, so they'll be wary of discriminating against people simply because they're born in China.[32] Efforts to learn the language, history and customs considerably weaken their claim.[33]

Rather than attempting to establish a right to protect culture in (fairly) large, globalized nations, let me briefly present what I consider to be the strongest case. Imagine an aboriginal group living on an island with no contact with the outside world. This is truly a homogenous population with a distinct culture and cultural change proceeds at a much slower rate. If anybody has a right to prevent immigration to protect their culture, then these people do.

I am rather uneasy with this case, given its tragic history and too familiar present day consequences. As I mentioned above, history is filled with brutal examples of forced assimilation and genocide, particularly of aboriginal groups. Still, let me attempt to abstract from the reality of conquest and colonization and simplify the case. A group of pacifists want to migrate to the island. They don't want to displace the original inhabitants and their presence, for the most part, won't interfere with their livelihood. Furthermore, immigrants into the territory respect the community's rules and attempt to learn the language (though the first generation may do so somewhat unsuccessfully). The character of these pacifists helps narrow the cause of concern: the only risk to the group will be cultural change.

Now, predictably, immigration will alter the culture. Perhaps at first, the aboriginals and newcomers will keep to themselves, but eventually they will begin to trade. Technology will be incorporated. Some will become friends, others may start families. Languages will change, perhaps with some language or languages becoming dominant. We need to ask ourselves whether the *right to protect culture* is reason for these aboriginals to exclude the pacifists.

I should stress that I am simply discussing the right to protect culture. Groups will continue to have a right to resist forced assimilation and the appropriation of their natural resources, and a right to continue to enjoy self-determination and autonomy, including a form of self-government. It might be argued that access to one's cultural tradition is a necessary precondition for self-determination and autonomy. This is probably true in the case of aboriginal cultures which have been destroyed in a short period of time, usually by the threat of violence—the Ik come to mind here, as do Canadian First Nations and American Indians. But it's not clear why cultures that change as a result of dialogue, contact with other cultures and experimentation wouldn't be able to exercise full autonomy.[34]

Assuming that cultural change will not be coerced, what should we make of this example? First, there is a tendency to regret the loss of cultures themselves, not just what they mean to individuals (though this is part of it). Perhaps there is an analogy to biodiversity and the value we place in species. Even if we have little use for a species, we tend to think that it's a bad thing if it's exterminated. There is something compelling about this idea—we mourn the loss of many cultures. Still, the analogy breaks down. The rate of cultural change is far higher than biological evolution and is unavoidable. If we accept this argument, we would have reason to prevent internal cultural change. Thus, this argument, if successful, would give grounds for preserving a culture against the will of its members. Liberals can't accept this, even if they could make sense of it.

If we reject this argument, then the strongest reason these aboriginals have for preventing immigration is that they value their culture in its present state: they prefer their way of life and don't want it to change, at least not at the rate that immigration would spur. This poses a difficulty, given that in order to reach this decision, they ought to have some knowledge of what they are rejecting.[35] If their decision isn't simply based on ignorance or fear of strangers, it requires some knowledge of the outside world and its benefits (and harms). They need to know exactly what the change entails.

A well-informed aboriginal group would rightly be suspicious of strangers and their supposed gifts. They might well decide that the best way to prevent forced assimilation would be to altogether prevent strangers from inhabiting their territory. They might hold that they rightfully own their land and can decide who enters simply on those grounds. But would they argue that this decision expresses their right to protect their culture?

I believe that they could consistently argue this *only if they rejected other ways the outside world affects their culture*. If they borrow technology, entertainment, legal and social reform, telecommunications or other wonders of the modern world, they have considerably weakened their case. Their situation becomes much more like that of the Icelanders, and the right to protect culture ceases to be a strong ground for exclusion. They have a case for control over their institutions and integration policy, so they can continue to enjoy what they value about their culture. They have the right to protect themselves from belligerent colonizers. Perhaps they would make an informed decision to reject the outside world. In this case, they can also justifiably exclude immigrants. But this case is at best a rare one in today's world.

The use of exclusion to protect general culture is a dubious project, even if we can make sense of it. This isn't to invalidate more positive efforts to promote culture, perhaps through public funding and education. Forms of government—regional autonomy, for example—can be used for these purposes. Nationalists who want to preserve their culture should examine these alternatives. This leads us to questions about morally permissible means of minority integration. But I won't attempt to answer these here.

V. Conclusion

I have concluded that the right to protect culture, either societal or general, is a poor reason for excluding immigrants. In fact, *protecting* culture at all is a rather odd notion—we can trace most of what we value about cultures to migration, exchange, intermarriage and intermingling. Even—or especially—languages, the focal point of many nationalists, are a complex amalgamation of many tongues. Almost all of the things we value—art, law, technology, food, religion—have roots in other cultures, either contemporary or historical. In fact, the greatest danger to a culture is homogeneity; diversity allows us to adapt and thrive in a rapidly changing world. Of course, culture shouldn't be imposed on people. Forced assimilation, however common in the past, is morally unacceptable. But the attempt to protect culture, by excluding people and ideas, has many parallels with forced assimilation: it robs people of potential riches that they may wish to adopt.

Alex Sager, University of Calgary

Notes

1. I am grateful to Dennis McKerlie, Dave Mellows, and Kai Nielsen for detailed comments on drafts of this paper, as well as to the two anonymous referees for their helpful suggestions. I would also like to thank the participants of the North American Society for Social Philosophy.

2. Joseph Carens, "Migration and Morality: A Liberal Egalitarian Perspective," in *Free Movement*, ed. B. Barry and R. Goodin (University Park: PA: The Pennsylvania State Press, 1992), 40.

3. Though immigrants make up roughly 1 percent of Japan's population, including a long-term Korean minority, Japan also depends on a sizeable force of guest workers.

4. Will Kymlicka, *Multicultural Citizenship: A Liberal Theory of Minority Rights* (New York, NY: Oxford University Press, 1996), 125.

5. Throughout this paper, I remain neutral about the question of "open borders," forcefully put forward by Carens and others. My aim is to show that the right to protect culture isn't good grounds for limiting immigration. There may or may not be other grounds. Joseph Carens, "Aliens and Citizens: The Case for Open Borders," *Review of Politics* 49

(1987): 251–73. Philip Cole, *Philosophies of Exclusion* (Edinburgh: Edinburgh University Press, 2000).

6. Aristide R. Zolberg makes a compelling case for this, at least regarding the Unites States, in *A Nation by Design* (Cambridge, Mass: Harvard University Press, 2006), 11.

7. One example would be in favoring ethnic migrants abroad as in the case of Jews, Albanian Greeks, etc.

8. For example, one of the main objectives of *The Canadian Immigration and Refugee Act* is "to permit Canada to pursue the maximum social, *cultural* and economic benefits of immigration." (my emphasis)

9. John Rawls, *Political Liberalism* (New York: Columbia University Press, 1996).

10. Kymlicka states, "Such diversity is the inevitable result of the rights and freedoms guaranteed to liberal citizens, particularly when combined with an ethnically diverse population. This diversity, however, is balanced and constrained by linguistic and institutional cohesion; cohesion that has not emerged on its own, but rather is the result of deliberate state policies." Will Kymlicka, *Politics in the Vernacular* (New York, NY: Oxford University Press, 2001), 25. Societal culture is sometimes called "public culture," for example by Rawls and David Miller.

11. Beyond that, every individual is multicultural in many ways, with diverse loyalties and projects with many origins.

12. Kymlicka, *Politics in the Vernacular*, 215.

13. Of course, they generate considerable tensions and sometimes violence, especially if refugees end up competing for scarce resources. The fact that refugees are often restricted to squalid camps for years, wholly dependent on the UNHCR and its donors, generates its own set of problems—e.g., many of the Taliban emerged from the Pakistani refugee camps formed during the USSR invasion of Afghanistan. In the case of armed conflict, conflicts may spill over borders. But the problems have little to do with a "common language or societal institutions." It's an issue of extreme scarcity in states that are often unable to adequately provide for their own populations, along with the threat of violence.

Generally, refugees pose a special set of problems, and the main target of Kymlicka's arguments are so-called "economic" immigrants. Among these, the right to asylum—despite the increasing efforts of liberal states to curtail it—is well entrenched in international and state law. Most liberals accept the duty to provide asylum for those fleeing from persecution (though there are legal and moral debates about what this means).

14. I would argue that we do have obligations to assume considerable burdens given the sheer amount of misery in this world, but won't press this point here.

15. There is considerable empirical work on the economic effects of immigration, often ideologically charged. The general conclusion seems to be that immigration is, on the whole, good for the economy, and slightly bad for low-income workers. See Roger Lowenstein, *The New York Times Magazine*, "The Immigration Equation," July 9, 2006 for an account of some of the main, U.S. players in this debate: http://www.nytimes.com/2006/07/09/magazine/09IMM.html?ei=5090&en=8b2c5c0a2ceea8e0&ex=1310097600&partner=rssuserland&emc=rss&pagewanted=all (verified January 23, 2007).

16. See Thomas J. Espenshade and Gregory A. Huber, "Fiscal Impacts of Immigrants and the Shrinking Welfare State" in *The Handbook of International Migration: The American Experience*, ed. Charles Hirschman, Philip Kasinitz, and Josh De Wind (New York, NY: Russell Sage Foundation, 1999), 360–70 for references to some of the literature on the comparative use of social services of immigrants. This is a complicated area, fraught with methodological difficulties and ideological bias, where groups of immigrants and locals differ sharply in their impacts on different levels of government. Many of these studies are quite limited, focusing on impact in a specific area and not necessarily saying much about net costs and benefits. As well, the fiscal impact of immigration doesn't necessarily imply a moral point—e.g., the exclusion of immigrants if net costs exceed net benefits. Research, as well, suggests that part of the problem with the net earnings of immigrants can be traced to systematic discrimination, suggesting that host societies are at fault. See, e.g., Grace-Edward Galabuzi, *Canada's Economic Apartheid* (Toronto: Canadian Scholars' Press Inc, 2005). Needless to say, the issues are complex.

17. One of my referees pointed out the more general possibility that there are good economic reasons for thinking that immigration will be largely self-regulating, especially if the host country has strong institutions of private property. Chain migration, where new residents tell their families and friends to come, is a major factor in migratory flows and provides information about the job market. Once the capacity to absorb migrants is reached, people would stop coming or migrate to areas with greater opportunities (rates of emigration are less well known and more rarely reported, but circular or serial migration are common; a significant number of immigrants eventually return to their country of origin). The argument that immigrants would overwhelm a state neglects the possibility that migration would be, to a large extent, self-correcting.

18. Samuel Huntington, "The Hispanic Challenge," *Foreign Policy* (March/April 2004).

19. Britain, I suppose, is Anglo-Protestant (Anglican culture), but it isn't the United States, and for obvious historical reasons it is probably quite far apart on some grounds. We could ask why the emergence of a Hispanic-Catholic culture is a bad thing—will it really prevent Anglo-Protestants from continuing to enjoy their cultural goods? After all, are multinational states so bad—for example, Canada, Switzerland, and Belgium?

20. Huntington, "The Hispanic Challenge."

21. http://www.census.gov/prod/2003pubs/c2kbr-29.pdf (verified January 23, 2007).

22. This is generally meant as an Anglo-Saxon protestant culture, whether or not this accurately reflects U.S. demographics.

23. There are many questions about the justice of this integration process. For example: Are immigrant minorities entitled to funds to maintain their languages and customs? To what extent do our major institutions need to accommodate differences? I will not attempt to answer these here.

24. For example, what's remarkable about abortion debates in the United States is not that a few extremists blow up abortion clinics; it's that the majority of people who oppose abortion are committed to doing so through proper legal and political channels.

25. Parekh, Bhiku, *Rethinking Multiculturalism* (Cambridge, Mass: Harvard University Press, 2000).

26. I am using the word "nation" to refer to group of people who share a common identity, usually in terms of language, history, religion, ethnicity and/or culture (broadly speaking). As in the case of Quebec, not all nations have their own states.

27. Elspeth Guild gives a telling example from the UK Home Office. In a two week period, the home office issued a press release boasting about the high level of work permits issued (108,825), while at the same time praising its success in reducing the number of asylum applications by 11 percent. After all, the home office went on to say, most of the asylum seekers are "really" economic immigrants. This apparently contradictory attitude reflects class—only comparatively wealthy professionals are eligible for work permits—and also race. Elspeh Guild, "Cultural and Identity Security," in *International Migration and Security: Opportunities and Challenges*, ed. Elspeth Guild and Joanne van Selm (New York, NY: Routledge, 2005).

28. For a discussion of democratic racism, see Peter S. Li, *Destination Canada* (Oxford: Oxford University Press, 2003).

29. McKenzie King is often quoted here. "The policy of the government is to foster the growth of the population of Canada by the encouragement of immigration. The government will seek by legalization, regulation, and vigorous administration, to ensure the careful selection and permanent settlement of such numbers of immigrants as can advantageously be absorbed in our national economy .

> There will, I am sure, be general agreement with the view that the people of Canada do not wish, as a result of mass immigration, to make a fundamental alteration in the character of the population. Large-scale immigration from the orient would change the fundamental composition of the Canadian population. (Canada, House of Commons Debates, 1 May 1947: 2644–6)

30. These are basically conditions required for citizenship in many countries—a grasp of the language, history, customs, etc. I should note that this example reflects what most immigrants do—they attempt to integrate, as best they can, insofar as they're allowed.

31. What's often overlooked in philosophical debates about immigration is that it's not necessarily the first generation of immigrants who are most significant: it's their children and grandchildren, who generally integrate and often dissolve into the mainstream population, if allowed. This is a major source of conflict in Europe right now. Guest workers and their children were excluded from the major institutions and continue to be subjected to racism, both explicit and implicit. Second, third and fourth generation children of immigrants now ask why they continue to be marginalized, especially when confronted with the liberal rhetoric of equality. The problems in countries which traditionally encouraged integration—the U.S., Canada, Australia—tend to be less explosive. For example, much of the rhetoric on immigration in the U.S. centers around national security, not culture.

32. We should be cautious, however. At least some cultural choices are quite voluntary. Amartya Sen writes: "The same person can be, without any contradiction, an American citizen, of Caribbean origin, with African ancestry, a Christian, a liberal, a woman, a vegetarian, a long-distance runner, a historian, a schoolteacher, a novelist, a feminist, a heterosexual, a believer in gay and lesbian rights, a theater lover, an environmental activist, a tennis fan, a jazz musician, and someone who is deeply committed to the view that there are intelligent beings in outer space with whom it is extremely urgent to talk (preferably in English)."

Though he's discussing group identity, this clearly involves culture, where many of these characteristics are voluntary. Amartya Sen, *Identity and Violence: The Illusion of Destiny*. (W.W. Norton & Company, Inc.: New York, NY, 2006), xii–xiii.

33. Furthermore, as liberals, they will be uneasy about any policy that says you are eligible if you change your values, your religion, and so on, even if there were a way of establishing this. These policies have existed historically—for example, forcing Jews to convert to Christianity to enter certain professions.

34. I thank one of my referees for pressing me on this point.

35. This point holds more generally: it's irrational to reject the influence of a culture if we don't have at least some understanding of what this entails. This isn't to say that we can't prefer something because it's ours or we're used to it—these are perfectly good reasons, in many cases. But aversion to strangers and their customs, simply because they're strangers and different from us, is xenophobia, not a justified preference to retain the familiar.

Individuals and Relational Beings: Expanding the Universal Human Rights Model

P. J. Lomelino

Abstract: Currently, the universal human rights model relies on the notion of individual human rights. According to Michael Ignatieff, this is based on the fact that universal human rights are necessarily individual rights. However, there are cultures in which persons define themselves as relational beings (firmly believing that the foundation of their value as persons rests in their being an integral part of a larger whole rather than their being identified as an individual self). Thus, the problem arises as to whether universal human rights can apply to such persons. In this paper, I will argue that Ignatieff is mistaken; there can be (both theoretically and practically) collective human rights. Moreover, respect for human agency requires us to incorporate collective human rights into the universal human rights model so as to make these rights applicable to all human beings–individuals and relational beings.

I. Introduction

With the implementation of the 1948 Universal Declaration of Human Rights,[1] the groundwork was laid for what has come to be known as the Universal Declaration model of rights—a model that is intentionally restricted to individual human rights.[2] Underlying this model is the theoretical assertion that universal human rights are necessarily individual rights and, consequently, cannot encompass collective rights.[3] However, in restricting the universal human rights model to individual rights, proponents fail to recognize that there are those in the global community who define themselves as relational beings (firmly believing that their value as persons rests in their being an integral part of a larger whole rather than on their being individuals).[4] In this paper, I will argue that the universal human rights model must necessarily be expanded to include collective rights.[5] Although others have argued for the inclusion of collective rights, my argument differs in that it draws on the importance of the descriptive difference between the various definitions of 'person' within our global community as an additional motivation for expanding the current universal human rights model.

In order to conclude this, I will begin by briefly explaining the difference between individual and collective rights. After doing so, I will introduce the notion of relational beings and why I believe that collective rights must necessarily be included. Next, I will address what I believe are the strongest objections to my argument for the necessity of incorporating collective rights. And, lastly, I will close by leaving the reader with a few examples of how collective rights can be incorporated into the universal human rights model.

II. Collective Rights

What Are Collective Rights?

Prior to arguing for the need to include collective rights, it is necessary to respond to the following questions: What are collective rights, and how do they differ from individual rights? The answer to these questions is best framed in an explanation of what has come to be referred to as "generations of rights." In order to distinguish between the various types of rights, some draw a distinction between what is often referred to as three generations of rights. This reference to *generations* of rights is not meant to imply that second generation rights stem from first generation rights, for example. Nor is it meant to imply that each generation is wholly separate, having no relation with other generations. Nor is it meant to imply that third generation rights, for example, replace the previous generations of rights.[6] Instead, many who argue for the inclusion of third generation rights (myself included) believe that such rights must necessarily be recognized along with first and second generation rights in order for the protection of human rights to be universally applicable (though the justification for such arguments differ, as I will explain later in this paper).

Among the three generations of rights, first generation rights are directed towards preserving persons' liberty and, as such, are aimed towards protecting individuals from the state. Examples of first generation rights can be found in Articles 3 through 21 of the Universal Declaration of Human Rights and include such rights as the freedom of speech and the right to a fair trial. Since such rights are directed towards protecting individual liberties, first generation rights are indisputably individual rights.

Second generation rights also fall within the realm of individual rights. These rights are aimed at equality and provide economic, social and cultural rights for individuals. In general, these rights impose state's obligations to persons, such as the requirement of the state to provide protection against poverty, malnutrition, illiteracy and unemployment. As Jeremy Waldron explains, "Though these are thought to be more radical claims requiring a more interventionist state, they remain essentially individualistic in their content, inasmuch as it is the material welfare of each man, woman and child that is supposed to be secured by these provisions."[7] Within the UDHR, Articles 22 through 27 are directed towards these second generation rights.

Simply put, third generation rights are those rights that are not protected by the previous generation of economic, social and cultural rights, such as the right to self-determination, freedom from genocide, and the right of peoples to development.[8] Whereas first and second generation rights deal with individual rights, third generation rights equate with collective rights (aiming at protecting communities of persons as opposed to the individual). As such, these rights are meant to protect groups from tyranny by the majority[9] (meaning those who hold a majority of the power which may not always align with their being the majority in number). This protection may be needed between nations (such as the protection against colonialism) or within a nation (such as the protection of a minority against genocide). The importance of these rights can be seen by the atrocities that arose in Nazi Germany (with the persecution of the Jews), Apartheid (which illustrates that the majority need not be in numbers), and in Darfur (where genocide continues today). Certainly, most (I would hope—all) of us acknowledge that these are all instances of human rights violations. In doing so, it is important to note that these violations were directed towards particular groups and not specific individuals. With such tragedies in mind, we can begin to see the need for incorporating third generation rights into the human rights model.[10]

Within the current discourse regarding third generation rights, the classification of these as *collective* rights rests on the fact that they are designed to protect "non-individualized goods."[11] Although this is most certainly true, I wish to expand the basis for classifying such rights as collective. In addition to their protection of collective goods, collective rights also (importantly) encompass the idea that there are some persons in the global community who place their locus of value as persons on their being part of a larger whole (in other words, they are who I shall refer to as "relational beings," a point that I discuss in more detail later in this paper).

Recognizing Collective Rights

It is important to note that many who want to reject the inclusion of collective rights into the universal human rights model oftentimes still recognize the importance of collective rights. For example, both Jack Donnelly and Michael Ignatieff[12] accept the importance of such rights as the language and religious rights of minorities and the right to self-determination (the right that provides peoples with the ability to exercise their will as a collective to "determine their political destiny in a democratic fashion and be free from systematic persecution").[13] In recognizing the importance of such rights, however, each presents a different argument as to why these rights should not be recognized as part of the universal rights model. According to Donnelly, such rights are already recognized and protected in the Universal Declaration model, which rests on individual rights.

Yet, as I will later argue, there are some collective rights that are not covered by the current model. On the other hand, Ignatieff's argument leaves room for the conclusion that collective rights are important. Nonetheless, he argues that such rights should not be construed as universal human rights. I will also be addressing his argument later in this paper. For now, what is important to note is that despite the fact that many recognize the importance of collective rights, they do not accept the conclusion that these should necessarily be included in the universal human rights model.

Standard Arguments for Including Collective Rights

Prior to addressing the definition of 'person' that I believe motivates the conclusion for the need to incorporate collective rights into the universal human rights model, let me take a moment to address two common arguments in support of this conclusion. (Later, I will take the opportunity to explain how my argument differs from these.) The first argument rests on the Aristotelian belief that the individual can only thrive to the extent to which society thrives.[14] Hence, for example, the right to development is a necessity since it enables the larger society to flourish, thereby creating the necessary fertile ground for the individual's flourishing.

A second argument in support of collective human rights is that they are necessary in order to respond to the larger problems that face our global community. As Carl Wellman points out, "[A] third generation of human rights (collective rights) is required to achieve a coordinated response on a worldwide scale to those threats to human rights arising from the global interdependence of all peoples and nations."[15] For example, in recognizing that we are a global community, we now recognize the importance of equity among nations and, as a result, the need for the right to development arises.

III. Relational Beings and the Need to Include Collective Rights

Introducing the Notion of a Relational Being

Although I agree with both of these standard arguments, I also believe that together they represent an incomplete justification for the necessity of including collective rights in the universal human rights model. In order to understand what I believe is missing, let me begin by introducing the notion of a 'relational being.' It is this type of being, I will argue, that is currently excluded from the Universal Declaration model.

In "Can One Size Fit All? Indic Perspectives on the Declaration of Human Rights by the World's Religions,"[16] Christopher Key Chapple introduces the term "dividuals." Despite Chapple's good intentions in defining such persons, I will forgo utilizing the term "dividuals" as it hints at a type of dividedness. Nonetheless, his point is profound and one worth expanding upon. Hence, in doing so, I shall refer to those who define themselves as part of a larger whole as "relational beings."

In addressing the concept of a relational being, Chapple turns to Indic values, according to which the value of being a person lies in being an integral part of society.[17] Within the traditional Hindu caste system, the priority of family and social roles is exemplified by the fact that fulfilling one's role in the caste system is paramount. Although he acknowledges that the current caste system violates human rights, he points out that Hindu values and human rights can be mutually supportive. However, he also points out that human rights must extend beyond merely applying to the lowest caste members. In addition to making sure that individual rights protect the lowest caste, Chapple argues that human rights would have to recognize and protect the role of families and societies:

> Though the loose collection of movements and ideas that now refers to itself as Hindu would in principle support the ideas of the Universal Declaration of Human Rights, it would remain suspicious of any ideology that would seek to undermine the primacy of the family, advocate particular forms of worship, or cede any autonomy to non-local economic entities.[18]

Although he does not phrase it as such, it is important to note that Chapple is calling for a broader conception of human rights that relates to relational beings as well as individuals. By emphasizing the primacy of family, religious worship, and the autonomy of local economic entities, he is emphasizing human rights as applicable to persons who are part of something larger than themselves as individuals; he is emphasizing the need for recognizing collective human rights.

An additional example of relational beings can be found in John Berthrong's, "Human Rights and Responsibilities: A Confucian Perspective on the Universal Declaration of Human Rights"[19] in which he presents a similar argument regarding relational beings but this time in the context of Confucian values. Although Berthrong does not utilize the term "relational being" his discussion of Confucian values illustrates another tradition in which persons are defined by their relationships to a larger whole. As Berthrong points out, Confucians gauge human flourishing based on one's relationships, beginning with one's relationship with one's family and extending to one's relationship with the world. As Berthrong explains,

> We are persons because we live in community, beginning with our families of origin but expanding in concentric circles out to the widest horizons of the human social order and now to the fragile ecology of the entire planet.[20]

From a Confucian perspective, then, the Western model of human rights is too narrow. Based on traditional Western thought, human flourishing emphasizes the individual, and although important relationships are recognized as constituting part of this flourishing, these are not the foundation (as in Confucian thought).

Consequently, cultures that address the human flourishing of persons as relational beings are excluded from the discourse.

The Need for Collective Human Rights

So, how does the idea of a relational being relate to the need for incorporating collective human rights? What is important to note is that all of the generations of rights are important because they deal with claims on behalf of persons. In explaining human rights, Jeremy Waldron states:

> But the idea of rights is a claim about value: whatever its provenance, the life of a given person is *hers, and it feels important to her*, from the inside as it were. The idea of rights involves a determination to reflect that feeling of importance in the respect we offer to one another as a fundamental basis of our life together.[21]

Yet, as Berthrong has explained, some persons (whom I have been referring to as "relational beings") conceive of human flourishing solely in relation to the relationships that they have with others. Thus, ironically, the basis for individual human rights (of respecting what an individual values) necessarily includes the idea that there are those who place the value of being a person on one's relation with a larger whole. Of course, rights do not respect all that one values (for some may have values that do not align with human flourishing). However, among what we do value and the ways in which these things are necessary for human flourishing, surely one's conception of where one places one's value as a person (whether on being an individual or a relational being) is of the utmost importance. As such, and because there are those who place this locus of value on their relation to a larger whole, the human rights model must include protections that recognize these important relationships. In other words, it must incorporate collective human rights.

Differing Definitions of 'Person'

In arguing that the universal human rights model must necessarily be expanded to include differing definitions of 'person' (or what I have also been referring to as differences in where one identifies that locus of value of 'person'), some might raise the objection that those who define themselves as relational beings are simply mistaken. It is important to note that this objection rests on the normative claim regarding how we ought to define 'persons.'[22] However, universal human rights deal with the state of affairs in the world as it stands. As a result, it is necessary to look to descriptive claims regarding 'persons.' Regardless of how one thinks we ought to define 'persons,' the fact of the matter is, when we look at the global community, people's definitions differ—some define 'person' as individual, while others define 'person' as relational being. Given that the current Universal Declaration model includes only first and second generation rights, it is apparent that it rests on the normative claim of 'person' as an individual rather than looking to the global community and recognizing that this definition is not universal.[23]

IV. How the 'Relational Being' Relates to the 'Relational Self'

In my discussion of relational beings, some may be reminded of the Feminist concept of the "relational self." This is no coincidence; yet, as I will explain, my concept of a relational being extends beyond the idea of a relational self.

As a means of providing a more realistic notion of the self than had been previously touted in traditional political and moral philosophical theories, Feminists introduced the notion of 'the relational self.' Within traditional philosophical theories, the self was thought to be an atomistic individual—one who, in essence, stands alone, able to autonomously formulate one's desires, intentions and actions.[24] In response to this claim, many Feminists introduced the notion of the relational self to indicate that persons are always necessarily in relationship with others.[25] Instead of acting as isolated individuals within the world, individuals are integrally connected to others by means of various valuable relationships while, at the same time, being able to question and re-evaluate these relationships.[26]

Previously, I referred to "relational beings" as those who place the value of 'person' on the role that one plays in one's important relationships with others. Because the relational self encompasses the idea that one is always in relation with others and that these relationships influence one's definition of the self, this conception of the relational self seems to be an example of a relational being. Yet, the examples that I used from Hinduism and Confucianism point to a slightly different being. Whereas the Feminist relational self focuses on the importance of the individual to continually re-examine and re-define her relationships, the examples from Hinduism and Confucianism focus on what is seen as the inherent interrelatedness between persons in comprising a group. The implications of this difference are that the definition of 'person' as relational self is adequately represented in the individualist framework of first and second generation rights, while the definition of 'person' as relational being is not and hence, in addition, requires third generation rights.[27]

V. Addressing Objections

Ignatieff's Argument: Human Rights Are Necessarily Individual Rights

In response to my argument for including collective rights as part of the universal human rights, many argue that we should not do so. Among the most adamant protesters is Michael Ignatieff. In his book *Human Rights as Idolatry*,[28] Ignatieff argues that universal human rights must necessarily be restricted to individual rights. According to Ignatieff, there is a reason that the universal human rights model has excluded collective rights. As he asserts, "it is a mistake to water down the individualism of rights discourse" in an attempt to "make human rights more palatable to less individualistic cultures."[29] In support of this claim, he appears to present two arguments. First, he argues that collective rights are important *because* they serve to protect individual rights. Thus, "the ultimate purpose and justification of collective rights is not the protection of the group as such but the protection of the individuals who comprise it."[30] For example, the collective rights to language and worship serve to protect an individual's right to speak his chosen language and to practice his chosen religion.

Second, Ignatieff concludes that human rights are necessarily individualistic based on the argument that individual human rights should trump collective rights where these conflict. To illustrate, he presents the example of the group right to language, explaining, "the group right to language . . . must not be used to prevent an individual from learning a language besides the language of the group."[31] Using these two arguments: (1) that collective rights serve to protect individual rights, and (2) that individual rights necessarily trump collective rights, Ignatieff insists that all human rights exist, in essence, to protect individuals. This, in turn, is supposed to lead to his overall conclusion that universal human rights can *only* be individual rights.

However, it does not necessarily follow that universal human rights (as assignable to individual persons) can only be assigned to persons who consider themselves to be individuals. In fact, we can grant (and most certainly would want to grant) Ignatieff's two claims regarding individual and collective rights without arriving at his conclusion. First, it is true that the enforcement of collective rights provides the necessary groundwork for supporting individual rights. Certainly, the collective right to language protects the individual right to speak whichever language one chooses. Second, I agree that (in cases in which individual and collective rights conflict) individual rights should trump collective rights. Hence, for example, it is a human rights violation against those in the lowest Hindu caste system to be systematically oppressed. Thus, we need not reject collective human rights in order to allow individual rights to trump, nor do we need to do so in order to recognize that collective rights support individual rights. For example, we can order human rights so that individual rights take precedence over socioeconomic and collective rights (where these conflict).[32] Moreover, incorporating collective rights into the model in a hierarchical fashion highlights the supportive role that collective rights play with regards to many individual rights.

Donnelly's Argument: Collective Rights Are Unnecessary

In response to my argument, some who wish to reject the idea of collective human rights insist that there is no need to incorporate collective human rights because the interests that are supposedly protected by collective rights are already protected by the system of individual human rights. This is Jack Donnelly's argument in "The Universal Declaration Model of Human Rights: A Liberal Defense."[33] According to Donnelly, "issues that some see as matters of 'collective rights' are addressed by liberals and by the Universal Declaration model primarily through individual rights." Specifically, he argues that the Universal Declaration model's commitment to non-discrimination and to freedom of association can be seen as protecting the interests of groups, making it unnecessary to incorporate collective rights.[34] For example, the commitment to non-discrimination is reflected in a set of civil liberties (such as freedom of expression, belief and assembly) that serve to protect the interests of individuals as members of groups (and, in this way, Donnelly asserts, as groups themselves).[35] In addition, others have argued along a similar vein, insisting that such interests as protecting communal ownership of environmental resources can be protected by a system of individual rights whereby joint ownership is recognized as a protection for individuals who jointly come together to own property, much like in our American legal system.[36]

Yet, even if we grant that many of the provisions in the Universal Declaration on Human Rights can be utilized to protect the interests of groups, excluding third generation rights is still problematic. As I have previously argued, rejecting collective rights disregards the foundational belief system of those in the global community who define themselves as relational beings (and as a result marginalizes these persons). As Jennifer Jackson-Preece points out, the UDHR's reference to the principles of equality and nondiscrimination makes "no mention of special minority rights" (such as "the rights to culture, language, and education").[37] Without including third generation rights, the Universal Declaration model overlooks an entire population of persons, which is a crime given that this model is supposed to apply to the global community as a whole.

To give an example of the importance of third generation rights, consider the case of the Gojami-Amhara of Ethiopia, who believes that the land is communally shared and not individually owned.[38] This idea of communal ownership is one aspect of a centuries-old tradition in which persons are considered to be, most importantly, relational beings in a communal relationship with the land. For them, the narrow framework of respecting individual property rights (even when jointly combined) cannot address this important relationship.

Collective Rights Are Not Human Rights

Although I have argued for the necessity of incorporating collective human rights, some might argue that these rights are not human rights and thus do not belong in discussions about universal human rights. Human rights are those rights that one has simply because one is human. However, "a people are not the same as a human being."[39] Therefore, it seems odd to refer to collectives as having human rights.

This point is worth addressing since my argument is for necessarily considering collective rights as universal *human* rights.

In response, it should be noted that this concern reflects the ideology of individualism that I am arguing is not universal. In order for one to argue that human rights cannot be assigned to collectives one must adhere to the belief that such rights are necessarily and only assignable to separate individuals. Yet, as L. W. Sumner points out:

> [T]here is nothing in the logic of rights which restricts them to individuals. Some rights, such as the right not to be assaulted or killed, belong to individuals simply as such, but others, such as the right to religious holidays or services in one's native language, can be held by individuals only as members of an ethno-cultural group. Even individual rights, therefore, need not define their holders as abstractions isolated from their social contexts. Furthermore, nothing seems to prevent us from taking a further step and attributing some rights (of self-determination or cultural survival, for example) to ethno-cultural groups as wholes, where the right cannot be decomposed into the separate rights of several members of the group.[40]

Thus, from a conceptual standpoint, it seems plausible to assign rights to collectives. What rights call for is a subject, and, as Sumner points out, there is no reason to believe that this subject cannot be a group. The fact that this group is a group of human beings seems sufficient for considering collective rights as human rights.

Although it is beyond the bounds of this paper to go into more detail about alternative conceptions of rights, it is interesting to note that Martha Minow and Mary Lyndon Shanley introduce the notion of 'relational rights.' Briefly, "a conception of relational rights and responsibilities . . . would not regard 'rights' as belonging to individuals and arising from the imperative of self-preservation, but rather would view rights as claims grounded in and arising from human relationships of varying degrees of intimacy."[41] In stretching beyond the narrow confines of the ideology of the atomistic self, thinking of rights as relational rights enables us to conceive of how collective rights are human rights. Moreover, from a practical standpoint, it is important to note that collective rights have been put into practice. For example, Belgium has granted collective human rights to "three cultural communities that are identified on the basis of language" in its constitution.[42]

VI. Proposals for Incorporating Collective Rights

Having argued for the necessity of collective rights as universal human rights, incorporating collective rights into the universal human rights documents can take one of many possible forms. First, one could incorporate the suggestion by Richard McKeon (a member of the American delegation for drafting the Universal Declaration of Human Rights). According to McKeon, in order to be applicable to diverse cultures, the UDHR (which relies on individual human rights) could expand human rights to also encompass third generation collective rights. Doing so "would add more specific rights for social, cultural or national groups as collectives to the first two iterations of civil-political and socioeconomic rights, seeking a balance between individual and collective rights."[43] Based on this revised model, first generation rights would trump second and third generation rights where these conflict.[44] As Chapple's example of the Hindu caste system illustrates, it is necessary to protect individual rights when they conflict with collective rights. Nonetheless, this necessary hierarchy need not lead to the conclusion that third generation rights be excluded from the Universal Rights model. As Waldron explains, "[T]here does not seem to be any logical or ethical difficulty with this approach [of creating a hierarchy of generations of rights], provided of course that the rights of the group are always asserted against some larger entity rather than against its own individual members."[45]

Notably, collective rights have been included in some of the international legislative documents that comprise the 1966 International Human Rights Covenants. For example, the International Covenant on Civil and Political Rights recognizes the right to self-determination (Article 1), as well as cultural, language and religious community rights (Article 27).[46]

> Article 1: All peoples have the right to self-determination. By virtue of that right they freely determine their political status and freely pursue their economic, social and cultural development.
>
> Article 27: In those States in which ethnic, religious or linguistic minorities exist, persons belonging to such minorities shall not be denied the right, in community with the other members of their group, to enjoy their own culture, to profess and practice their own religion, or to use their own language.

Within this document there is no explicit hierarchy between individual and collective rights. Instead, the protection of these rights is upheld by the provisions set forth by the Charter of the United Nations, which provides for the International Court of Justice to settle disputes.[47] The recognition of collective rights is also apparent in the United Nations, "International Covenant on Economic, Social and Cultural Rights," in which Article 1 provides for the protection of the right to self-determination. Once again, the same provision for protection is provided as in the Civil and Political Rights covenant.[48]

In both McKeon's proposal (of explicitly stating a hierarchy between individual and collective rights) and the example set forth by the International Rights Covenants (in which collective rights are included, with disputes settled by an international court) the important end result is that collective rights are officially incorporated into the universal human rights model. In doing so, the door is open for the representation of those whose definition of 'person' differs from the Western conception of the individual.

VII. Conclusion

In this paper, I have argued that the reliance on the Universal Rights model of individual rights is mistaken and must necessarily be expanded to include collective rights in order for universal human rights to be applicable to all members of the global community. In its reliance on a Western conception of 'person' as individual, the current universal human rights model has restricted itself to first and second generation individual rights. Yet, as I have argued, once we recognize that some persons define themselves as relational beings (placing the locus of value on their relationship to a larger whole), it becomes apparent that we must expand the current model to necessarily include third generation collective rights. Only in this way can the universal human rights model be universally applicable to all persons in the global community.

P. J. Lomelino, University of Colorado

Notes

1. United Nations, "Universal Declaration of Human Rights" (New York: UN, 1948). Article available at: http://www.un.org/Overview/rights.html.

2. Jack Donnelly, "The Universal Declaration Model of Human Rights: A Liberal Defense," (2001) http://www.du.edu/humanrights/workingpapers/papers/12-donnelly-02-01.pdf.

Some might object that the Universal Declaration of Human Rights was introduced as a normative and not a legally binding document. However, many argue that the Declaration's prominent existence over the past nearly sixty years has enabled it to become "binding under customary law" (Adamantia Pollis and Peter Schwab, "Human Rights: A Western Construct With Limited Applicability" in *Human Rights: Cultural and Ideological Perspectives*, eds. Adamantia Polis and Peter Schwab (New York: Praeger Publishers, 1979), 1–31.

3. Refer to Section II below for my explanation as to how Donnelly perceives collective rights.

4. In drawing a distinction between individuals and relational beings, I am by no means implying that individuals do not place importance on their relationship with others within a group (whether that group is the family, a religious tradition or a society). Rather, the distinguishing feature between individuals and relational beings is the primary locus from which one is valued as a person; whereas individuals believe that the individual self is the locus of value, relational beings believe that the locus of value is one's relationship to others and/or nature.

5. Despite the UDHR's use of 'human being,' I have chosen to use the term 'person.' In doing so, I draw on the philosophical distinction between human beings and persons, whereby the former is a biological term and the latter is a moral one. My utilization of this distinction in no way is meant to imply that only persons have human rights, for I agree that

such rights are necessarily applicable to all human beings. Instead, given that my argument focuses on the agency of persons in defining themselves as such, it seems more appropriate in the given context to isolate my discussion to 'persons.'

6. Carl Wellman, "Solidarity, the Individual and Human Rights," *Human Rights Quarterly* (2000): 639–57.

7. Jeremy Waldron, "Rights" in *A Companion to Contemporary Political Philosophy*, ed. Robert E. Goodin and Pettit Philip (Cambridge, Mass.: Basil Blackwell, 1993), 578.

8. P. R. Baehr, "Controversies in the Current International Human Rights Debate," *Human Rights Review* (October–December 2000): 7–32.

9. My thanks to Ajume Wingo for making this further clarification.

10. Moreover, there have been instances in which groups have tried to exercise such rights, such as the Catalonia's secession from Spain.

11. Waldron, "Rights" 578.

12. Donnelly, "The Universal Declaration Model of Human Rights: A Liberal Defense." See also Michael Ignatieff, "Human Rights as Idolatry" in *Human Rights As Politics and Idolatry*, ed. Amy Gutman (Princeton, N.J.: Princeton University Press, 2001), 53–98.

13. Paul R.Williams and Francesa Jannotti Pecci, "Earned Sovereignty: Bridging the Gap Between Sovereignty and Self-Determination," *Denver Journal of International Law* (2004).

14. Aristotle, "Politica" in *The Basic Works of Aristotle*, ed. Richard McKeon (New York: Random House, Inc, 1941), 1127–324.

15. Wellman, "Solidarity, the Individual and Human Rights."

16. Christopher Key Chapple, "Can One Size Fit All? Indic Perspectives on the Declaration of Human Rights by the World's Religions" in *Human Rights and Responsibilities in the World Religions*, ed. Joseph Runzo, Nancy M. Martin, and Arvind Sharma (Oxford: Oneworld Publications, 2003), 178–85.

17. In his referring to "Indic values," I grant that Chapple is by no means implying a mistaken homogeneity within India regarding values but instead is referring to a particular Hindu tradition within India.

18. Ibid., 184.

19. John Berthrong, "Human Rights and Responsibilities: A Confucian Perspective on the Universal Declaration of Human Rights" in *Human Rights and Responsibilities in the World Religions*, ed. Runzo, Martin, and Sharma (Oxford: Oneworld Publications, 2003), 199–205.

20. Ibid., 204.

21. Waldron, "Rights," 582. In his article, Waldron argues for collective rights but from an individualist standpoint. I address this later in the paper.

22. Although it is beyond the bounds of this paper to address personhood arguments, one should note that arguments for the definition of 'person' as individual reflect Western thought. It is my belief that, once one steps outside of this framework, one will recognize that arguments for the definition of 'person' as relational being are equally justified.

23. The fact that the UDHR relies on a Western conception of 'person' should come as no surprise, given that those from cultures in which 'person' is defined as relational being were absent from the delegation that drafted that document (i.e., Native Americans, Africans, Muslims).

24. John Rawls, *A Theory of Justice* (Oxford: Oxford University Press, 1971); Robert Nozick, *Anarchy, State and Utopia* (Cambridge: Harvard University Press, 1974).

25. Lorraine Code, "Second Persons," in *Science, Morality, and Feminist Theory*, ed. Marsha Hanen and Kai Nielsen (Calgary: University of Calgary Press, 1987); *Relational Autonomy: Feminist Perspectives on Autonomy, Agency and the Social Self*, ed. Catriona Mackenzie and Natalie Stoljar (Oxford: Oxford University Press, 2000).

26. Samantha Brennan, "Recent Work In Feminist Ethics," *Ethics* (July, 1999): 858–93.

27. In response to my argument for third generation rights, Feminists (such as Susan Moller Okin) are quick to point out that a reliance on group rights overlooks the gender inequalities within groups. Hence, she warns that we must be careful to identify these inequalities. As will become apparent later in this paper, I will argue for a necessary hierarchy between individual and group rights. An advantage of this proposal is that it provides the means by which to address the gender inequalities within groups once we have located them, thus providing a means by which to both incorporate collective rights and address Okin's concern. Susan Moller Okin, *Is Multiculturalism Bad For Women?* ed. Joshua Cohen, Matthew Howard, and Martha C. Nussbaum (Princeton, N.J.: Princeton University Press, 1999).

28. Ignatieff, "Human Rights as Idolatry."

29. Ibid., 66.

30. Ibid., 67.

31. Ibid.

32. This suggestion comes from Richard McKeon and is one that I discuss in further detail later in the paper.

33. Donnelly, "The Universal Declaration Model of Human Rights."

34. Ibid., 18.

35. Ibid., 19.

36. My thanks to John Rowan for introducing this objection.

37. Jennifer Jackson-Preece, "Human Rights and Cultural Pluralism: The 'Problem' of Minorities" in *International Human Rights in the 21st Century: Protecting the Rights of Groups*, ed. G. Lyons and J. Mayall (Oxford: Rowman & Littlefield Publishers, Inc, 2003), 49–71.

38. Within their article, Pollis and Schwab present this example to illustrate the need for expanding universal human rights to include collective human rights. However, I have taken this line of argument farther in arguing that the underlying basis for this expansion rests on differing conceptions of the self (differences in how one defines the importance of being human—whether as having the primary focus as the individual or as a person in specific relation to others) (Pollis and Schwab, 9).

39. This is the way in which Wellman explains the objection. In response, he argues that the idea of protecting collections of individuals is implicit in the first and second genera-

tion rights that already appear in international human rights law. Thus, he argues that the necessary legal groundwork has already been laid for considering third generation rights as human rights. See Wellman, "Solidarity, the Individual and Human Rights," 653.

40. L. W. Sumner, "Rights" in *The Blackwell Guide to Ethical Theory*, ed. H. LaFolette (Oxford: Blackwell Publishing, 2000), 296.

41. Martha Minow and Mary Lyndon Shanley, "Relational Rights and Responsibilities: Revisioning the Family in Liberal Political Theory and Law," Hypatia, (Winter 1996): 4–29.

42. K. VanderWal, "Collective Human Rights: A Western View" in *Human Rights in a Pluralist World: Individuals and Collectives*, ed. J. Berting, P. R. Baehr, J. Burgers, C. Finterman, B. de Klerk, R. Kroes, C. van Minnen, and K. VanderWal (London: Meckler, 1990), 90.

43. Berthrong, "Human Rights and Responsibilities."

44. For a suggestion as to how one might be able to implement into law ways to define a group and its claims, see Wellman (656).

45. Waldron, "Rights," 578.

46. United Nations, "International Covenant on Civil and Political Rights" (New York: UN, 1966). Article available at: http://www.ohchr.org/english/law/ccpr.htm.

47. United Nations, "Charter of the United Nations" (New York: UN, 1945): Chapter XIV. Article available at: http://www.un.org/aboutun/charter.

48. United Nations, "International Covenant on Economic, Social and Cultural Rights" (New York: UN, 1966): Article 1. Article available at: http://www.ohchr.org/english/law/cescr.htm.

Can Arms Be Sold Responsibly in the Global Market?

EDMUND F. BYRNE

Abstract: Corporate social responsibility (CSR) research has ignored the arms industry, in large part because of political assumptions that tie this industry to nation-state sovereignty. Bypassing this obsolescent Westphalian world-view, I examine the US arms industry on the basis of CSR requirements regarding the environment, social equity, profitability, and use of political power. I find the arms industry fails each of these four CSR requirements. In response to the assertion that the arms industry should not be subject to CSR requirements because it is crucial to national defense, I point out that many arms manufacturers are post-Westphalian entities more powerful in their own right than many nation-states. So they should be held responsible for the foreseeable consequences that flow from use of their products, both under civil law and, where applicable, under international human rights standards.

In an effort to expand corporate concerns beyond profitability, many business ethicists promote corporate social responsibility (CSR). CSR involves ethical standards that limit a company's profit-seeking activities so as, for example, not to harm the environment, or people, or political institutions. Views differ as to whether CSR standards should be binding on management. I think they should, at least in those instances commonly addressed in law in which a corporation puts artefacts in the world that cause foreseeable and preventable harm.[1] This is preeminently the case of a corporation that produces weapons used for military purposes. But few CSR studies address the arms industry directly.

This lacuna is due largely, I believe, to centuries-old assumptions about political sovereignty which give a nation-state absolute control over war and weapons. Left unchallenged, these assumptions exonerate the arms industry of all responsibility for what is done with its products. But an appeal to sovereignty should not exempt the arms industry from CSR because, as critical international relations scholars tell us, the paradigmatic nation-state with absolute sovereignty is becoming a null class,[2] even as the quasi-sovereignty of MNCs is increasing and at times causes negative externalities.[3] Those who believe in the imaginary world of a nation-state, however, still think in terms of absolute sovereignty, so would vilify any claim that an industry devoted to "national defense" could possibly be involved in fundamentally (not just incidentally) unethical activity.

This Hobbesian if not Machiavellian ideology is no guarantor of arms industry ethics because (1) the primary beneficiaries of nation-state arms procurement are not citizens needing protection but private corporations needing revenue and (2) many weapons are neither sold to nor used by nation-states. To show the moral significance of these assertions I will assess the CSR status of the arms industry, especially its US component, with regard to (1) environmental quality, (2) social equity, (3) profitability, and (4) use of political power. I will conclude that corporations in the arms industry violate these CSR standards and so for the sake of human well-being should be subject to external regulation.

In working through this agenda, I will address only obliquely two important background considerations. One of these involves a distinction between Westphalian and post-Westphalian political arrangements. The first term derives its meaning from the Treaty of Westphalia (1648) which made nation-states sovereign entities uniquely empowered to use and control violence. This Westphalian doctrine is confounded today by many powerful non-state entities, thus inviting introduction of the term post-Westphalian. A second consideration involves a bevy of issues regarding causation. I posit a causal connection between the manufacture and distribution of arms on the one hand and harm effected by their use on the other hand. The kind of causal connection I have in mind embraces conditions necessary to the outcome (a but-for condition) but otherwise is not directly derived from any philosophical theory about causality or about ethical grounds for assigning responsibility. Rather, it looks to legal scholars' discourse regarding grounds on which to assign liability for harm done or foreseeable, including in particular an agent's role in increasing such harm's probability and thus the risk of its occurring.[4] The import of this discourse is exemplified by a jurisdiction's finding some artifacts to be so constructed that their potential for facilitating harm justifies defining and policing them as deadly or dangerous weapons or destructive devices.[5] In other words, the law of agency is presupposed where linkages between arms and harm are asserted in what follows.

With regard to the CSR environmental requirement, first of all, modern weapons of war often cause harm to the environment. Under some possible set of circumstances they could conceivably benefit the environment, though I fail to see how. Then, again, it is possible that war-caused harm to the environment might not be irreversible. It is difficult to imagine, though, that anyone would seriously claim that war making endeavors as such are not harmful to the environment.

The extent of environmental damage a weapon might cause depends in large measure on the level of military technology it involves and the attitude one has about the economically bankrupt notion that the environment has no owner so may be used at no cost to the user. Moreover, the scope of harm caused by a weapon extends beyond the effects of its actual use in war to numerous places where it is produced, tested, stored, or disposed of. Nuclear, chemical, and biological weapons have all had devastating effects on the environment.[6] So also has artillery testing. The extent of these negative externalities, due primarily to large weapons systems but also to small arms and conventional weapons, has been documented by various ecological groups.[7] Does this mean, however, that an arms manufacturer or trader should be deemed responsible for the environmental degradation traceable to the weapons it makes or sells? Given that there already exist legal theories and institutions whereby one could establish such causal connections, I endorse the affirmative without argument and turn to the more widely discussed issues regarding how weapons used militarily violate human rights, sometimes catastrophically.

The arms industry, secondly, would fail a CSR social equity requirement. For, especially if its proponent embraces a normative stakeholder theory, CSR requires that a corporation's products and services not unduly cause harm to people. Often understood locally, this social equity requirement must be understood to apply globally wherever the arms industry's products are located.

It is a fact that horribly detrimental wars are occurring today in many places, and extant international standards of warfare are of limited use, especially as to noncombatants. So at the very least the human community needs to adopt additional norms that will extend protection on an emergency basis to those who are most vulnerable in these unprecedented conflicts, especially civilians and indentured child soldiers. This is clearly the position of organizations seeking to maintain and expand civil society as a counter-force to government prerogatives; and many corporations are in agreement with this stance, at least as it applies to their own workplaces. Mindful, then, of the old maxim about what is good for goose and gander respectively, I here address just the dangers inherent in the small arms bazaar. Small arms include handguns, carbines, assault rifles, rocket-propelled grenades, light mortars, and shoulder-fired missiles. It may be consoling to know that these weapons account for only $10 billion worth of the $850 billion/year of military expenditures. But compared to this benefit the costs are overwhelming, as follows.

There are presently an estimated 500–550 million small arms in circulation around the world. Their easy availability facilitates conflicts and heightens their severity and longevity. Small arms, moreover, are involved far more often in violations of human rights and humanitarian laws than are such major conventional weapons systems as planes and helicopters. Indeed, according to one study, small arms were the only weapons used in 46 of 49 major conflicts in the 1990s, in which 80–90 percent of those killed were civilians (as compared to 5 percent in WW I), and are the single most important cause of the upsurge in refugees.[8] Besides, because small arms are comparatively light, they can be used by children, over 300,000 of whom under the age of 18 are now serving as soldiers.[9]

Appalled by these data, a large coalition of NGOs is seeking to stem the tide of human rights violations effected with small arms by holding users, traders, and authorizing governments accountable. One key reason to hold arms traders accountable is because governments, especially the US, choose not to be accountable. For example, the US did not sign the 1997 treaty banning land mines, and it just recently (July, 2006) blocked a long planned "Control Arms" treaty. Meanwhile, certain non-state actors, namely corporations, already ban possession and use of weapons wherever they exercise control. Some prohibit possessing a weapon at a workplace without explicit permission; others ban weapons outright with no mention of exceptions. At least one company in the arms industry, General Dynamics, is no less restrictive with regard to weapons on its premises.

Some corporations, then, ban weapons. Some states in the US seek to make such bans mandatory. Gun rights organizations are striving to invalidate workplace weapons bans. In their fervor regarding gun rights, however, they are ignoring the even more fundamental capitalist values of ownership and property rights. And those exercising these rights are not just ordinary owners, they are politically powerful organizations whose wealth and influence may surpass many nation-states. As such, they exemplify a major component of a post-Westphalian world: politically powerful non-state actors. So perhaps their arms control policies can be emulated by other actors, both state and non-state, who have no less of a need to protect their interests and their people.

The arms industry, thirdly, would fail a CSR profitability requirement. Considering the multi-billion dollar revenues some defense contractors take in, it might seem foolish to contend that the arms industry is not profitable. But in general it is not. For to a great extent this industry depends for much of its working capital on government funds obtained through taxation. The amounts it receives are impressive, but are they earned?

During the years 1997 to 2003 the Department of Defense (DOD) worked with a budget totaling over $900 billion. Over half went to thousands of private contractors via some 2.2 million contracts. Eighty percent went to just 737 contractors, all but a hundred of which are American-owned. The fifty biggest contractors got more than half the money, and the top ten got 38 percent.[10] Only one of these companies, Science Applications International, won its contracts through, in Pentagon terms, "full and open" competition. More commonly, the way to win contracts involves campaign contributions and lobbying expenditures.[11]

So in what sense are these companies profitable? If one thinks of profit as the desired result of risking capital to develop and market goods and/or services, then the arms industry is not profitable. A free-market conservative who eschews managerial responsibility for any CSR objective other than profit would, then, be especially disappointed. But a Keynesian economist who favors government subsidies to tweak the market might not find this intrusive funding source fatal to a claim of profitability. So the CSR profitability requirement might arguably be waived if the arms industry's output is politically justified because needed by the government for the sake of national defense. But this is an untenable position considering, fourthly, how the arms industry uses political power.

Arms industry output is friendly neither to the natural environment nor to social equity, and can be considered profitable only by changing the meaning of government subsidies. The issue, then, is whether these failings can be discounted because weapons providers are inseparable from government and its sovereign responsibilities. I say no, because (1) arms makers are not just docile servants of a nation-state and (2) the claim that they are requires endorsing a Westphalian world view that has become increasingly counterfactual.

In a Westphalian world people support "national defense" expenditures as long as they are persuaded that their government is acting as a sovereign and is obliged to fight an enemy they clearly recognize as such. In the US, by contrast, neither condition is as straightforward today as it was during the Cold War era, in part because the enemy is not a super-state as was the USSR but an unbounded, stateless enemy, and in part because the defense industry seems more powerful than its nation-state customer. For, this customer's obsession with military supremacy is utterly dependent on the industry and is maintainable only at a level of spending that risks leading the country into a major financial crisis. So why do American taxpayers let their government expose them to such great risk?

Two reasons are lack of effective participatory democracy and lack of relevant information. Another is fear—a deliberately inculcated fear that enables the US government to spend more on "national defense" than do all other countries combined.[12] Especially since 11 September 2001, the US government has labeled the object of this fear terrorism and declared an open-ended war against it. Congress has fully funded this war, and the media (with few exceptions) have adopted the counter-terrorism rhetoric without assessing how well it corresponds with "facts on the ground." Not doing so, however, leaves hidden an agenda that has more to do with marketing than with impending mayhem. To uncover this agenda one needs some familiarity with the history of defense spending in the United States, including in particular the ideological rupture brought on by the end of the Cold War.

The end of the Cold War quickly deflated the moralistic anti-communism raison-d'etre for US arms expenditures. So arms manufacturers had no adequate response to the ethically appealing call for a "peace dividend" that would shift resources from weaponry to civilian priorities. They sought new rationales, e.g., recasting groups in less developed countries as villains, and the Clinton administration touted business reasons to bolster the DOD budget. But arms sales declined. Not for another decade would there be another cornucopian rationale, namely, the open-ended war on terrorism. Consider, then, how anti-communism once played this role and then became ineffective.

World War II turned some US businesses into massive providers of military supplies and services—what President Eisenhower famously labeled a "military-industrial complex." Its mission was to spend government money to defend capitalism even as its foe spent about as recklessly in defense of communism, resulting in a combined annual debt of $600 billion when the Cold War ended. Who benefited from this indebtedness? In the US it was the weapons industry, but very much at the expense of many people, especially in the Southern Hemisphere.

During the Cold War years, 1945 to 1991, 125 different hot wars were fought in less developed countries, resulting in the deaths of 40 million people, mostly civilians. In the 1960s former auto executive Robert McNamara expanded the market for weapons by "rationalizing" the US arms industry to maximize production of "uniform" products that were sold largely on credit. This soon necessitated replacing the gold standard with a floating US dollar; but in the 1980s the global arms manufacturing industry approached $1 trillion per year in sales, with some $140 billion of this total going to third world countries. US sales to buyers in developing countries grew over the next decade to the point that they now account for well over 50 percent of all arms transfer agreements made globally,[13] regardless of all the challenges to human rights that this entails.[14] Meanwhile, defense contractors have also been expanding sales of commercial products, including those with a dual use.[15]

During the Cold War era the Western bloc fairly rigorously monitored exports of dual use technologies to countries behind the Iron Curtain. This mechanism was abolished in 1992, and two years later thirty-three co-founding countries, including Russia and some of its former satellites, signed the Wassenaar Arrangement, a voluntary regime of after-the-fact reports on conventional arms sales (semi-annually) and of sales of dual-use technologies (frequency depending on the sensitivity of the items sold and to whom).

Meanwhile other treaty and statutory regimes that were supposed to regulate US arms exports remained in place.[16] But how effective are they? During the Cold War the West routinely subordinated smaller nations' claims to sovereignty to the global task of containing one monolithic state. This bipolar worldview provided a credible Westphalian rationale for keeping major weapons systems directly or indirectly under US control but putting them to use wherever a threat was identified. Now that this global menace is no more, by what rules are weapons to be bought and sold? In the absence of a Westphalian answer to this question, post-Westphalian answers have arisen. Whether perceived as such or not, these answers amount to government acquiescence in corporate priorities. This can be seen from the following examples.

1. The International Military Education and Training (IMET) program was set up to introduce potential weapons users to available products on a try-before-you-buy basis. If a participating country is short of funds Congress has taxpayers make up the difference.[17] How trainees will use these weapons is seldom an issue, even if they come from countries at war or with abominable human rights records.

2. In 1997 the US House of Representatives unanimously adopted an "Arms Sales Code of Conduct" that would have allowed sales only to cooperative democratic countries that respect their citizens' human rights, are not aggressive towards other states, and participate fully in the UN Register of Conventional Arms. This legislation was killed in conference committee. Meanwhile the US Foreign Military Sales (FMS) program facilitates distributing weapons of all kinds, usually gratis, to "friendly" (i.e., strategically useful) countries.

3. Bypassing US arms control statutes has become an art. In spite of seemingly prohibitive legislation, weapons have been sent to coup-governed Pakistan, exporters ship arms to terrorist states and regimes that violate internationally recognized human rights, a financial institution can participate in weapons sales provided it is not "directly involved" in a transaction, and human rights violators in Afghanistan can have military assistance by virtue of a "notwithstanding any other provision of law" clause in a 2001 funding bill.[18]

4. In October 2005, to squelch a growing movement that seeks to hold weapons manufacturers liable for arms-related harm, two-thirds of the members of each Congressional body voted for The Protection of Lawful Commerce in Arms Act, exempting the arms industry from liability, and the President promptly signed it.

5. On the international level, especially at the UN, various efforts to establish meaningful arms controls have so far been frustrated. Four years before the "Control Arms" treaty was blocked, a limited-scope UN Conference on the Illicit Trade in Small Arms and Light Weapons in All Its Aspects had also failed. These setbacks, in turn, mirror the fact that the UN Security Council, whose permanent members are major arms exporters, has never fulfilled its responsibility under Article 26 of the UN Charter to submit plans to the UN "for the establishment of a system for the regulation of armaments."

One constant in all this is a commitment to bolstering the arms industry, regardless of who gets hurt or how badly. Perhaps it is a jungle out there, as gun lobbyists say, but the unhampered distribution of weapons is surely not a civilizing factor. Indeed, the process of distributing weapons has become so complex that the respective roles of government agencies and private contractors are blurred. Hobbes would perhaps understand how this could be; but he would surely understand even more clearly the need to impose order on the chaos and assign responsibilities. This has been done to some extent in the wake of 9/11, but only on the basis of a simplistic rationale.

Although their country had for years had military bases all over the world, had often interfered in the internal affairs of other countries and had often encountered opposition, Americans saw themselves as the innocent victims of the terrorist acts committed on their soil. The US administration expanded this anecdotal understanding into a Manichean global bipolarity and set people's sights on fighting terrorists (rather than communists) everywhere. The national debt has since been mounting steadily, and the country is becoming ever more dependent on the willingness of foreign creditors to "stay the course." Yet as before during the Cold War era, companies that do business with and through the DOD are benefiting. In one important respect, however, the present state of affairs is different because it involves what Marx might have seen as an inversion of the master-slave relationship.

Among the many contractors that do business with the DOD there are now just a few really major players: two giants, Boeing and Lockheed Martin, and two other major contractors that want to remain independent, Raytheon and Northrop Grumman.[19] This consolidation was effected via mergers with other contractors the cost of which was paid by taxpayers and by the thousands of American workers who were the victims of outsourcing to China and Saudi Arabia just a few years after Boeing and others had emphasized job maintenance in the 1992 election campaign. The most important of these mergers involved Boeing's purchases of Rockwell International's space and engine divisions in 1996 and of McDonnell Douglas in 1997. As a result of these and other related changes at Boeing, this company is now the largest US arms exporter (60 percent of its sales are to other countries). It so controls the Export-Import Bank that this institution is commonly referred to as the "Bank of Boeing," and its business connections with China have given it the single most important influence on US-China policy.[20]

To investors in and (surviving) employees of these companies, their control over how and where the US government will spend its defense dollars must seem on the whole a good thing. Victims of US military adventures, including its taxpayers and its troops abroad, may not agree. But few even seem to notice that all these intertwined causes and effects are bringing a post-Westphalian political community into being. Defense contractors claim to be ethical in all their business dealings.[21] Their customer, though, is reportedly both corrupt and incompetent as it goes about funding them. According to a recent evaluation of its practices, the DOD is vulnerable to contracting fraud, waste, and abuse (mismanagement) by virtue of weaknesses in each of five areas: "senior leadership, capable acquisitions workforce, adequate pricing, appropriate contracting approaches and techniques, and sufficient contract surveillance."[22] Because of these weaknesses, no one in the Pentagon is held accountable when production glitches inflate projected budgets far beyond initial estimates. And contractors are paid regardless of their performance. This has led some members of Congress to call for better oversight.[23] But both government and media spokespersons divert attention from such problems by focusing rhetorically on the military's salvific mission.

In short, the US national treasure is being expended for the sake of a comparatively small sector of the population, namely, people who benefit directly or indirectly from policies that commit two-thirds of the discretionary federal budget to "national defense." Local opposition may arise if some nearby base is being considered for closing. But generally speaking the American people let militaristic rhetoric trump moral concerns. Thus does the mantra of national defense drown out serious concern about why discretionary tax-derived funds are so heavily concentrated on the arms industry. If an elected official should happen to wonder about this, industry spokespersons point out that they not only protect people but give them good jobs. Perhaps so, but whatever employment the industry provides could be accomplished just as well by subsidies to other industries and, in any event, the actual number of citizens employed is minimized by offsets (on site manufacturing) and outsourcing to client buyers abroad.

Neither capitalist nor communist, if principled, could defend this boondoggle in the name of national defense. But so long as the world and its inhabitants do not go up in a mushroom cloud, Americans seem unperturbed by the many lesser cataclysms effected in their name—by, e.g., smart bombs, computer guided missiles, and helicopter gun ships. This moral blindness is understandable considering how carefully it is being crafted, partly by politicians and media but perhaps even more by arms industry advertisers and lobbyists. In some quarters this might even be thought of as a criminal conspiracy. But Westphalian mythology diverts people's attention from the efforts of peace-oriented NGOs to impose humanitarian values on the military weapons industry. Considering how poorly this industry performs with respect to either the CSR profitability requirement or the CSR use of political power requirement, then, a company in the arms industry should not be immune from liability by virtue of its relationship to a sovereign state.

The arms industry is in violation of CSR standards regarding the environment, social equity, profitability, and use of political power. This being the case, should an arms manufacturer be able to disavow its CSR inadequacies by simply pointing to government priorities?

In a blueprint Westphalian nation-state, the government exercises hegemony over violence whether within or beyond its borders. In practice, though, there are complications. In the US one must acknowledge a constitutional right to bear arms, which renders the government's designations of friends and foes irrelevant in the absence, say, of some felonious behavior or terrorist connections. This suggests that in the domestic market US arms manufacturers are not merely agents but are principals in the provision of weapons to users. Similarly, given the seemingly deliberate defects in US controls over arms transfers, these manufacturers are also principals in the provision of weapons to users abroad.

So whether the venue of liability is within or beyond the nation-state, no corporation based in the United States is acting responsibly if it unhesitatingly transfers weapons to any group that can pay even if the transfer should have been blocked by political operatives. For these weapons are ordinarily intended to serve as means to power and wealth over the bodies of anyone who stands in the way. In short, token political oversight is no substitute for authentic cost-benefit analyses and human rights standards that take peoples' lives and well-being into account. If this were done in all seriousness, at least small arms manufacturers and traders would be seen for what they are and what they intend to be: facilitators of death and destruction.

Edmund F. Byrne, Indiana University, Indianapolis

Notes

1. Aditi Gowri, "When Responsibility Can't Do It," *Journal of Business Ethics* 54 (2004): 33–50. One social response to such concerns is the Socially Responsible Investing movement. A common legal response is to impose strict liability on manufacturers of certain products on the grounds that they are in the best position to make their products safer to use. Such legal constraints are called for because the "do no harm" principle so familiar to moral philosophers is too easily dissipated in a complex corporate setting. See in this regard Lawrence E. Mitchell, *Corporate Irresponsibility* (New Haven: Yale University Press, 2001); M. David Ermann and Richard J. Lundman, *Corporate Deviance* (New York: Holt, Rinehart and Winston, 1982); and compare Christopher D. Stone, *Where the Law Ends* (New York: HarperCollins, 1975).

2. Andrew Linklater, *The Transformation of Political Community: Ethical Foundations of the Post-Westphalian Era* (Columbia, SC: University of South Carolina Press, 1988).

3. To economists, an externality is any effect of a transaction between two parties on a third party who is not involved in the carrying out of that transaction. If the externality is a benefit it is positive; if it is a cost, it is negative. Some consider only externalities from one market to another (e.g., reduction of fish population due to pesticide runoff from a farm). As I use this term it extends beyond identifiable markets to anything of value, human or not, even if not readily quantifiable.

4. See Anthony Honoré, "Causation in the Law," *Stanford Encyclopedia of Philosophy*, 8 Nov. 2001, rev. 12 Oct. 2005, online at http://plato.stanford.edu/entries/causation-law/. See also Christopher Hitchcock, "Probabilistic Causation," ibid., 11 July 1997, rev. 6 Sept. 2002, online at http://plato.stanford.edu/entries/causation-probabilistic/.

5. See "Deadly Weapon" in Wikipedia at http://en.wikipedia.org/wiki/Deadly_weapon. For a detailed elaboration of the processes by which potential for harm is estimated, see Kristin Shrader-Frechette, *Risk Analysis and Scientific Method* (Boston: D. Reidel, 1985), esp. chap. 5.

6. Gert G. Harigel, "Chemical and Biological Weapons: Use in Warfare, Impact on Society and Environment," Nuclear Age Peace Foundation, 2001, online at http://www.wagingpeace.org/articles/2001/11/00_harigel_ebw.htm; Ruben Mnatsakanian, "A Poisoned Legacy," *Our Planet* 8:6 (March 1997), online at http://www.ourplanet.com/imqversn/86/sakan.html.

7. Normand Gariépy, "Lac Saint-Pierre, Quebec," UNESCO Biosphere Reserves in Canada, No. 13, March 2001, online at http://www.biosphere_canada.ca/publications/newletters-bulletins/13/art.1.htm; Jurgen Brauer, "The Effect of War on the Natural Environment," 2000, online at http://www.aug.edu/~sbajmb/paper-london3.PDF; Nancy L. Peluso and Michael Watts, ed., *Violent Environments* (Ithaca: Cornell University Press, 2001); Cynthia G. Wagner, 2003, "War Crimes Against Nature: Groups Raise Call to Arms Against War on the Environment," *The Futurist* 37:3 (May–June 2003).

8. Michael Klare, "The Kalashnikov Age," *Bulletin of the Atomic Scientists* 55:1 (Jan/Feb, 1999): 18–22.

9. Tracy London, "Small Arms and Corporate Social Responsibility: Emerging International Norms and a Program for Advocacy" (2005): 1, online at http://www.ploughshares.ca/libraries/WorkingPapers/wp051.pdf.

10. These top ten contractors and the amounts of their contracts over FY 1998–2003 were (not counting joint venture income): Lockheed-Martin ($94 billion), Boeing ($81.6 billion), Raytheon ($39.9 billion), Northrop Grumman ($33.9 billion), General Dynamics ($33.2 billion), United Technologies ($17.8 billion), General Electric ($10.6 billion), Science Applications International ($10.5 billion), and Newport News Shipbuilding ($8.8 billion), which is now owned by Northrop-Grumman.

11. These were General Electric ($88.million), Lockheed Martin ($71.5 million), Boeing ($64.4 million), and Northrop Grumman ($61.2 million). See Larry Makinson, "Outsourcing the Pentagon: Who Benefits from the Politics and Economics of National Security?" 29 Sept 2004 (The Center for Public Integrity), online at http://www.publicintegrity.org/pns/report/aspx?aid=385.

12. The US defense budget came to $538–548 billion in 2004 but grows to $765.5 billion if one includes other defense-related expenditures that are funded outside the Department of Defense, e.g., in the Department of Energy (nuclear weapons) or the Veterans Administration. That year total expenditures for defense in the rest of the world came to $509 billion. See Stockholm International Peace Research Institute (SIPRI), *SIPRI Yearbook 2005: Armaments, Disarmament and International Security* (Oxford: Oxford University Press, 2005), 310; Jurgen Brauer and Nicholas Anglewicz, "Two-Thirds on Defense," *Tom Paine*, 10 June 2000, reposted on Global Policy Forum website; Winslow Wheeler, "Just How Big Is the Defense Budget?" *CounterPunch*, 19 Jan 2006, online at www.counterpunch.org/wheeler.01192006.html.

13. Richard F. Grimmett, "Conventional Arms Transfers to Developing Nations, 1997–2004," Report for Congress, U.S. Congressional Research Service, Library of Congress, 29 Aug. 2005, online at http://www.fas.org/man/crs/RL32547.pdf.

14. Frida Berrigan and William D. Hartung, "U.S. Weapons at War 2005: Promoting Freedom or Fueling Conflict?" World Policy Institute, June 2005, online at http://www.worldpolicy.org/projects/arms/reports/wawjune2005.html.

15. A dual-use technology is by definition developed for and identified with a military use but can also be used for a non-military purpose. The Internet is in fact an example. So too is high resolution spy-satellite technology which, though developed by the Cold War principals to secretly keep track of one another's activities, has many non-military uses.

16. In addition to the Nuclear Nonproliferation Treaty (effective 1970), which the US had signed, there were US statutes in place to regulate munitions exports, including the Arms Export Control Act, covering State Department oversight of defense items, and the Export Administration Act of 1979, covering Department of Commerce oversight of dual-use goods, software, and technology (some 12,000 applications per year). Licenses are required for items on the Commerce Control List, the United States Munitions List, and the Nuclear Regulatory Commission Controls, all supplemented with ad hoc oversight provisions. See U.S. Department of State, Bureau of Nonproliferation, "An Overview of U.S. Export Controls," online at http://www.exportcontrol.org/, click on 'Export Control'.

17. William D. Hartung, "Corporate Welfare for Weapons Makers: The Hidden Costs of Spending on Defense and Foreign Aid," *Policy Analysis* No. 350 (12 Aug. 1999), online at http://www.cato.org/pubs/pas/pa350.pdf.

18. The statutes at issue are: Sections 116 and 502b of the Foreign Assistance Act of 1961; Section 508 of the FY2002 Foreign Operations Appropriations Act; Section 40 of the Arms Export Control Act of 1976, 22 U.S.C. sect. 2778(b), as amended 1996; and the Leahy Amendment to the Foreign Assistance Act and the Defense Appropriation Act. Regarding financial institutions' involvement, see Amnesty International, TransArms, "Dead on Time—Arms Transportation, Brokering and the Threat to Human Rights" (10 May 2006): 5 and 35, online at http://web.amnesty.org/library/index/engact30082006.

19. Post-9/11 contractors may also provide new products and services to the newly established Department of Homeland Security (DHS), which the Bush administration initially opposed but then learned to love. DHS buys purportedly safety-enhancing products from companies whose top personnel come increasingly from the DHS, where they earned far less than now in the private sector. Another newcomer is the foreign-based but largely American owned arms manufacturer (e.g., the UK's BAE Systems) that challenges so-called Buy America rules and the domestic/foreign distinction by locating a plant in the US and/or buying US companies (*New York Times*, 16 Aug 2006, 18 and 19 June 2006, 27 Sept 2005).

20. Boeing Aircraft's relationship with the US government is a paradigm of the industry as a whole. Though also a producer of commercial products, it depends on DOD for a large percentage of its revenues. (In 2004 it derived profits of $623 million from revenues of $12.96 billion, 57 percent of which [$7.4 billion] came from sales of military aircraft and weapons systems [Associated Press, 28 April 2004].) Given this dependency, it relies heavily on lobbyists, whose contract-seeking practices have periodically immersed the company in scandal, e.g., during the Reagan administration and more recently when a last-minute amendment to the Pentagon's appropriation bill, passed in December 2001, authorized an Air Force 10-year lease of a hundred 767 commercial jets at $20 million per jet to use as refueling tankers. The total cost, including back-and-forth conversion costs, would have exceeded that for purchasing the aircraft outright. Opposition intensified, some key personnel at Boeing and at DOD were dismissed or imprisoned, and Boeing and its competitors began formulating plane replacement proposals. Other proposals include continuing to purchase C-17 cargo planes ($200 million each) even though no more are needed and installing (as yet unreliable) antimissile interceptors in Poland to knock out (hypothetical) incoming missiles from Iran. See *New York Times*, 22 and 24 May 2006; *Mobile Press-Register*, 13 June 2006; G. Parrish, "US Arms Exporters: Boeing," *Mother Jones Mojowire*, 1999, online at http://www.motherjones.com/news/special_reports/arms/boeing.html.

21. Defense Industry Initiative, "The Defense Industry Initiative on Business Ethics and Conduct: 2005 Annual Report to the Public," online at http://www.dii.org/.

22. US Government Accountability Office, "Global War on Terrorism: DOD Needs to Improve the Reliability of Cost Data and Provide Additional Guidance to Control Costs," Report to Congressional Committees (Sept. 2005), 2 online at http://www.gao.gov/new.items/d05882.pdf

23. Leslie Wayne, "Late and Costly: Pentagon Still Pays," *New York Times*, 11 July 2006, C1+.

Part 2:

Cosmopolitanism and Liberalism

State Consent vs. Human Rights as Foundations for International Law: A Critique of Allen Buchanan's Cosmopolitanism

Jordy Rocheleau

Abstract: The traditional view that legitimate international law is founded on the consent of the states subject to it has come under increasing attack by liberals, such as Allen Buchanan, who argue for a cosmopolitan order in which the protection of human rights norms is legally foundational. The cosmopolitan argument presupposes that human rights would be better preserved by doing away with the requirement of state consent. However, state consent is seen to be necessary for protecting the rights of individuals in weaker states and preserving global stability. The requirement of state consent preserves individual rights better than attempts to assert non-consensual liberal norms as international law, such that the internationalist system is more legitimate than the cosmopolitan on the latter's own terms.

I. Introduction: State Consent vs. Cosmopolitan Rights

International law has traditionally been viewed to be legitimate insofar as the states subject to it voluntarily consent to its norms. This view has come under increasing attack by cosmopolitan liberals who define international legitimacy in terms of the preservation of human rights, making state consent neither sufficient nor necessary for legitimate law. Although I have sympathy for cosmopolitan concerns, I qualifiedly defend the traditional international consent view after assessing the influential cosmopolitan view of Allen Buchanan.

On the state consent model, legitimate law is created through the voluntary agreement of states. This consent may take the form of explicitly signed treaties or the tacit acceptance and observance of common law norms. The United Nations Charter System is based on this consent model. The charter, itself signed by almost all of the world's states, proclaims in article 2 that "the Organization is based on the sovereign equality of all of its members."[1] The stipulation that international law only becomes legitimate through consent preserves the sovereignty of members, by protecting them from subjection to laws to which they object. Although treaties sometimes distribute rights unequally between states, these inequalities are voluntarily accepted. On this model, the consent of states is necessary and sufficient for the legitimacy of international law. Legitimated by procedure, the system and individual laws do not need to conform to any substantive moral principles.[2]

The consent theory appeals to common modern, liberal legal ideals. The sovereign equality of states seems to foster autonomy and democracy. In a sense, international law, in which parties explicitly sign on to the system and its rules, satisfies social contract conceptions of justice much better than domestic law. By protecting national sovereignty, the international consent model seems to address communitarian concerns. Furthermore, since state consent forms the basis of current international law it gains support from legal absolutists and pragmatists for whom maintenance of the stability of the current system trumps moral concerns.

However, this internationalist view of global legal legitimacy has been widely critiqued by cosmopolitan liberals. The most systematic critique to date is that of Allen Buchanan, who, in his work *Justice, Legitimacy and Self-Determination*, argues that the legitimacy of the international legal system does not depend on consent by states but rather on its protection of basic human rights of life, liberty, equality, and political participation.[3] Buchanan argues that a "Natural Duty of a Justice" requires that international institutions be designed to protect these rights. The system's legitimacy, that is its worthiness of being applied and enforced, depends to a large extent, if not entirely, on its accomplishment of this fundamental task. Buchanan uses this justice-based theory of international law to argue that the system could be made more legitimate by doing away with the consent requirement:

> It is a credible commitment to the protection of human rights, not consent, that confers political legitimacy. Consent of the governed . . . is not necessary for the justified exercise of political power, whether within individual states or in the workings of international legal institutions. Nor is it sufficient.[4]

Similar views have been defended by other liberal cosmopolitan theorists such as Thomas Pogge[5] and Henry Shue.[6] Furthermore, while cosmopolitans have repeatedly criticized Rawls's *Law of Peoples* for its derivation of international norms from a hypothetical contract between peoples rather than individuals, Rawls limits this contract to minimally decent states which can agree upon basic human rights. Thus, Rawls can be seen as part of a cosmopolitan liberal trend that would replace the consent model of legitimacy with one in which constitutional adherence to fundamental rights takes precedence.[7] I will take Buchanan's theory as paradigmatic of cosmopolitan approaches to international law. By analyzing and criticizing this influential proposal, I hope to raise a cautionary challenge to the liberal chorus supporting cosmopolitanism and show the power of the much maligned international consent view.

II. The Liberal Argument for a Cosmopolitan International Law

I want to assess in more detail Buchanan's argument for circumventing the state consent model. His cosmopolitanism ultimately rests on the moral principle of the equality of persons, "the obligation each of us has to treat every person with equal concern and respect."[8] Furthermore, he argues that there is a collection of identifiable, though perhaps not precisely determinable, basic human rights, including rights to life, liberty, legal equality, and resources for subsistence. Belief in basic human interests and an equal right to their realization, Buchanan notes, is not premised on a particular metaphysical doctrine but rather supported independently by an array of philosophical and religious views about human nature and morality. Since rights are unlikely to be achieved without international norms and institutions which protect and foster them, it follows that human beings should attempt to establish and support an international legal system to do this. As Buchanan puts it, "equal consideration for persons requires helping to ensure that they have access to institutions that protect their basic human rights."[9] Buchanan acknowledges that international law may have other goals besides the preservation of rights, such as international peace and security. However, he argues that preserving rights must be one of its main purposes. Thus, international law gains legitimacy insofar as it preserves basic rights and loses legitimacy insofar as it fails to do so. Although there is much potential for debate about the existence and meaning of human rights and natural duties, I accept Buchanan's basic premise that there are human rights and that international law gains legitimacy insofar as it preserves them.

Buchanan's cosmopolitanism rests on a second premise: that the consent of states adds nothing to the legitimacy of international law. That is, he seeks to argue that international agreement among state actors has no intrinsic value that warrants its institutionalized protection by the international system. This second key premise in the argument for replacing the system of international law as a voluntary system is also well founded, I suggest. States lack moral agency and inherent moral worth, such that their preservation is not a significant goal of the international community separate from its contribution to the rights and well being of individuals.

Buchanan rightly rejects nationalistic and communitarian arguments for state sovereignty. If national cultures must be protected, it is because they are of such importance that individuals have a right to them. However, it is implausible to think that cultural preservation is the only or most important right. It would be strange to assert that individuals' interest in being part of a self-determining nation is more basic than their interest in life, liberty, and opportunities to pursue their own life plan. This is to say that national sovereignty is morally derivative of basic human rights.

Furthermore, states do not map one to one onto culturally homogeneous nations, so *state* sovereignty does not necessarily foster *national* self-determination. If the state is multinational, the law may reflect only the politically dominant nation or a non-nationalistic compromise. The large number of authoritarian, undemocratic states would seem to fail to represent any semblance of societal self-determination. As Buchanan notes, "State consent is of dubious moral significance in a system in which many states often do not represent all or even most of their citizens or take their basic interests seriously."[10] So, a right of national self-determination, if anything, tells *against* a general right of sovereign state authority.

Buchanan takes pains to preempt legal positivist and legal absolutist objections to his project. Namely, he attempts to counter the view that international law just is, by definition, the rules that the states of the international community agree to. Buchanan replies that positivism, properly understood "is a view about what the law is, not about what it should be," and that it is therefore "entirely neutral as to whether moral reasoning can determine how the law ought to be."[11] That is, although law at any given time may in fact be composed of positive rules, this does not show that the rules ought to be exactly what they are or that the system is legitimate. For example, if business law is or came to be constituted by the rules that businesses agree to, this would not mean that this system should be accepted as legitimate rather than changed and replaced for the good of humanity.

Although I will shortly take exception to the scope of the conclusions that Buchanan draws from this critique of state sovereignty, I take it that the second step of Buchanan's argument is well founded. The consent of states, unlike the preservation of human rights, does not in and of itself confer legitimacy upon international law. So far, we can reconstruct Buchanan's cosmopolitan argument as follows:

(1) International law increases in legitimacy insofar as it furthers basic human rights.[12]

(2) State consent adds nothing to the legitimacy of international law separate from its furthering of other ends such as human rights.

Premises 1 and 2 make clear that human rights preservation is more fundamental to international law than state consent. Thus they seem to imply the conclusion that state consent should be replaced by the adherence to basic rights as the fundamental criterion for legitimate international law. However, this does not follow from these premises alone. The argument requires a last step, a claim that state consent is not itself required for the preservation of human rights or other fundamental goals of international law besides human rights preservation:

(3) The requirement of state consent does not promote human rights or other conditions for legitimacy.

Indeed, Buchanan goes on to argue for this third premise, making the case that the requirement of state consent has undermined human rights and failed to contribute to the legitimacy of the international system. He joins other critics of existing international law in arguing that the consent model describes as legitimate the results of self-interested bargaining between flawed state actors. The sovereign equality system gives too much deference to illiberal states, allowing them to veto or opt out of human rights norms and prevent humanitarian intervention. Buchanan suggests that given the number of undemocratic, non-rights-respecting states, human rights can be furthered by moving away from states' sovereign consent and equal voting rights: "[A]t this point in time—when a robust human rights culture is not firmly rooted in many states—state majoritarianism is not the most reliable mechanism for protecting human rights."[13]

Buchanan adds that "[He], for one, would be much more comfortable if the members of the European Union had the power to determine the character of international law than if the UN General Assembly did."[14] Furthermore, Buchanan suggests that because "the most powerful states in the system today have much better than average records in human rights,"[15] it is not only desirable but also feasible for liberal powers to take steps outside the UN Charter's sovereign consent system to establish an international law that better respects human rights. These legitimate norms would emerge through "the creation of a treaty-based, rule-governed intervention regime composed of the more democratic, human rights-respecting states that would operate outside the strictures of the UN Charter-based intervention regime."[16]

It is this third premise, that state consent does not effectively contribute to human rights preservation, that I think is suspect. Although I support a human rights basis for international legitimacy in principle, and reject any inherent moral demand for national sovereignty, I argue that the state consent model should be preserved because it actually preserves human rights better than feasible alternatives. My argument, then, insofar as it is about what institutional norms are most effective, will take the form of a rule-utilitarianism. It is a consequentialism in which the preservation of human rights, rather the maximization of utility, serves as the ultimate good. International norms are right, as Buchanan suggests, insofar as they as they foster human rights. However, in practice this ideal theory implies the superiority of the consent system to Buchanan's cosmopolitanism.

III. State Consent and the Human Rights Costs of Hegemony

There is little dispute about whether rights are furthered by respecting the sovereign rights of consent held by liberal democratic states. Their power to accept or reject international norms helps to preserve their own culture of internal respect for rights and foster popular sovereignty, and presumably it should contribute to the legislation and enforcement of international norms which protect rights everywhere.[17]

The debate is over whether recognition of the sovereign equality of illiberal, undemocratic states furthers human rights. I defend this counterintuitive thesis.

The norm of state consent protects individual human rights in a manner similar to the norm of non-intervention. Armed intervention, even against flawed states, results in more loss of life, liberty, and opportunity than non-intervention. Illiberal states should not be invaded or bombed, not because there is an inherent value in maintaining dictatorships but because war's destruction and the resulting national and international instability generally outweigh any expected humanitarian benefits.[18] I take it that the aftermath of the U.S. invasion of Iraq has been particularly illustrative of the validity of the presumption against armed intervention.

Yet it is not obvious that giving illiberal states the right to consent to or opt out of international norms promotes human rights. One might argue that avoiding the bloodshed and destabilization of military intervention is one thing but recognizing the equal sovereignty of illiberal states before international law is another. Merely denying rights to consent to or veto international norms would not seem to directly endanger life or liberty. Furthermore, the very assertion of human rights norms as laws would theoretically put pressure on illiberal states to improve their records. Public criticism, diplomatic pressure, and economic coercion short of military intervention might can give teeth to human rights laws.

Nonetheless, I argue that the consent of illiberal states to international norms does have practical benefits in preserving rights, much like the norm of nonintervention. First, the exclusion of illiberal states from norm formation invites imperial assaults of the rights of the world's least well off individuals. This is because even liberal states tend to make decisions which favor their own citizens to the detriment of the rights and well being of foreign citizens. Liberal states are behind direct rights violations in the form of colonial domination as well as primarily responsible for international economic norms which undermine and indirectly violate human rights. One need only look at the extent of collateral damage in interventions by the United States and its coalitions, not to mention the intentional killing of noncombatants and abuse of prisoners, for evidence that liberal states cannot be trusted of their own accord to protect the rights of the world's citizens. Liberal states, along with the illiberal, are prone to violating rights out of self-interested calculation or irrational fears. If the international legal system were to do away with the state consent requirement and assert liberal rights norms as fundamental laws, this would risk giving a blank check to the world's powers to implement imperial programs in the name of cosmopolitan rights. In response to Buchanan, while it is plausible to think that everyone in the world would do well to have the rights accorded to citizens of the European Union, it isn't the case that everyone would do well to live in a world ruled by the European Union.[19]

Buchanan acknowledges that the prevention of imperialism in the form of "predation" of weak states by strong states is one reason for recognizing state sovereignty and the right of state consent to norms. If strong states can easily colonize the weak, then the basic human right of equality is undermined.

However, Buchanan counters that "it is not at all clear that adequate constraints on predation can only be achieved by a requirement that all norms must enjoy state consent."[20] He suggests making the rules prohibiting aggression clearer and instituting safeguards regarding intervention. However, the institutional change that he mentions—including "weaker states" in the "permanent membership of the Security Council" so that "they could veto decisions that would authorize the more powerful states to intervene"[21] is odd—since it would give precisely the sort of power to non-rights respecting states that Buchanan takes pains to criticize. Vetoes of humanitarian intervention by non-rights respecting states are exactly what Buchanan designs his legal proposal to circumvent, so he would render his own proposed safeguard ineffective. Buchanan gives us little argument and no assurance that abandoning the Charter norm of sovereign equality and state consent would not lead to predation.

Furthermore, "predation"—that is, full scale invasion and occupation—is only the most extreme example of a risk to the international community in circumventing state consent. Recognition of a legal regime which bypasses state consent would legitimate the imposition of norms which purport to spread human rights but place disproportionate burdens on poor states. The threat of invasion is one way of coercing weaker states to adhere to such norms, but other sanctions might be used as well. The assertion that giving liberal powers the authority to write and enforce international norms would not result in the exacerbation of imperialist domination is implausible.[22]

IV. Consent, Illiberal States, and Human Rights Law

What then, of the argument that the requirement of sovereign consent protects human rights violations and thus comes at too high a price? I argue that there is reason to think that providing consent and voting rights to illiberal states will *not* lead to the rights violations imagined by their detractors. There are several reasons for this. First, even authoritarian rulers share interests with their people and thus tend to support international legislation which furthers rights at home, for example promoting economic growth and regulating environmental degradation.

Furthermore, even when authoritarian rulers do not share the interests of their populations—such as workplace and welfare rights—they must present themselves as furthering national interests, such that they may find it difficult not to sign international human rights legislation on such matters. This is to say that participation in the process of international public legislation encourages authoritarian states to endorse international norms more favorable to human rights than their own worst inclinations and practices. Law requires public defense of one's view, and it is difficult to defend human rights abuses. The weaknesses of dictators' arguments in the face of international ridicule are presented for all to see.

In addition to these humanizing effects of public reason, self-interested motives also lead to rational compromises in international law. While illiberal authoritarian regime A may be inclined to violate the rights of its minority groups and regime B may do the same, each A and B also have an interest in stopping this abuse by the other party. Thus, they will tend to compromise on human rights norms despite their own tendency to abuse them. It is for such reasons that the majority of the world's states, including the illiberal, are signatories to the Universal Declaration of Human Rights and the Geneva Conventions despite their mixed records regarding the stipulations of these documents.

One might object that such unprincipled compromises tend to lack compliance. Indeed, I just acknowledged that human rights norms are regularly violated. Cosmopolitans will conclude that the internal violations of human rights by illiberal states, from restrictions on speech to caste systems to genocide, are much more egregious than the threats of imperialism masquerading as human rights. Am I not ignoring evidence of massive rights abuse by illiberal states while I exaggerate the dangers of a relatively benign liberal hegemony?

In response, I argue that a realistic consideration of international law's limits illustrates that no significant improvement in human rights preservation could be made on a cosmopolitan model. Today, the most egregious violations of human rights—genocides and other cases of severe discrimination, restrictions on freedom, and material deprivation—can be understood as crimes against humanity which violate international law consented to under the U.N. Charter system. States are subject to sanctions for violating the norms to which they have consented. That the threat of material sanctions carries some force is exhibited by the pains taken by most states to argue that they are not in violation of international law. Such massive rights violations occur because the international system's minimal human rights laws are not effectively enforced. A more cosmopolitan international law would not change this. Most human rights violations would remain unpunished because of the limited resources and will of even rights-respecting states, much as occurs under the sovereign consent model.

A cosmopolitan international system would only be advantageous to the extent that the consent model prevents the effective recognition and enforcement of more rigorous human rights not currently recognized in international law—such as political freedoms, gender equality, workplace rights, and subsistence provision. However, in a world in which illegal genocides go unchecked, it is not feasible that more stringent human rights norms would be enforced. The most probable attempts at enforcement would be selective cases which coincide with the national interests of the great powers most capable of conducting forceful intervention or economic coercion. But such inconsistent, unilateral enforcement is not only unfair but also, because of its nationalistic, *realpolitic* motives, unlikely to genuinely further human rights. Indeed, despite the importance of human rights generally, it is questionable whether an attempt to enshrine and enforce any that do not have widespread national agreement is worthwhile. This concern will be discussed below as illustrative of the fundamental importance of stability in international law.

Before discussing stability arguments, I want to respond to a second objection, which is that my argument for national consent presupposes a false dichotomy in which we must either acknowledge the absolute sovereignty of illiberal states or completely ignore the views and concerns of their citizens. Buchanan argues that there are ways of fostering the inclusion of the world's citizens without granting their governments legitimacy and sovereignty rights to make or reject international norms. International law, he avers, would be best democratized by fostering individual citizen participation in its formulation rather than giving representation to illiberal state governments.[23] However, he doesn't specify how international law could be democratized in a way that bypasses states. Perhaps it would involve giving voting rights to non-governmental representatives, for example spokespersons from groups such as women's, labor, and minority rights organizations.

Although greater involvement by such players in international legislation would have benefits, as a democratic replacement for state consent it is flawed and impractical. There are so many individuals and groups that the process of consultation would be incomplete and arbitrary. Most of the world's people, who either lack ties to vocal non-governmental organizations or whose NGOs are not selected for participation, would have little connection to the political process. Territorial boundaries are the most systematic way to give world representation to individuals. Representation under any other rubric, be it nationality or field of labor, will involve both massive exclusion and imposition of arbitrary categories. As flawed as states are, they serve an important practical mediating role between the individual and international law, which is not easily replaced by other structures. The advantages of having international laws which are agreed to by the powers that effectively govern territories can generally be summarized as benefits of "stability," a concept I turn to now.

V. Stability, Legitimacy, and the Necessity of State Consent

In addition to preventing domination and ensuring that international norms are responsive to the needs of weaker states, the consent model has the virtue of reducing conflict and fostering international stability. Stability, I argue, is necessary for the preservation of human rights, and therefore the international system is more legitimate to the extent that its principles promote stability. Unfortunately, stability is rarely defined and too often functions as a catch-all phrase for consequentialist considerations in international policy debates. I suggest that there are four different forms of human rights-preserving stability fostered by state consent that would be undermined by the institutionalization of a cosmopolitan rights system.

First, having international norms which are widely consented to reduces occasions for conflict, thereby preserving peace. If international law includes norms that many states disagree with, and can be argued to be in violation of, then causes for war multiply. Any state found to violate human rights—for example denying democratic participation, equal rights for women, or civil liberties—becomes a potential target for the use of force. The states targeted for invasion themselves develop strong incentives to arm themselves and threaten violence. Although international peace is not sufficient for the preservation of human rights within states, it is necessary. War inevitably involves massive rights violations, killing civilians, causing soldiers to be forced to fight, and undermining the economic infrastructure necessary for basic subsistence and economic opportunity. An international law consented to by the large majority of the worlds' states, even if it fails to protect some human rights, is likely to prevent conflict better than an international system founded on provocative assertions of expansive rights.

Further adding to the stability of the consent model are considerations of reciprocity and incentives for legal obedience. A legal system is only effective when it is generally observed. Each party obeys in part on the expectation that others will do the same. If parties know that others are inclined to break the rules, and if the rules are broken so frequently that most violations go unpunished, then the world community is likely to view the rules cynically. The only incentive for states to obey the law becomes moral integrity, which, given the combination of self-interested and irrational motives for states to break rules, is a weak foundation for international responsibility. That is, when the law is not widely consented to, expectations of reciprocity are lost, and even rights-respecting states are likely to cheat. Legal norms which are widely consented to, by contrast, have a better chance at being generally obeyed and thus creating the expectation of reciprocity. Once again, human rights are better preserved by a legal system which does not impose a cosmopolitan standard on the world community.

A third practical, stability consideration in favor of the consent model of legitimacy is that consent represents a clear framework for generating public norms, which may then form a predictable background for international diplomacy and trade. One of the purposes of international law is to develop a system of cooperation based upon stable and predictable rules. Doing away with state consent would lead to greater legal uncertainty. Whereas state voting is a straightforward procedure for producing legislation, the nature and scope of non-consensual human rights legislation would be indeterminate. One need not be skeptical about human rights to recognize ambiguity in what they entail. A system in which liberal states occasionally and unpredictably assert and enforce rules against illiberal states would again lack the stable system of expectations that effective law must provide. This uncertainty would create insecurity and undermine rational state planning to satisfy the needs of citizens.

A final reason to recognize sovereign equality and base international law upon state consent is the benefits of cooperation between states. State governments, by definition, exercise power over their territories. We already discussed the high costs and unlikely success of attempting to enforce norms in states in which they are not supported by the people who control military power and political institutions. Furthermore, the major problems which face the world cannot be solved without international cooperation, including that of illiberal states. The great challenges to security and human well being—ethnic and territorial conflicts, international terrorism, nuclear weapons proliferation, failed states, global climate change, famine, and the AIDS epidemic—all require international solutions. Indeed, it is impossible to imagine major progress in these areas which does not involve many undemocratic, rights-abusing states, especially the nuclear powers Russian, China, and Pakistan.

Now, presumably, any cosmopolitan would agree that getting illiberal states on board in solving such problems is a good idea. The question is whether this cooperation must be enshrined in law. Liberal states might cooperate with Russia and Pakistan to catch terrorists and must work with China to prevent nuclear proliferation in Asia without recognizing the sovereignty and voting rights of these states. However, cooperation is less likely to be stable if is not based on mutual respect and assurances. A workable international system will have to involve cooperation on a shared understanding between liberal and illiberal states. Establishing the basis for future cooperation to reduce rights violations is another reason that liberal states should not declare as law human rights norms rejected by foreign powers.

Arguing for states' right to consent to or opt out of international norms is not, of course, to say that illiberal practices should not be criticized and that liberal states should not try to encourage illiberal states to consent to more demanding rights norms. It is only to say that the assertion of an international legal regime not agreed to by many or most states would be detrimental to the preservation of the very human rights norms that liberals aim to achieve.

The necessity of accommodating existing illiberal regimes and practices is tacitly acknowledged by Buchanan. He argues that other than the derivation of the ideal goals of the international system, the theory of international law must focus on non-ideal principles about how to best realize these moral goals in light of current power structures and institutional realities. As Buchanan puts it "nonideal theory's task is to guide our efforts to approach those ultimate targets, both by setting intermediate moral targets . . . and by helping us to determine which means and processes for achieving them are morally permissible."[24] To this end, he argues that currently accepted international norms should continue to be treated as legitimate international law, and though he urges that new states should be accepted as legitimate international actors only if they respect human rights, he argues for grandfathering in all existing regimes, whether they respect rights or not.[25] Buchanan rightly notes that such concessions to injustice are necessary to promote the end of best achieving moral goals on balance. In their sober moments, then, most international theorists recognize that the assertion and enforcement of human rights norms over and against the sovereign equality of states is necessarily exceptional and occasional. Cosmopolitan theorists should heed these realist insights before suggesting the rejection of the consent model of international legitimacy.

Buchanan is right to reject "Legal Absolutist" arguments that international law simply means that which has been agreed to by states.[26] Such arguments are either question-begging or presume the intrinsic value of state consent without argument. However, Buchanan fails to take seriously the argument that legitimate law must secure a stable system of peaceful cooperation with reciprocal expectations. Otherwise law becomes, at best, empty moral exhortation and, at worst, the basis of ongoing conflict, with arbitrary and unpredictable enforcement. If legitimacy requires a stable system of generally recognized norms, and if this is to be achieved through state consent rather than the implementation of liberal human rights norms, then legitimacy is furthered by the consent model.

VI. Reply to Objections and Conclusion

At least three important objections to the consent theory of legitimacy should be addressed before I conclude. First, states frequently consent under duress, such that their international treaties and votes can hardly be called voluntary, rational expressions of their own best interest, much less their considered views about what is morally right. States may be pressured by outright threats of aggression or a combination of economic sticks and carrots. In rejecting the consent requirement, Buchanan concludes that, "To hold that 'consent' under duress bestows legitimacy is absurd."[27]

On one hand, I would note that the consent model has traditionally rejected as illegitimate any treaties or votes resulting from the direct threat of force. Consent in pressured but uncoerced situations can be argued to rightly express considered judgment about a state's best interest in current circumstances. Although such consent may be a non-ideal form of legitimacy, to call it absurd is overstated; it would imply the rejection of much contract law as we know it. On the other hand, Buchanan's use of international coercion to reject state consent is paradoxical. If states are subject to coercion, other parties to international agreements, such as non-governmental organizations, are subject to it as well. Furthermore, the coercion that undermines state consent is usually imposed by precisely those powerful states which in Buchanan's system would be the principle architects of international law. If, under today's consent system, the world's powers are succeeding in coercing smaller states to agree to laws that are bad for their citizens, we can conclude that if we were to implement a cosmopolitan system in which weaker, illiberal states are denied rights of consent, international domination would be considerably exacerbated.

A second objection to my case for a politics of consensus in order to preserve human rights is that my argument leads to inconsistencies at the national and international levels.[28] That is, my argument for the virtues of political consent for protecting the rights of the governed implies that each state should be democratically organized internally to prevent the abuse of citizens by their states.[29] However, the universal prescription of democracy at the state level implies a cosmopolitan norm which states ought not to be free to ignore. Does my rule-consequentialism of human rights preservation not imply that the world community should require states to be liberal and democratic?

My response relies on the difference between justice and legitimacy, on one hand, and national and international legitimacy on the other. Justice involves meeting best practice political principles, including democracy and respect for rights. Legitimacy only requires that a state be warranted in exercising power. Although it might seem that unjust states are always unwarranted in exercising power, in many cases a government's abdication of power would be worse—that is, would undermine human rights to a greater extent—than its continued exercise of its flawed governance. Such states are unjust but legitimate. I acknowledge that a similar point applies at the international level. If a system were in place whereby one powerful force, say the United States or NATO, effectively legislated and enforced norms worldwide in a way which generally preserved human rights throughout the world, albeit with loss of local autonomy, and if this system could not be replaced without the system devolving into anarchy or domination by a more abusive power, then this non-consensual system would have legitimacy. However, in the world that we are in, we have a more or less functional system of international cooperation, and there is no available alternative that offers sufficient stability and justice to make efforts to implement it legitimately.

The second point is that the decision about internal, national, state legitimacy, which involves a state's authority to govern its own people, is a different matter than its external legitimacy, that is, whether it warrants the respect of the international community as a sovereign, voting member. Government X lacks legitimacy if its ceasing to exercise power would better protect human rights. However, if X's flawed government continues to remain in control of the territory, there are practical reasons for continuing to maintain international dialogue with this power in order to improve the situation in the territory and foster international stability. Thus it can make sense to recognize even unjust and internally illegitimate governments as legitimate international players. The key point is that although my argument commits me to recognizing the general value of democracy at all levels, it does not require that at the higher levels, entities are excluded for their lack of democracy at the lower level. Such exclusion repeats the error made within the undemocratic state.

The greatest objection to the consent model is that if consent is considered necessary for legitimate law, then illiberal, "rogue" states could veto or opt out of human rights norms, preventing international progress and even allowing human rights catastrophes. By contrast, the cosmopolitan view underpins the growing consensus among international scholars and activists that the international community has not only a legitimate right but also a moral duty to enforce basic human rights norms against their most egregious violators. My argument to this point might seem to imply an absolute respect for state sovereignty, denying any international jurisdiction in the affairs of non-consenting states. This would in principle require the world to remain passive in the face of genocide if the perpetrator has not signed a treaty against it or otherwise accepted its prohibition.

However, one need not go this far to support the general norm of state consent. Another option is simply to follow current practice in international law by recognizing a handful of peremptory, *jus cogens* norms which hold certain crimes against humanity to be illegal regardless of what states consent to and vote in favor of. These notably include the illegality of genocide and aggressive war.[30]

I would caution against expanding the list of norms which are considered peremptory. The institutionalization of rights norms bypassing or overriding state consent has diminishing returns and increasing risks. It undermines the international system by increasing conflict, uncertainty, and hegemony. State consent provides a realistic and stable set of norms in light of current interest and power structures. This system has yielded considerable human rights-preserving treaties which can be used to sanction states' worst practices. The cosmopolitan theory that international law is legitimate insofar as it promotes human rights, in practice, implies a presumption in favor of acknowledging and enforcing the system of sovereign state consent.

Jordy Rocheleau, Austin Peay State University

Notes

1. United Nations, "Charter of the United Nations, 1945," Appendix D in Michael Byers, *War Law* (New York: Grove Press, 2005).

2. As an anonymous reviewer noted, the standard of consent could be considered a moral constraint on law, although, as I will show, the strongest case for the consent standard is pragmatic rather than principled.

3. Allen Buchanan, *Justice, Legitimacy and Self-Determination* (New York: Oxford University Press, 2004).

4. Ibid., 234.

5. Thomas Pogge, *Realizing Rawls* (Ithaca, NY: Cornell University Press, 1989) and Pogge, "An Egalitarian Law of Peoples," *Philosophy and Public Affairs* 23 (1994): 195–224.

6. Henry Shue, *Basic Rights, Subsistence, Affluence, and U.S. Foreign Policy*, 2nd edition (Princeton: Princeton University Press, 1996).

7. John Rawls, *The Law of Peoples* (Cambridge, MA: Harvard University Press, 1999).

8. Buchanan, 27.

9. Ibid., 88.

10. Ibid., 234.

11. Ibid., 21.

12. Because matters besides human rights preservation—particularly peace and security—can also affect the legitimacy of the international system, (2) is not entailed by (1).

13. Buchanan, 319.

14. Ibid.

15. Ibid. Buchanan cites China and Russia as notable exceptions to this principle.

16. Ibid., 472.

17. However, democracies might agree to violate the rights of foreign citizens, especially non-democracies, as I argue below.

18. For examples of this pragmatic argument against intervention, see Richard Miller, "Morality, Intervention, and Reality" in *Ethics and Foreign Intervention*, ed. Deen Chatterjee and Don Scheid (Cambridge: Cambridge University Press, 2003), 215–50, as well as the chapter on intervention in Michael Walzer, *Just and Unjust Wars* (New York: Basic Books, 1977), 86–108.

19. In fact, in cases of extreme differences in national wealth and power, the same rules and privileges may not provide for equally good standards of living. For example, free trade benefits those who already have the wherewithal to participate in the market. Rules of warfare which prohibit intentional targeting of innocents but are permissive toward collateral damage privilege powerful states over the weak.

20. Buchanan, 311.

21. Ibid.

22. The argument that new efforts to erode state sovereignty threaten to increase global inequality can also be found in Bennedict Kingsbury, "Sovereignty and Inequality," *European Journal of International Law* 9 (1998): 599–625; and Jean Cohen, "Whose Sovereignty? Empire Vs. International Law," *Ethics & International Affairs* 18 (2004): 1–24.

23. See Buchanan, 322–7.

24. Ibid., 61.

25. Ibid., 261–88.

26. Ibid., 307–8. Jean Cohen's critique of new cosmopolitan legal proposals raises concerns regarding the threats of hegemony and the undermining of international cooperation that I second here. However, she slips into begging the question in favor of state sovereignty when she states that "international law has to be based on a set of political relationships between states to which sovereignty is ascribed within a common framework, based on shared political norms, involving mutual recognition, balance, and institutionalized

cooperation." (Cohen, 20) While I agree with this conclusion, one must defend the value of a system of state equality for individuals, rather than presuppose it as the form of international politics.

27. See Buchanan, 304.

28. I am indebted to John Rowan for raising this instructive challenge to my position.

29. I will not try to defend my position with the technical point that general consent is impossible at the state level where the governed number in the millions. My position is open to the objection that arguments very similar to my own would show that a majoritarian democratic voting system with political rights best secures human rights and therefore should be realized everywhere, again contradicting my cosmopolitanism.

30. Byers, 6.

Cosmopolitanism and Global Public Health

JAN SUTHERLAND AND ELAINE GIBSON

Abstract: In this paper we examine a nation's obligations to report infectious diseases under the World Health Organization's new International Health Regulations. We argue that acceptance of the Regulations signals a concrete turn to cosmopolitan citizenship in the area of health. But we also show that the new global health regime and its economic consequences raise ethical tensions for both the conceptualization and practice of cosmopolitanism. Specifically: 1) using global public heath as a lens makes visible how current conceptions of cosmopolitan theory are not truly in conversation with those who are the subject of their concern; and, 2) focusing on global public health illustrates the limits of present cosmopolitan citizenship. In matters of virulent pathogens, nations are required to be good global citizens by protecting citizens of other states in the absence of a framework by which other states bear some of the costs that such global citizenship demands.

I. Introduction

Despite their long history and the persistent institutional trace of their presence, cosmopolitan worldviews have had little impact on the conceptual pre-eminence of the nation state as the primary site of citizenship and political obligation.[1] Recently, however, the realities of globalization have led to increased efforts to understand how we may yet conceive of global citizenship. International trade and the movement of capital have undermined and perhaps, in some sense, erased national boundaries in important ways. The flight of capital and jobs has generated conflict in western nations, which have seen the departure of significant portions of their manufacturing and service sectors to developing nations, while compulsory participation in global economic restructuring has often forced developing nations to compromise on labour conditions and a living wage for their citizens. National governments and legal systems have tolerated but not adequately addressed the new global shift. The impact of globalization on the economy has motivated theorists to argue for moral cosmopolitanism; however, no one would argue that economic restructuring has yet fostered actual cosmopolitan citizenship.

In this paper, we look at a specific instance of the tension between national autonomy and the demands of global participation, one that seems to be actually fostering a kind of moral cosmopolitanism. Specifically, we look at a nation's obligations in public health emergencies due to outbreaks of infectious disease with respect to the World Health Organization's (WHO) new International Health Regulations (IHR). Globalization has been enabled through new information technologies. In the area of health and epidemiology, the use of technology allows reporters, minor officials, and members of non-governmental organizations (NGOs) to interact with bodies at an international level, thus bypassing national systems. The instantiation of technology seems broadly conducive to cosmopolitanism in that it allows actors to bypass the nation state.

We argue that the widespread acceptance of the new WHO regulations is to some extent a concrete turn to cosmopolitan citizenship in the area of health, one enabled by the structures of epidemiology and information technologies. But we also show that the new global health regime and its economic consequences raise ethical tensions for both the conceptualization and practice of cosmopolitanism. Specifically: 1) using global public heath as a lens makes visible how current conceptions of cosmopolitan theory are not in conversation with those who are the subject of their concern; and, 2) focusing on global public health illustrates the limits of present cosmopolitan citizenship. In matters of virulent pathogens, nations are required to be good global citizens by acting to protect citizens of other states in the absence of a framework by which benefiting states bear some of the costs that such global citizenship demands.

We first discuss the legal regime of the IHR, with particular attention to the role of information technologies in facilitating the effectiveness of the new Regulations. Cosmopolitanism seems an ideal lens with which to view both the changing legal regime and the actions of people in response to recent pathogenic crises. Focusing on cosmopolitan theory, in particular on the work of Kwame Anthony Appiah, we demonstrate that an incomplete sense of cosmopolitanism on the part of wealthier nations imposes severe burdens on poor nations. We also hope to show the ways in which full moral cosmopolitanism can be a boon to motivating nations' compliance with the IHR.

II. The Global Health Regime

International Health Regulations

The legal instrument governing global public health is the International Health Regulations administered by WHO. First issued in 1969 (IHR, 1969),[2] revised in 2005 with the new version in force as of 2007 (IHR, 2005),[3] the IHR aim to balance preventing the international spread of disease with minimizing effects on international trade and travel. The Regulations apply to all 192 member states of the World Health Assembly.[4]

The IHR (1969) require member states to report to WHO only three diseases—cholera, plague, and yellow fever—which occur within their national boundaries. The IHR (1969) outline steps that affected countries must take to prevent the international spread of disease, including hygiene measures at national points of entry. They also outline the maximum allowable measures that unaffected nations are allowed to take to secure the health of their citizens, including instituting trade and travel restrictions on goods and citizens from affected countries. David Fidler argues that IHR (1969) are a reflection of Westphalian governance principles where primacy is given to the principles of sovereignty, non-intervention, and consent-based international law.[5] Sovereignty is protected by the vesting of responsibility on the nation-state to notify WHO of any event of concern. Absent notification, WHO is without legal authority to act.

The actual impact of the IHR (1969) has been less than stellar. Despite clear obligation, nations often did not report outbreaks of disease for fear of economic repercussions. As India found out when it experienced a limited outbreak of the plague, excessive sanctions and over-reaction can have serious effects on a nation's economy.[6] The limited scope of the diseases covered has also been a serious issue. The IHR (1969) have been ineffective during the HIV/AIDS crisis as they were during the recent SARS crisis. Through much of the outbreak of SARS in 2002/2003, China did not cooperate with WHO. Unquestionably, China's response aided the international spread of the disease, but it was wholly within its legal rights: SARS was not a reportable disease.

Given the failure of the IHR (1969) and against the background of newly emerging and re-emerging infectious diseases during the 1980s–1990s, the IHR have been revised. The IHR (2005) are less concerned with national sovereignty, more interventionist in orientation, and allow non-state actors to play a key role in global health surveillance. Significant changes include the responsibility of countries to report not just specified diseases but "all events which may constitute a public health emergency of international concern" to WHO within 24 hours.[7] WHO is also authorized to act on information from non-governmental sources,[8] which is a significant shift from hewing to national sovereignty. Drawing from a broader array of public health information sources will greatly enhance the ability of WHO to mobilize its resources to intervene in situations where timeliness is a necessity.

Global Health Surveillance

As the recent SARS epidemic showed, efficient and effective global health surveillance can prove invaluable in containing potentially devastating pathogens. Information technologies, as part of a global public health surveillance system, are used to track outbreaks, analyze data, and communicate the results worldwide. One of the most striking developments information technologies have brought about is the ability of non-governmental actors to extend the reach of more traditional information sources in global surveillance.[9]

A sterling example of information technologies application in global health surveillance is the Global Public Health Information Network (GPHIN). An internet-based early warning system developed in Canada and in operation since 1998, it has become a key component of WHO's efforts to detect and track infectious diseases. GPHIN is an automated search engine that continuously monitors a variety of information sources including websites, news wires, local online newspapers, public health email services and electronic discussion groups.[10] GPHIN tracks information about specific topics such as disease outbreaks, emergence of infectious diseases, contaminated food and water, and safety of products, drugs, and medical devices. As of 2006, it operates in seven languages with plans to add more languages and, thus, increase its reach.[11]

By 2004, approximately 40 percent of outbreak early warnings that WHO received came from GPHIN. It was GPHIN officials who first noticed reports of an unusual respiratory infection occurring in Guangdong Province, China in 2002 which heralded the presence of SARS as a global health concern. Accurate information alone, however, will not prevent diseases from spreading. Public health bodies must have the ability and the authority to act in such circumstances. With respect to international heath threats, an international public health body such as WHO can only act within its permissible legal scope and, in the case of infectious diseases, the legal regime that empowers WHO is the IHR.

Both revisions to the IHR and the demonstrated usefulness of information technologies in global health surveillance have tipped the balance away from a primary concern with state sovereignty to prevention of the spread of infectious diseases:

> The new IHR's information and verification provisions mitigate the consequences of non-compliance with notification obligations because WHO will, in all likelihood, learn of disease events through other sources, triggering the information verification and dissemination processes. . . . In short, the information and verification provisions provide global health governance over state sovereignty.[12]

Whereas IHR (1969) adhered to Westphalian principles of sovereignty and non-intervention, IHR (2005) can be seen as an expression of post-Westphalian sensibilities: there is less regard for sovereignty, more willingness to impose requirements on matters formerly viewed as internal to the nation, and the ability to rely on information provided by non-governmental sources. Given their effect on state sovereignty, the status of IHR (2005) as a voluntarily assumed international obligation is notable. We believe this commitment indicates a shift towards post-Westphalian health governance that requires deeper analysis. The post-Westphalian shift preceded IHR (2005) and must be seen as its expression rather than its cause. It is worth noting that SARS occurred under the jurisdiction of the IHR (1969) yet, as observed by the editors of *The Lancet Infectious Diseases*:

During the severe acute respiratory syndrome (SARS) outbreak of 2003 all affected member states, with the exception of China, openly reported outbreaks and cooperated with WHO despite having no legal obligation to do so. This remarkable situation signified that a fundamental change had taken place in global public health governance—the shift in the political, economic, and technological climate had brought about new ways of thinking for public health.[13]

III. The Global Health Regime and Cosmopolitan Concerns

Cosmopolitan Theory and Global Health

Cosmopolitan moral theory is an ideal lens through which to look at the IHR (2005) as a shift in conceptions of political citizenship in the area of health. Simply put, germs do not respect borders and it is incumbent on all to lessen the possibility of international spread of disease. Global citizenship is a concept made real in the case of infectious diseases: with respect to virulent pathogens, we really do share one world, and technological systems such as GPHIN have made the rapid movement of disease visible to us. Insofar as the IHR (2005) are an expression of post-Westphalian public health governance, they are also, to some degree, an instantiation of cosmopolitan ideals.

As we understand it, cosmopolitan theory holds that all humans, despite the many and varied differences amongst us, belong to a single community. As such, we have moral obligations to assist others in need even though we may never meet them. The content and extent of those obligations varies between theories; we are not so much concerned with the specific content of the theories as the discourse in which they are framed. We draw primarily on recent work by Kwame Anthony Appiah and on problems framed most famously by Peter Singer.

Thomas Pogge takes the core of cosmopolitanism to be as follows:

> Three elements are shared by all cosmopolitan positions. First, *individualism*: the ultimate units of concern are human beings, or persons—rather than, say, family lines, tribes, ethnic, cultural, or religious communities, nations or states. . . . Second, *universality*: the status of ultimate unit of concern attaches to every human being equally. . . . Third, *generality*: this special status has global force. Persons are ultimate units of concern for everyone—not only for their compatriots, fellow religionists, or such like.[14]

Consistent with Pogge, Kwame Anthony Appiah writes:

> There are two strands that intertwine in the notion of cosmopolitanism. One is the idea that we have obligations to others, obligations that stretch beyond those to whom we are related by the ties of kith and kind, or even the more formal ties of a shared citizenship. The other is that we take seriously the value not just of human life but of particular human lives.[15]

Individuals are the locus of moral concern and, irrespective of our geographic distance, we have mutual moral obligations to alleviate suffering where it is in our power to do so.

These basic principles appear to underlie Peter Singer's intuitions in his much discussed "Famine, Affluence and Morality." As a utilitarian, Singer judges the rightness of an action by its effects on aggregated welfare. He offers us a situation where you see a child drowning in a shallow pool. If you go into the pool to rescue the child, you will destroy the expensive suit you are wearing. Do you have a duty to rescue the child at the expense of the suit? Surely you do have such a duty because the death of a child is much worse than the loss of a suit. Singer extracts the following principle: *If we can avoid a greater harm by sacrificing some lesser thing, then we should do so.* We can disagree with how far the Singer Principle (as it has come to be known) should extend but it does give some content to the duty to aid. Moreover, Singer claims that distance is morally irrelevant with respect to the duties to aid others: "it makes no moral difference whether the person I help is a neighbor's child ten yards from me or a Bengali whose name I shall never know, ten thousand miles away."[16] Without entering into the extensive debates that Singer's essay has generated, we can at least say that these two bare principles—that we have a duty to aid humans in need and that that duty is not blocked merely by distance[17]—are central to cosmopolitan morality.

It is fairly easy to see how cosmopolitan moral theory can provide a description of the requirements of IHR. The IHR codifies a moral responsibility that we all have to look out for the welfare of others with respect to the global spread of infectious diseases. We must ensure that the harm of infectious diseases is minimized even if doing so causes us some financial or reputational harm. We are not here implying that nations do or will accept the obligations of the IHR (2005) on primarily moral grounds. Pragmatism based on the knowledge that virulent pathogens know no boundaries is of itself a compelling reason to accept the IHR (2005). Nevertheless, the global response to the SARS crisis would seem to indicate that people are prepared to take these obligations seriously for both pragmatic and moral reasons. Irrespective of the possible consequences, nations did not stand on their legal rights and private citizens undertook voluntary quarantine.

While we acknowledge that the response to SARS is to some degree consistent with moral cosmopolitanism, we want to use the international health context to challenge the commitment of the developed world to a robust moral cosmopolitanism. When viewed through the lens of global health and epidemiology, the construction of moral cosmopolitan theory in the developed world in fact reveals our continued lack of community with the global poor.

Problems with Cosmopolitanism

Appiah patterns his cosmopolitan theory on a conversational model. From conversations with others we learn both what we have in common and to accept diversity.

He urges "that we should learn about people in other places, take an interest in their civilizations, their arguments, their errors, their achievements, not because that will bring us to agreement, but because it will help us get used to each other."[18] While it is impossible to always agree on values, through conversation we can learn to respect each other across our differences. Increased understanding across differences will make strangers less strange and foreigners less foreign:

> [e]ngagement with strangers is always going to be engagement with particular strangers; and the warmth that comes from shared identity will often be available. . . . I care about some people in other places, people whose oppression would engage me particularly, just because I have read their philosophical writing, admired their novels, seen them play spectacular games of tennis on the television. . . . When a stranger is no longer imaginary, but real and present, sharing a human social life, you may like or dislike him, you may agree or disagree; but, if it is what you both want, you can make sense of each other in the end.[19]

Appiah does not believe that we need a shared perspective or a body of shared norms in order to care about each other. What we need is a willingness to engage.

With respect to obligations, Appiah believes that basic needs required for human flourishing ought to be met, but he imposes four constraints on these obligations. First, the primary mechanism for ensuring human flourishing is the nation-state. Thus, we have a special responsibility to the life and justice of fellow nationals. We also have a duty to ensure that other states meet the needs of their citizens. If they do not, we "share the collective obligation to change them" and if through lack of resources they cannot, "providing resources can be part of that collective obligation."[20] Second, our obligations do not require us to do more than our fair share. Appiah allows that it is difficult to specify what our fair share is and to specify how we are to respond to the unmet needs that arise because others fail to do their fair share.[21] Though Appiah does not state it, it follows from his view that it is supererogatory for those who do more than their fair share—they are truly beneficent. And, in response to those who advocate a strict application of the Singer Principle, Appiah offers a third constraint:

> [W]hatever our basic obligation, they must be consistent with our being . . . partial to those closest to us: to our families, our friends, our nations; to the many groups that call upon us through our identities, chosen and unchosen; and, of course, to ourselves. . . . This constraint is another that the [Singer Principle] theorists are indifferent toward. They think that it is so important to avoid the bad things in other lives that we should be willing to accept for ourselves, our families and friends, lives that are barely worth living. This third constraint interacts, I think, with the worry that I expressed about the second. For, if so many people in the world are not doing their share . . . it seems to me I cannot be required to derail my life to take up the slack.[22]

Finally, as a general constraint, Appiah argues that there are many different values in the world and our obligations must take note of that.

> What would the world look like if people always spent their money to alleviate diarrhea in the Third World and never on a ticket to the opera. . . . Well, it would probably be a flat and dreary place. . . . Not all values have a single measure. . . . Would you really want to live in a world in which the only thing anyone ever cared about was saving lives?[23]

We are particularly struck by this last sentence. We would hazard that for a significant number of the world's population, the answer is that they would very much like to live in a world where people were wholly obsessed with saving lives because theirs is one of the lives that could be saved. Appiah is clearly addressing those of us in the developed world—we who are fortunate enough to be born in a place that allows us to consider going to the opera a significant value. He is not addressing those whose basic needs are not being met.

One might rightly remark that Appiah's vision of cosmopolitanism is made of pretty weak stuff. Basically, our primary obligations are to ourselves, and to our family, friends, and fellow nationals, leaving little, we suspect, to assist others deeply in need. Secondly, we are encouraged to first attend to the needs of the needy near who are likely not so needy as those living in extreme poverty in the developing world. And while we have some financial obligations to the poor, we are only obligated to do our fair share despite knowing that others are not doing theirs and knowing that the ultimate consequence is that people will fail to have their basic needs met.

Appiah seeks to provide reasons why we in the developed world should be motivated to help the distant poor. Yet cosmopolitanism is about rights, duties, and benefits of world citizenship irrespective of geographical location: this is part of what makes it an apt theory for discussing global public health. With respect to global pathogens: 1) distance is simply not an issue when infectious diseases can spread so rapidly, and 2) we expect citizens and nations to undertake measures to prevent the global spread of disease. But Appiah's theorization is from the perspective of the well off. This is made obvious when we switch to the perspective of the global poor and ask whether they would be morally obligated to report a health event of possible international significance.

Let us ask how Appiah's constraints on cosmopolitan morality would apply in the case of a poverty-stricken nation in Africa facing an outbreak of a reportable infectious disease. They know that if they do not report the disease, some of their fellow citizens will die and the disease may spread worldwide killing many others. They also know that if they do report the disease, trade and travel restrictions will have a devastating effect on the economy of the country, hampering their efforts to meet the basic needs of its citizens. If they are followers of Appiah's theory, should they report the disease?

It is not obvious to us that they would be morally obligated to report the threat to the WHO. First, in meeting their obligations to their families, friends, and compatriots, they would have to balance the loss of life attributable to the disease outbreak and the loss of financial resources that would result from travel and trade sanctions. One fact that they might take into account is that the baseline premature mortality rate of the country might be very high due to respiratory or diarrheal diseases endemic to the country but not subject to IHR reporting. The nation's citizens are already dying and the devastation to the economy from trade and travel restrictions could mean that the lives of the citizens would be "barely worth living." To suffer the possibility of restrictions on top of the human cost of diseases subject to the IHR and those not subject to the IHR is, perhaps, asking the country to do more than it could bear.

Perhaps, then, Appiah's view of cosmopolitanism is not adequately rigorous. What can we say about how the Singer Principle would apply in this set of circumstances? The Singer Principle holds that if one can avoid a greater loss by sacrificing something of lesser value, one should do so. And, unlike Appiah's conception, we should give no special consideration to those who are near to us. Here, it seems more likely that reporting to the WHO would be required but, again, it is not certain. To speak of greater and lesser harms requires conceiving of some kind of metric. For an impoverished disease-ridden nation, allowing the disease to spread to, say, North America may well be of lesser value than the devastating effects that trade and travel restrictions might have on the country. It might well be that North America could sustain the loss of lives and damage to its economy better than the impoverished nation could sustain the loss of lives and damage to its economy that reporting would bring about.

The affected nation might receive economic assistance from wealthier countries to soften the blow, but on Appiah's theory (which, we believe, accurately reflects the views of most developed nations) that assistance would come under the heading of beneficent aid. That it would be beneficent shows that Appiah and his theory are out of conversation with those his constraints would affect.

While Appiah agrees that we should be able to justify our actions to those who are affected by them,[24] Gerald Cohen's comments on Rawls's incentive argument seem equally applicable to Appiah. Rawls permits inequalities in wealth when they act as an incentive for the talented to work harder and produce more. In so doing, the talented are made rich but the inequalities also benefit the least well off and so are justified. Cohen argues that this argument violates a condition of community. Cohen notes that the incentive argument seems plausible when it is presented in third person terms, arguing that the rich and talented will not be as productive if they are not given incentives. However, when the argument is put in first person terms—"I will not work as hard or be as productive unless I am given incentives and thus you will be worse off"—the lack of a sense of community becomes apparent. As Cohen says, the incentive argument is:

> generally presented in thoroughly third person terms and relatedly, as though no question arises about the attitudes and choices of the rich people it mentions. When,

> by contrast, we imagine a talented rich person himself affirming the argument, the background issues of equality and obligation come clearly into view, and, if I am right, the rich are revealed to be out of community with the poor in respect of the economic dimensions of their lives.[25]

Could Appiah really justify going to the opera to someone who faces the prospect of dying of a diarrheal disease that is treatable but untreated? The fact that such justifications would, even if utterable, fail indicates that Appiah is not truly in conversation or community with those who are desperately needy.

In matters of global public health we expect poorer countries to act in ways that take the interests of the developed world into account and to act out of a sense of cosmopolitan obligation. But the way we frame one of the central questions of the theory—why should we help the distant needy—often cannot withstand a shift in position. When considered from the position of the "distant needy" the following question becomes glaring: Why should poor nations take measures to protect our interests when we consider them as so distant from us that we generally treat them merely as the recipients of beneficent aid? Cosmopolitanism ought to be capable of bidirectionality but it appears as though, as currently constructed, it is not.

IV. Moving Pathogens and Static Theory

Moral Distance and Moving Pathogens

That what justice requires is for us to overcome distance in our responses to others is very familiar in our moral language. Overcoming distance is seen as one of the key problems in motivating moral actions towards those with whom we are not in intimate relationships. Indeed, the subtitle to Appiah's book is *Ethics in a World of Strangers*; Deen K. Chatterjee's volume is entitled *The Ethics of Assistance: Morality and the Distant Needy*;[26] and Cheah and Robbins's book is titled *Cosmopolitics: Thinking and Feeling beyond the Nation*.[27] In each case, motivating moral attitudes beyond our kith and kind is taken to be one of the central problems.

The issue we wish to raise is whether the trope of moral distance is an adequate discourse in which to conceive cosmopolitan obligations in regulating potential global health epidemics. The language of distance is at the same time the language of place. Given Appiah's audience, the language of distance assumes obligations from those securely placed in the developed world towards distant others in the developing world. But epidemiologists have alerted us to the fact that the most appropriate way of understanding diseases is in terms of vectors and the rapid movement of pathogens that are never stably enough located such that they can be securely contained in a place. In parallel, the key feature of globalization is rapid movement.

AIDS theorist Cindy Patton discusses the dynamic between fixed places and movement in the context of epidemiology in her essay "Performativity and Spatial Distinction: The End of AIDS Epidemiology."[28] Patton marks a distinction between the older notion of tropical medicine, which was centered in a place, and the relatively newer concept of epidemiology, which tracks movement. Tropical medicine addressed problems European colonizers experienced when they went out to distant places:

> A tropical disease is always proper to a place, to a *there*, but only operates *as disease* when it afflicts people from *here*. . . . Tropical disease is contained by virtue of already being *there*, in the 'tropics': even if he could not always get well, the colonist could always go home.[29]

Epidemics are different as they are not bound to specific and stable places. Epidemics are located in mobile bodies. Movement is a key feature of an epidemic and tracking it requires a vectoral analysis.[30]

> Declaring an epidemic depends on an expectation: in its perpetual movement, pathology becomes visible against a background state of health. These migratory sites of pathology can at any times be linked. This framework requires a vectoral imagination, since movement is always outward from the center.[31]

Tropical medicine addressed illnesses that were stable and identified with particular locations. Epidemics, on the other hand, require connecting bodies to spaces and the movement of bodies to new spaces:

> Bereft of a stable *place* of pathology, epidemiology must constantly construct and correlate populations and subpopulations in order to make epidemics visible, hence the interest in technologies of "surveillance" (descriptive) and "sentinel studies" (predictive).[32]

Patton argues that viewing diseases as either fixed in places or located in mobile bodies has led to particular strategies to manage diseases. The diseases of tropical medicine were contained by place; they could be avoided by staying away from that place or by use of immunization, which gave one the ability to enter into diseased spaces and remain healthy. Epidemics, on the other hand, must be "confined and policed" and the eradication of diseases occurs through cures or through "isolating the disease and vectoral bodies from healthy bodies."[33]

Information technologies like GPHIN make epidemic vectors visible by connecting incident reports. The strategies outlined in the IHR to manage infectious disease fit the epidemic model of confinement and policing that Patton discusses. IHR (1969) permit measures such as quarantine, health certificates, port of entry protocols, and so forth to keep the infectious disease from spreading. IHR (2005) permit non-governmental actors to play a significant role in disease management at the expense of national autonomy and they permit the use of information technologies to police nations into reporting. These measures are meant to limit the movement of virulent diseases. The IHR recognize that the danger comes from the movement of a pathogen from a source of infection into different spaces. If not contained, the disease will emanate from that carrier and infect yet more potential carriers. Containing the *movement* of pathogens is, in fact, the *raison d'être* of the IHR.

Cosmopolitan Commitments and the Costs of Infectious Disease

Bridging distance is articulated by contemporary cosmopolitan theory as a paramount problem, yet the will to bridge distance is simply not a problem with respect to infectious disease. Obligations to take into account the health of others is built into the IHR because, for the most part, it truly is in everyone's interest to prevent the international spread of infectious disease. Yet there remains a serious problem in the full 'cosmopolitanization' of infectious disease management: nations are expected to act in ways that limit the international spread of infectious disease despite the economic losses associated with openness and transparency. While nations can receive financial assistance in tracking and containing the disease under IHR (2005), they are expected to bear the losses from trade and travel sanctions on their own; economically we are not citizens of the world engaged in a common project but, rather, independent nations whose primary obligations are to our compatriots. To perhaps overstate it, when infectious diseases can affect the developed world, notions of global citizenship account for why developing countries ought to report an outbreak of infectious disease and take whatever steps are necessary to contain it, and they are expected to do this despite the often crippling economic losses the country will experience. These actions are clearly beneficial to the nations as yet unaffected by the disease but the actions of the affected nations are seen neither as beneficent nor as aid. However, once the disease is contained and the damages tallied, economic parochialism returns and developing nations are left on their own; they become again the distant others about whom we are again trying to grasp the extent of our obligations. If help is given, it is constructed as beneficent aid.

As we argued above, Appiah's cosmopolitan theory is at risk of not being able to show why morality requires that developing nations fulfill their obligations to report—his constraints allow for too much partiality and for too much distance from the seriously destitute conditions in which some people live. The Singer Principle may not be able to deal with the asymmetry of global infectious diseases where the less well off are expected to undertake actions that benefit the (often) better off despite catastrophic harms to the affected nation. A problem shared by both views is an implicit commitment to an us-them dynamic. In both views, this dynamic is expressed in terms of what are our (the rich) obligations to them (the poor). There is still a distance between us and them that accounts of moral motivation are expected to bridge.

Global public health has shed the us-them dynamic; it is clear in this context that we really are one world. The international spread of infectious diseases is a global health threat and WHO has taken steps to address it as such. The IHR set out a structure designed to prevent the movement of pathogens by containing the disease and limiting the vectors of transmission. During the SARS epidemic, many countries were willing to act as good global citizens by subjugating their national autonomy for the benefit of other nations while private citizens voluntarily quarantined themselves to minimize risk to others. We do, then, have some sense of what a health crisis requires. Yet the developed world fails to acknowledge the economic consequences of reporting as part of the costs of global disease containment and that reimbursing economic harms may be part of cosmopolitan obligations.[34]

Technology, Epidemiology, and Cosmopolitan Obligations

As we quoted above, the editors of *The Lancet Infectious Diseases* claimed that the response of nations to the SARS crisis showed that a "fundamental change had taken place in global public health governance—the shift in the political, economic and technological climate had brought about new ways of thinking about public health."[35]

The political climate has indeed shifted in terms of public health. IHR (2005) expresses a commitment by member states to take seriously the threat of global pathogens. Because the Regulations state that WHO, and not the affected country, decides when an event of international significance is occurring,[36] they undercut national sovereignty. They require nations to develop core capacities to respond to health emergencies.[37] They permit WHO to rely on non-governmental sources of information bypassing national reporting systems. All of these indicate a shift towards a global notion of citizenship in the matter of public health as infectious diseases are no longer something that occur "over there."

The technological climate has been important for rethinking public health because it mirrors and makes real to us the epidemiological concern with rapid movement. Technologies have created new means of surveillance. We are acquainted with global diseases for the most part not through getting the disease but rather through the reporting of disease surveillance. The combination of technology and epidemiology has shifted the international health landscape to take seriously the rapid movement of pathogens.

However, the economic climate has not kept pace with the requirements of a just system of public health, despite promises made regarding economic globalization. Not only are health systems of many countries woefully inadequate; these same countries are also expected to bear the economic hardships of infectious disease. When help is given, the discourse remains that of beneficent aid. Economic globalization has not manifested itself in any meaningful way with regard to the requirements of global citizenship so necessary in the area of public health.

Our motivation for cosmopolitanism requires that we feel the rapid movement of disease as a global threat. Our knowledge of that rapid movement in the west is acquired primarily through electronic surveillance systems and conveyed to us through the technologically sophisticated institutions of the media. If part of the motivational force of epidemiology is via information technologies, this raises an additional issue of why it is that that motivation should extend to those with far less access to those technologies than people in the developed world. In creating a motivational structure that promotes moral cosmopolitanism rather than further coerced participation in structures of globalization that only benefit the developed world, we in the developed world must take seriously the full range of our cosmopolitan obligation with respect to infectious disease. Surely part of that obligation is to share the economic burdens of reporting.

Jan Sutherland and Elaine Gibson, Dalhousie University

Notes

1. This work has been supported through a Social Sciences and Research Council of Canada Collaborative Research Initiative Grant titled "The Role of Technology in the Production, Consumption and Use of Health Information: Implications for Policy and Practice" (ACTION for Health). A version of this paper was read at the North American Society for Social Philosophy Conference in 2006. For helpful feedback, the authors wish to thank Sue Campbell, members of the Health Law Institute, John Rowan, and anonymous reviewers of this journal.

2. *International Health Regulations* (1969), 3rd ed. (Geneva: WHO, 1983) [hereinafter called IHR (1969)].

3. *Revision of the International Health Regulations*, WHA Res. 58.3 (23 May 2005) [hereafter called IHR (2005)]. IHR (2005) came into effect on June 15, 2007.

4. While beyond the scope of this paper, it should be noted that countries can put reservations on their obligations under international treaties.

5. David Fidler, *SARS, Governance, and the Globalization of Disease* (New York: Palgrave Macmillan, 2004), 25.

6. Unwarranted trade and travel sanctions resulted in economic loss to India of over $2 billion USD. R. Cash and V. Narahimhan, "Impediments to Global Surveillance of Infectious Diseases: Consequences of Open Reporting in an Open Economy," *Bulletin of the World Health Organization* 78:11 (2000): 1360–3.

7. IHR (2005) Article 6(1).

8. Ibid., Article 9(1).

9. Fidler, 62.

10. Ibid., 67.

11. Public Health Agency of Canada, "'Early Warning' System Traces Global Public Health Threats 24/7" (news release) 2004-11-17, available at http://www.phac-aspc.gc.ca/media/nr-rp/2004/2004_gphin-rmisp_e.html.

12. D. Fidler and L. Gostin, "The New International Health Regulations: An Historic Development for International Law and Public Health," *Journal of Law Medicine and Ethics* 34 (2006): 90.

13. Editors, "Infectious Diseases: A New Public Health World Order," *The Lancet Infectious Diseases* 4 (1994): 475.

14. T. Pogge, "Cosmopolitanism and Sovereignty," *Ethics* 103 (1992): 48.

15. K.A. Appiah, *Cosmopolitanism: Ethics in a World of Strangers*, (New York: W.W. Norton, 2006), xv.

16. P. Singer, "Famine, Affluence and Morality," *Philosophy & Public Affairs* 1:2 (1972): 231–2.

17. We are aware that Singer is counselling impartiality here but we take a more minimal version of the point.

18. Appiah, 78.

19. Ibid., 98–9.

20. Ibid., 163.

21. Ibid., 165.

22. Ibid., 165.

23. Ibid., 166.

24. "[O]ne such inescapable obligation is this: when you do something that harms someone else, you must be able to justify it." Appiah, 151.

25. G. A. Cohen, "Incentives, Inequality, and Community," in *Equal Freedom: Selected Tanner Lectures on Human Values*, ed. Stephen Darwall (Ann Arbor: University of Michigan Press, 1995). The significance of Cohen's remarks were made clear to us by Christine Koggel in *Perspectives on Equality: Constructing a Relational Theory* (Lanham, MD: Rowman & Littlefield, 1998).

26. D. K. Chatterjee, ed., *The Ethics of Assistance: Morality and the Distant Needy* (Cambridge: Cambridge University Press, 2004).

27. P. Cheah and B. Robbins, eds., *Cosmopolitics: Thinking and Feeling Beyond the State* (Minneapolis: University of Minnesota Press, 1998).

28. C. Patton, "Performativity and Spatial Distinction: The End of AIDS Epidemiology" in *Performativity and Performance*, eds. Andrew Parker and Eve Kosofsky Sedgwick (New York, 1995), 173–96.

29. Ibid., 185.

30. Ibid., 187.

31. Ibid., 186.

32. Ibid., 186–7.

33. Ibid., 187–8.

34. See R. Cash and V. Narahimhan, 1365, for concrete suggestions for addressing the economic harms of reporting infectious diseases.

35. *The Lancet Infectious Diseases*, 475.

36. IHR (2005) Article 12.

37. Ibid., Annex 1.

Care Ethics and International Justice: The Cosmopolitanism of Jane Addams and Kwame Anthony Appiah

MAURICE HAMINGTON

Abstract: This article attends to an unnamed and often missing element of the cosmopolitanism discourse: care ethics. Developed out of feminist theory in the 1980s, care ethics privileges the relational, contextual, and affective aspects of morality. It is my suggestion that contemporary discussions of cosmopolitanism would benefit from integrating the moral commitments of care ethics. First, a definition of care ethics is offered followed by a delineation of themes of care in the cosmopolitan theorizing of an historical figure, Jane Addams, and a contemporary theorist, Kwame Anthony Appiah. Ultimately, the contention here is that cosmopolitan societies envisioned by Addams and Appiah cannot be exclusively founded on systems of justice (i.e., rights, principles, laws) but needs caring to provide the social cohesion necessary for organic international justice, as well as lasting peace.

The real challenge to cosmopolitanism isn't the belief that other people don't matter at all; it's the belief that they don't matter very much.
—Kwame Anthony Appiah

The Advocates of Peace would find the appeal both to Pity and Prudence totally unnecessary, could they utilize the cosmopolitan interest in human affairs with the resultant social sympathy that at the present moment is developing among all the nations of the earth.
—Jane Addams

I. Introduction

Although cosmopolitanism can trace its intellectual genealogy to the Ancient Greeks,[1] the current specter of increased international migration, rising disparity between the quality of life among rich and poor, as well as cultural conflicts in the face of calls for greater pluralistic tolerance have reinvigorated discussions surrounding world citizenship. This renewed interest in cosmopolitanism has manifested itself in numerous recent publications. Simply defined, cosmopolitanism posits a postnational identity employing the notion that one's moral obligations extend beyond national affiliation or social group loyalty. Of course, the nuances and moral implications of cosmopolitanism are far more complex. The current discourse on cosmopolitanism is encouraging in light of world events that reveal a fractionated world desperately in need of the means to make common cause. This paper will attend to an unnamed and often missing element of the cosmopolitanism discourse: care ethics. Developed out of feminist theory in the 1980s, care ethics privileges the relational, contextual, and affective aspects of morality. It is my suggestion that contemporary discussions of cosmopolitanism would benefit from integrating the moral commitments of care ethics. To make this point, I will begin by defining care ethics and then tracing themes of care in the cosmopolitan theorizing of an historical figure, Jane Addams, and a contemporary theorist, Kwame Anthony Appiah. Ultimately, the contention here is that a cosmopolitan society cannot be exclusively founded on systems of justice (i.e., rights, principles, laws). A structural approach is not enough. Interpersonal relationships built on trust and understanding knit societies together in ways rules or codes of conduct are incapable of. Caring is an important nonstructural component in maintaining social cohesion. This overlooked affective dimension is necessary to build a lasting and organic international justice, as well as lasting peace.

II. Care Ethics and the Socialization of Care

Care ethics emerged as an independent sphere of moral inquiry in the 1980s. It began as an outgrowth of the writings of a number of feminist theorists including Carol Gilligan, Nel Noddings and Joan Tronto.[2] It is a moral orientation that is less concerned with the adjudication of individual acts and more concerned with the maintenance of right relationships in particular contexts. In *Embodied Care*, I offered the following definition of care: "Care denotes an approach to personal and social morality that shifts ethical considerations to context, relationships, and affective knowledge in a manner that can be fully understood only if care's embodied dimension is recognized. Care is committed to the flourishing and growth of individuals yet acknowledges our interconnectedness and interdependence."[3] The interjection of embodiment notwithstanding, care ethicists attend to affectations, conditions, relations, and consequences. Phenomenologically, the one cared-for and the caregiver engage in a relationship marked by mutuality in terms of attentiveness and responsiveness. In this manner, care is an ethic that cannot be separated from epistemology—we care about that which we know and it is difficult to care for that which we have little or no knowledge of. Knowing and caring are intertwined.

Care ethics is paradoxically both a complex moral orientation and a very common sentiment. It is unlike other theories of morality, such as Kantian ethics or utilitarianism, in that it does not delineate universal norms of evaluation. Its complexity lies in its inability to be extricated from the context and relationships of individual lives. Care offers no simple rubric for ethical adjudication. Yet care is a common disposition that pervades the human condition and is thus easily overlooked as morally insignificant.

The identification of an ethic of care is one of the most significant innovations in moral philosophy of the latter part of the twentieth century. Care ethics challenges liberal assumptions about objectivity as well as the nature of moral agency. Rather than positing moral agents as thoroughly independent to make decisions based on principles or consequences, care ethics assumes that every moral agent is a social being existing in a web of relationships that constitute a context which impinges on ethical decision making. Although receiving mixed reactions from philosophers, care ethics galvanized a groundswell of research and writing by feminist theorists in a number of disciplines around the notion that rules and consequences do not exhaust the content of morality.

Care theory has undergone significant development over the past quarter century which is relevant to the present discussion of international justice. In the beginning, feminist theorists were mostly concerned with naming the previously unnamed, and thus care was sharply contrasted with existing accounts of morality, often categorized as "justice." This period of identity formation fostered a false dichotomy between notions of "care" and "justice" that theorists subsequently came to reconcile. It became clear that care ethics is not an alternative form of morality to other ethical approaches such as utilitarianism or Kantian ethics. Instead, care reframes moral questions around the particulars of a given situation and asks how they relate to one another. As Virginia Held describes, "There can be care without justice . . . [but] There can be no justice without care."[4] Her contention is based on the notion that care is such an essential aspect of human existence, albeit often overlooked, that even the most effective system of justice requires individuals to care for one another in a manner that rules, principles, duties, and rights can never entirely account for. Ultimately, care ethicists are not antithetical to the development and discussion of systems of justice, but they point out that such systems do not encompass all that which is moral.

Another aspect of the maturing field of care ethics is its growing concern for discussions of social and political philosophy. Much of the original work on care ethics focused on interpersonal care as manifested in the reciprocal relations of dyads, often idealizing mother-child relationships. Recently, the work of care ethicists such as Nel Noddings, Joan Tronto, and Virginia Held have turned to theorizing about care as more than a personal ethic. Their work can be said to socialize care.[5] Accordingly, care theorists are exploring the ways in which social institutions, policies, and practices can facilitate care. For example, in Nel Noddings's recent book, *Starting At Home: Caring and Social Policy*, she contends that liberalism lacks the resources to overcome the tension between freedom and equality. According to Noddings, "too much emphasis [is] placed on autonomy (as in Kantian ethics), but much liberal machinery depends on a rational decision-maker who bears little resemblance to real persons."[6] Addressing individuals behind Rawls's veil of ignorance, Noddings observes, "they literally do not know who they are, to what traditions they belong, what their social status or physical condition might be, or even what their personalities are like."[7] By contrast, real people are social animals situated in particular times and places as well as entangled in webs of relationships, most involving varying degrees of care. These relationships are not incidental to the decision making process. For care ethicists, situatedness is inseparable from knowledge formation, which in turn is inseparable from ethics.

Perhaps the continuity between care ethics and cosmopolitan ethics is becoming clearer. Cosmopolitanism emphasizes the connection between all peoples fostered by the effort to learn about one another. As Martha Nussbaum describes, cosmopolitanism entails an eagerness "to understand humanity in all its strange guises."[8] The cosmopolitan's interest in learning about diverse people resembles what Noddings refers to as the caring disposition of "engrossment" with the other.[9] In each case, morality grows out of an epistemic disposition of openness and interest in others. Given the move by care ethicists to address social and political systems, the time is ripe for cross discussions between care and cosmopolitan theorists. Currently, there is a general lack of explicit interaction between these two fields. For example, in the insightful anthology, *The Political Philosophy of Cosmopolitanism*, edited by Gillian Brock and Harry Brighouse, although a number of important considerations regarding cosmopolitan principles of international justice are made, none of the 15 authors makes a passing reference to care theory. By comparison, recent works by care ethicists Nel Noddings and Virginia Held on socializing care make no mention of cosmopolitanism.[10] This is not an indictment of either intellectual position, as individual authors can only address so much material. However, given the resonance between the two approaches, I hope this article can provoke more theorists to find fruitful connections. We will begin to explore the relationship between care ethics and cosmopolitanism through the work of Jane Addams (1860–1935).

III. Jane Addams's "Sympathetic Knowledge"

Jane Addams record of accomplishments is remarkable given the gendered social restrictions of her era. Addams helped to found the National Association for the Advancement of Colored People, the American Civil Liberties Union, and the Women International League for Peace and Freedom and was awarded the Nobel Peace Prize in 1931. Several recent biographies delineate her significant intellectual, social, and political accomplishments.[11] Addams is best remembered for organizing and leading the social settlement Hull-House in Chicago, one of the earliest and most recognizable of the 400 progressive era settlements in North America. Organized by ideal-driven progressives around the notion of supporting oppressed communities, social settlements are difficult to precisely describe because they were largely unaffiliated with one another and each took on the character and endeavors of their neighborhood. Hull-House, located amongst the squalor created by unprecedented immigrant growth on the west side of Chicago, was buzzing with people and local projects that included a kindergarten, adult education programs, birth control information dissemination, labor union organizing, and community performing arts programs.

What is often overlooked about Addams's extraordinary career and accomplishments was her extensive theoretical work that included a dozen published books and over 500 articles in both scholarly and popular journals. Recent scholarship has established Addams as the foremother of feminist pragmatist philosophy and as an important influence on the American pragmatist philosophers of her era.[12]

For our purposes, Addams is an intriguing figure to consider in terms of international justice because she was an early North American adopter of the philosophies of both care ethics and cosmopolitanism. Addams argued that morality could not be abstracted from the quality and degree of our knowledge of other human beings. To know about someone is to open up the possibility of caring for them. Addams referred to this moral approach as "sympathetic knowledge." According to Addams, knowledge, empathy, and action exist in dynamic relation to one another:

> Sympathetic knowledge is the only way of approach to any human problem, and the line of least resistance into the jungle of human wretchedness must always be through that region which is most thoroughly explored, not only by the information of the statistician, but by sympathetic understanding.[13]

Accordingly, anecdotes garnered from almost a half century of living at Hull-House accompany most of Addams's philosophical writings. When Addams wrote, her primary subjects were not the rich and famous, although she knew many of the politically elite people of her day. Her work addressed the poor, immigrants, elderly and adolescents from the Hull-House neighborhood. They were met as individuals with feelings continuous with those who would listen. Addams applied care ethics through reciprocal relationships with her neighbors and then through her writing was able to extrapolate and thematize that care to others. For example, Addams described local immigrant communities not as cases for charity or the object of sociological study. Instead, immigrant communities could learn, and be learned from, in a process of mutually beneficial exchanges that led to greater social cohesion, thus making democratic processes more effective.

Perhaps more important than her personal application of care ethics was her structuring of the Hull-House settlement as a caring institution—an inverted home where people from the neighborhood could enter and meet one another. The myriad of activities that took place at Hull-House, which ballooned to take up thirteen buildings and a whole city block, were designed to foster sympathetic understanding through meaningful social exchanges. For Addams, social progress would not occur without individual growth that came through social transactions. She used the term "lateral progress" to describe an inclusive brand of egalitarian, democratic social advancement.[14] Accordingly, she defined the function of the social settlement as bringing "the circle of knowledge and fuller life [to] men and women who might otherwise be left outside."[15] Despite serving thousands of people each day at its peak, Hull-House managed to remain a caring endeavor rather than an alienating bureaucracy.[16] In this respect, Addams not only theorized the possibility of socializing care but also enacted it.

Furthermore, Addams had a radical commitment to cosmopolitan ideals that went far beyond many of her fellow progressives. For Addams, cosmopolitanism was a phenomenon grounded in the multicultural experience of the big city:

> Because of their differences in all external matters, in all of the non-essentials of life, the people in a cosmopolitan city are forced to found their community of interests upon the basic and essential likenesses of their common human nature; for, after all, the things that make men alike are stronger and more primitive than the things that separate them.[17]

Addams came to a cosmopolitan outlook as an extension of her interactions in Chicago. She daily witnessed the conflict of cultures and subsequent resolutions that occurred in the city, and felt that much was to be gained from getting to know the rich diversity of people in her neighborhood. Here, Addams foreshadows the conclusions of Iris Marion Young who opposes attempts to formulate "ideal communities," suggesting that city life provides a non-utopian ideal of "being together of strangers in openness to group difference."[18] Addams and Young are comfortable with the plurality of "unassimilated otherness" found in the city.[19] Social justice in such an environment does not derive out of homogenization of the community, but rather through a group process respectful of all the voices within the community: in a word, cosmopolitanism.

Addams's commitment to cosmopolitanism can also be witnessed in her pacifism. She suggested that only through greater understanding between people of different cultures could international conflict be avoided, stating, "I believe the diversity of immigrants is a source of great strength to this country in regard to keeping peace and averting war."[20] Addams even went so far as to employ the term "cosmic patriotism" as part of her vision for social advancement.[21] Accordingly, our loyalty should be to the peace and justice of humanity, not to nation states created from the happenstance of history. Addams claims, "There arises the hope that when this newer patriotism becomes large enough, it will overcome arbitrary boundaries and soak up the notion of nationalism. We may then give up war, because we shall find it as difficult to make war upon a nation at the other side of the globe as upon our next-door neighbor."[22] Addams's argument can be summarized as based on the propositions that cosmopolitanism fosters sympathetic understanding, which in turn makes violent conflict less possible.

As a progressive, Addams viewed humanity as always learning and growing. For Addams, morality also grew: "To attain individual morality in an age demanding social morality, to pride one's self on the results of personal effort when the time demands social adjustment, is utterly to fail to apprehend the situation."[23] Addams found the social context calling for a cosmopolitan ethic not only to foster international justice, but domestic justice as well. Her rich notion of democracy entailed dialogue amongst diverse voices and positions but with the common aim of advancing society:

> We are learning that a standard of social ethics is not attained by traveling a sequestered byway, but by mixing on the thronged and common road where all must turn out for one another, and at least see the size of one another's burdens. To follow the path of social morality results perforce in the temper if not the practice of the democratic spirit, for it implies that diversified human experience and resultant sympathy which are the foundation and guarantee of Democracy.[24]

Addams's cosmopolitan philosophy offers no new principles, rules, or system of rights. It is not that Addams was opposed to such measures, as exemplified in her call for the formation of a precursor organization to the League of Nations.[25] Her approach to cosmopolitanism begins with the building of understanding through care ethics at the local level and extending it to the international arena. For Addams, cosmopolitanism provided an image of hope for how a diverse world could sustain itself.

IV. Kwame Anthony Appiah

Advancing in time almost a century from Addams's era, we find that political philosopher Kwame Anthony Appiah also seeks a robust notion of cosmopolitanism that recognizes its personal moral and imaginative dimension. Like Addams, Appiah does not explicitly identify himself as a care ethicist, and yet the characteristics of care can be found in his philosophy of cosmopolitanism. Appiah's definition of cosmopolitanism hints at his resonance with care ethics. He offers a two-part description. The first part is consistent with most cosmopolitan theorists in that he calls for a moral obligation to others that extends beyond familial, friendship, or national ties. The second part of his definition is an epistemic imperative that "we take seriously the value not just of human life but of particular human lives, which means taking an interest in the practices and beliefs that lend them significance."[26] Here Appiah echoes the use of particularism found in the work of care political theorist Seyla Benhabib who finds care ethics rooted in engaging "concrete others" rather than "generalized others" as is the case with traditional moral approaches. Benhabib claims that positing a concrete other "requires us to view each and every rational being as an individual with a concrete history, identity, and affective-emotional constitution. In assuming this standpoint, we abstract from what constitutes our commonality."[27] For Appiah, cosmopolitanism is an outgrowth of specific efforts at caring about the lives, customs, and cultures of particular people—concrete others. Without that concrete beginning, there is no material from which to build a sense of commonality.

Appiah applies the distinction between concrete and generalized others in responding to the criticism that cosmopolitanism can be "rootless" or not grounded in a particular communal or geographic identity. To this claim, Appiah rejoins that rootlessness is a cosmopolitan fiction engendered by notions of absolute universalism. Of course people will establish their home somewhere and thus make connections to the people, places and ideas of their own area. Appiah offers the notion of a "rooted" cosmopolitanism that acknowledges these local affiliations and loyalties but also welcomes the unknown other.[28] Here, Appiah uses particularism to remind us that we should not think of our encounters in strictly binary terms of known versus unknown others. Our rootedness or situatedness will always provide us with some basis for connection to others, if nothing else, through shared embodiment. Appiah writes, "engagement with strangers is always going to be engagement with particular strangers; and the warmth that comes from shared identity will often be available."[29] For Appiah, there is no such thing as a purely unknown other. We have some level of understanding with all other human beings despite powerful social forces that divide us. His cosmopolitanism asks us to attend to those commonalities while simultaneously and thoughtfully exploring the differences.

The psychic distance between others and ourselves is a crucial factor to caring. The more I perceive someone as an "other" the easier it is for me not to care. The less I identify with someone, the more abstract they are, and the easier it is to treat them as a caricature of their humanity and therefore the harder caring is. Any label we apply to a group of others—whether it be black, gay, Iraqi or communist—that allows me to put psycho/social distance between them and us makes that group more abstract. Appiah, like care ethicists, finds in the meeting of particular others the potential to dispel the otherness of those encountered. Appiah explains, "When the stranger is no longer imaginary, but real and present, sharing a human social life, you may like or dislike him, you may agree or disagree; but, if it is what you both want, you can make sense of each other in the end."[30] Appiah is describing a caring approach to cosmopolitanism that is not romantic or idealistic but reorients the encounter with an unknown other away from being a threat toward becoming an opportunity for learning, growth, and coalition. As such, meeting a stranger is potentially morally transformative. Similarly, care theorist Fiona Robinson describes how care transforms moral orientation:

> The ability to care about others involves not only learning how to be attentive and patient, how to listen and respond, but also how to rethink our own attitudes about difference and exclusion by locating that difference within relationships, thus dispelling the claim that any one person or group of persons is naturally and objectively "different."[31]

Appiah and Robinson are describing changes in the moral agents at the local, interpersonal level that can potentially support formal structures of cosmopolitanism.

Appiah and Addams agree on the importance of learning about one another through formal education as well as social encounters as a precursor to the moral development necessary for cosmopolitan ethics. Appiah encourages education for global understanding: "I am urging that we should learn about people in other places, take an interest in their civilizations, their arguments, their errors, their achievements, not because that will bring us to agreement, but because it will help us get used to one another."[32] This is a theme that is also strong in the work of Martha Nussbaum on global citizenship. According to Nussbaum, "The world citizen must develop systematic understanding of distant cultures and of ethnic, racial, and religious minorities within her own."[33] None of these authors is Pollyannaish about what such education can accomplish. Neither Addams nor Appiah is under an illusion that merely mixing diverse people will end international conflict, but they see the potential for improved dialogue when we understand one another. In this respect, cosmopolitanism is a tentative or progressive utopian ideal. It is worthy to strive for, but is not a panacea or achievable in an absolute manner, nor can it be forced.

Appiah, like Addams, employs the language of care ethics to describe cosmopolitanism. Care ethics does not posit the possibility of an ideal world of mutual friendship or love. As Appiah describes, "Adam Smith saw, to say that we have obligations to strangers isn't to demand that they have the same grip on our sympathies as our nearest and dearest. We'd better start with the recognition that they don't."[34] More realistically, care ethics finds an existential potential between knowing others and caring about others. If I know about someone and their situation, I just might care and it might fuel my imagination to extend that care to others. It is not a foregone conclusion that I will care; human existence is too fraught with variables for such a conclusion, but it is a possibility, one which offers hope for international justice.

V. Conclusion

I have suggested that there is a moral voice not being attended to in the current discussions over cosmopolitanism: care ethics. Although not explicitly identified as such, the voice of care can be seen in the works on cosmopolitanism written by Jane Addams and Kwame Anthony Appiah, but it can also be found in the work of Martha Nussbaum and several others. Care ethics describes an approach to personal and social morality that shifts ethical considerations to context, relationships, and affective knowledge. It is committed to the flourishing and growth of individuals, yet it acknowledges our interconnectedness and interdependence. I am not suggesting that discussions of human rights or international policies in pursuit of cosmopolitanism be suspended, but merely that care ethics can provide an important moral outlook that can supplement, extend, and bolster the work on principles and rights.

Without considerations of care, morality can sometimes appear formulaic and abstract. Cosmopolitanism, when founded solely on moral principles, has the potential for this kind of existential alienation. Catriona McKinnon, for example, proposes that the cosmopolitan ideal shared by most theorists is "A world in which some fundamental principles of justice govern relations between all persons in all places."[35] McKinnon goes on to present the moral requirement to achieve the cosmopolitan ideal with the remark that "any commitment to some fundamental principles of justice at the domestic level ought to be extended so as to generate principles of justice with cosmopolitan scope."[36] McKinnon offers a useful interjection of the need for hope in regard to what might be termed an impossible goal albeit that, when it comes to cosmopolitanism, the journey is as important as the end result. Her characterization of the cosmopolitan ideal and morality probably reflects accurately the mainstream understanding as equating principled justice with morality. But what of human caring? Is it enough to delineate and enact into law the necessary principles of a just society in order to have a moral society? Jane Addams argued that although rights-based political philosophy is important, it was part of eighteenth-century individualism and that modern times needed a more socially oriented, experiential ethic: "A man of this generation easily discerns the crudeness of that eighteenth-century conception of essentially unprogressive human nature in all the empty dignity of 'inborn rights.'"[37] For Addams, rights and principles, while useful, were not enough for a moral community. Morality had progressed to demand a stronger social consciousness. Appiah also warns against a strict attachment to principles, observing, "The temptation is to look for a rule book."[38] Both Addams and Appiah are appealing to a more contextual, relational element of building a cosmopolitan society.

Perhaps it is more than coincidence that neither Addams nor Appiah occupies the dominant identity position in modern Western society; neither is a heterosexual white male. While both are privileged intellectuals, their experience of crossing boundaries of inclusivity and exclusivity places them in a position to have epistemic insight into the power and potential of cosmopolitanism. It is intriguing that both of these border crossers chose to integrate elements of care ethics into their approach to morality. Perhaps those who stand outside of dominant systems of power, or at least those who have the imaginative resources to do so, can see the limitations of traditional ethical systems to change structures of power. Nevertheless, I hope more theorists of all identities will take up considerations of the integration of care ethics and cosmopolitanism.

Maurice Hamington, University of Southern Indiana

Notes

A condensed version of this article was presented at the 23rd International Social Philosophy Conference at the University of Victoria, August 3, 2006. The author would like to thank the participants of that session as well as the *Social Philosophy Today* reviewers for their insightful comments, which led to significant revisions.

1. Martha C. Nussbaum, *Cultivating Humanity: A Classical Defense of Reform in Liberal Education* (Cambridge: Harvard University Press, 1997), 53

2. Early works on care ethics include: Carol Gilligan, *In a Different Voice: Psychological Theory and Women's Development* (Cambridge: Harvard University, 1982); Nel Noddings, *Caring: A Feminine Approach to Ethics and Moral Education* (Berkeley: University of California Press, 1984); and Joan C. Tronto, *Moral Boundaries: A Political Argument for an Ethic of Care* (New York: Routledge, 1993).

3. Maurice Hamington, *Embodied Care: Jane Addams, Maurice Merleau-Ponty, and Feminist Ethics* (University of Illinois Press, 2004), 3.

4. Virginia Held, *The Ethics of Care: Personal Political, and Global* (Oxford: Oxford University Press, 2006), 17.

5. See Maurice Hamington and Dorothy C. Miller, eds., *Socializing Care: Feminist Ethics and Social Issues* (Langham, MD: Rowman & Littlefield, 2006).

6. Nel Noddings, *Starting at Home: Caring and Social Policy* (Berkeley: University of California Press, 2002), 71.

7. Ibid.

8. Martha Nussbaum, "Patriotism and Cosmopolitanism" in *For Love Of Country?*, ed. Joshua Cohen (Boston, MA: Beacon Press, 1996), 9.

9. Noddings, *Caring*, 19.

10. One of the few care theorists who explicitly does address cosmopolitanism is Fiona Robinson. See *Globalizing Care: Ethics, Feminist Theory, and International Relations* (Boulder, CO: Westview, 1999).

11. Recent biographies include: Victoria Bissell Brown, *The Education of Jane Addams* (Philadelphia: University of Pennsylvania Press, 2004); Katherine Joslin, *Jane Addams: A Writer's Life* (Urbana, IL: University of Illinois Press, 2004); and Louise Knight, *Citizen: Jane Addams and the Struggle for Democracy* (Chicago: University of Chicago Press, 2005).

12. See, for example, Marilyn Fischer, *On Addams* (Toronto: Wadsworth, 2004); and Charlene Haddock Seigfried, *Pragmatism an Feminism: Reweaving the Social Fabric* (Chicago: Chicago University Press, 1996).

13. Jane Addams, *A New Conscience and an Ancient Evil* (New York: The Macmillan Company, 1913), 11.

14. Jane Addams, "A Modern Lear" in *The Jane Addams Reader*, ed. Jean Bethke Elshtain (New York: Basic Books, 2002), 175.

15. Jane Addams, *The Second Twenty Years at Hull-House* (New York: Macmillan Company, 1930), 404.

16. For a study of the caring methods of Hull-House and how they influenced the first U.S. agency (The Children's Bureau) headed by a woman, see Robyn Muncy, *Creating a Female Dominion in American Reform 1890–1935* (New York: Oxford University Press, 1991).

17. Jane Addams, *Newer Ideals of Peace*, (New York: Macmillan, 1907), 17.

18. Iris Marion Young, *Justice and the Politics of Difference*, (Princeton, NJ: Princeton University Press, 1990), 256.

19. Ibid., 227.

20. Jane Addams, "Hearing Before the Committee on Military Affairs," in *Jane Addams on Peace, War, and International Understanding 1899–1932*, ed. Allen F. Davis (New York: Garland Publishing, 1976), 115.

21. Jane Addams, "Immigration: A Field Neglected by the Scholar," *Commons* 10 (January 1905): 9–19.

22. Addams, *Newer Ideals of Peace*, 19.

23. Jane Addams, *Democracy and Social Ethics*, (Urbana, Il: University of Illinois Press, 2002), 6.

24. Ibid., 7.

25. Jane Addams, Emily G. Balch, and Alice Hamilton, *Women at The Hague* (Urbana, IL: University of Illinois Press, 2003).

26. Kwame Anthony Appiah, *Cosmopolitanism: Ethics in a World of Strangers* (New York: W.W. Norton, 2006), xv.

27. Seyla Benhabib, "The Generalized and the Concrete Other: The Kohlberg-Gilligan Controversy and Moral Theory" in *Women and Moral Theory*, ed. Eva Feder Kittay and Diana T. Meyers (Lanham, MD: Rowman & Littlefield, 1987), 164.

28. Kwame Anthony Appiah, "Cosmopolitan Patriots" in *For Love of Country?*, ed. Joshua Cohen (Boston, MA: Beacon Press, 1996), 22.

29. Appiah, *Cosmopolitanism*, 98.

30. Ibid., 99.

31. Robinson, *Globalizing Care*, 164–5.

32. Ibid., 78.

33. Nussbaum, *Cultivating Humanity*, 69.

34. Appiah, *Cosmopolitanism*, 158.

35. Catriona McKinnon, "Cosmopolitan Hope" in *The Political Philosophy of Cosmopolitanism*, ed. Gillian Brock and Harry Brighouse (Cambridge: Cambridge University Press, 2005), 234.

36. Ibid., 235.

37. Jane Addams, *Newer Ideals of Peace* (New York: MacMillan and Co., 1907), 32.

38. Appiah, *Cosmopolitanism*, 11.

Liberalism and the Polygamy Question

JON MAHONEY

Abstract: Part I of this paper examines liberal toleration and its relevance to the debate on polygamy. The remaining sections consider Marci Hamilton's claim that polygamy should not be accommodated. Hamilton's position rests on three kinds of arguments which I call: 1) *the argument from public reason*; 2) *the argument from democracy*; and 3) *the argument from exploitation*. Each of these fails: 1) fails because Hamilton's conception of public reason is too restrictive; 2) fails because it rests on a procedural test which attempts to balance claims about rights against claims about the public good—and thus presupposes a flawed conception of rights; 3) is the most compelling of Hamilton's arguments but could be met in principle if one can show that the right design of background institutions can accommodate polygamy without sponsoring an exploitative form of marriage.

I. Introduction

In *God vs. the Gavel: Religion and the Rule of Law*[1] Marci Hamilton claims that were a liberal state to accommodate same-sex marriage, marriage law would be consistent with liberal equality and no citizens' rights would be undermined. By contrast, were a liberal state to accommodate polygamous marriage, marriage law would bend to religious convictions and expose some to a high risk of exploitation. I suspect that many liberals, though likely to quibble with some of the reasons Hamilton offers, will agree with her positions on same-sex marriage and polygamy. But liberals should not agree with Hamilton's position on polygamy.

This paper has two main parts. Part II examines liberal toleration and its relevance to the debate on polygamy. Part III considers Hamilton's claim that polygamy should not be accommodated. Hamilton's position rests on three kinds of arguments which I call: 1) *the argument from public reason*; 2) *the argument from democracy*; and 3) *the argument from exploitation*. Each of these fails: 1) fails because Hamilton's conception of public reason is too restrictive; 2) fails because it rests on a procedural test which attempts to balance claims about rights against claims about the public good—and thus presupposes a flawed conception of rights; 3) is the most compelling of Hamilton's arguments but could be met in principle if one can show that the right design of background institutions can accommodate polygamy without sponsoring an exploitative form of marriage.

II. Liberalism and Polygamy

Although the debate on polygamy implicates religious freedom there are at least two reasons for claiming the issue cannot be settled by one's convictions about religious toleration. One is that there may be those who wish to practice polygamy for exclusively secular reasons. An analysis of polygamy which focuses exclusively on those who favor it for religious reasons will thus be incomplete.[2] Secondly, in a liberal state which promotes marriage by coercively distributing resources in ways which affect how benefits and burdens are shared, prohibitions against polygamy implicate foundational liberal principles which extend beyond the issue of religious toleration. For instance, questions about equal access to goods coercively distributed by the state are relevant to the debate on polygamy.

Polygamy implicates a more expansive set of liberal ideals than is suggested by those who construe the debate on polygamy as one that centers on the topic of religious freedom. This point is especially important in the U.S. where the debate on polygamy has been framed in terms of whether Mormon polygamy ought to be accommodated on First Amendment grounds.[3] In *Reynolds v. United States*, the Supreme Court established the precedent for denying that polygamy should be accommodated on grounds of religious freedom. The Court reasoned as follows:

> Can a man excuse his practices to the contrary [of prevailing norms] because of his religious belief? [To] permit this would be to make the professed doctrines of religious belief superior to the law of the land, and in effect to permit every citizen to become a law unto himself.[4]

This claim is true but only because liberal toleration circumscribes the kinds of religious practices that are permissible within a liberal political society. However, the Court's reasoning is disingenuous; *no practice should be permitted on the sole grounds that its practitioners have a religious reason to engage in it*; all practices, religious or otherwise, should be subject to regulation and prohibition when they cannot be exercised in a manner compatible with a scheme of rights consistent with the liberty and equal standing of all. Any practice that is permitted by a liberal conception of toleration is permitted because it is compatible with liberal ideals; the reasons that motivate those who support the practice are relevant only because these reasons are evaluated in terms of their compatibility with liberal ideals; the religious or non-religious nature of the reasons advanced by defenders of a policy is beside the point.

In *Reynolds* the Court invokes a sound principle, namely, that having a religious reason does not exempt one from a law or policy, yet errs in applying this principle because it misconstrues the issues polygamous marriage raises for a liberal state. The real legal question in *Reynolds* isn't, 'Do personal religious convictions trump the Constitution?'—the answer to this question is, 'Of course they don't!'—but rather, 'Can a liberal state which sponsors monogamous marriage prohibit polygamous marriage?' The Court likely would have reached the same decision had it asked the right question—although arguably only because of animus towards a despised religious minority—but framing the issue in the correct way has a significant implication; it shows that liberals should examine polygamy in light of their positions on liberal values such as equality, public reason, and distributive justice; these principles are what justify the liberal conception of forms of marriage which may be sponsored by the state. The liberal position on which forms of marriage ought to be promoted isn't settled by the liberal conception of religious toleration; rather, it's settled by principles from which the liberal conception of religious toleration is derived.[5] Debates about polygamy tend to frame the issue in terms of accommodating a conception of marriage advocated by a religious minority, and this is a mistake.[6]

There is also good reason for construing the issue of polygamy as one that cannot be resolved by appealing to the liberal conception of freedom of expression. Liberals should insist that there is an important difference between, 'should polygamous cohabitation be tolerated?' and 'should polygamous marriage be included among the forms of marriage promoted as a good by the state?' Many liberals will oppose the prosecution of polygamous cohabitation engaged as a species of experimental living. Of course, prosecution of polygamous cohabitation may be supported on grounds other than that the cohabitation is polygamous (e.g., to protect the rights of children, to protect victims of abusive relationships, etc.).[7]

In liberal states which do sponsor marriage, toleration and freedom of expression should not serve as the sole basis for framing the issue of polygamy. Rather, the issue is really about whether the liberal state should be in the business of promoting the good of polygamous marriage along with the good of monogamous marriage. Liberals should ask, 'is polygamy an arrangement among persons and families which entitles members to state-sponsored benefits the non-married do not enjoy?'

III. The Argument from Public Reason

Hamilton claims that those who favor law and policies designed to prohibit same sex-marriage, at least in the United States, are typically motivated by religious convictions. On her view, this is problematic because a constitutional democracy founded upon liberal principles should prohibit any law or policy which rests solely upon religious convictions. For example, even if one's personal religious convictions favor prohibiting same-sex marriage this does not suffice as a justification for law and public policy measures designed to deny same-sex couples benefits that heterosexual couples can secure by means of marriage:

> The religious have every right to contribute their religious viewpoints to the public debate and to try to persuade leaders and fellow citizens that their ideas about social problems have merit. . . . But they do not have the right . . . to mold public policy to their beliefs and their beliefs alone.[8]

In another passage, Hamilton notes the similarities and differences between those who support prohibitions against same-sex marriage and those who favor accommodating polygamy:

> The issue of polygamous marriage presents both a different and a similar issue. In the case of polygamous marriage, there are very few religious sects that advocate the practice. They are small in number and even smaller in political power; they lack the close relationships with those in power that the same-sex marriage opponents enjoy. Nor do they argue that the law should reflect their religious teaching. . . . Rather, they argue that the First Amendment gives them the right to practice polygamy, despite the laws against it. In the end though, the two sets of arguments by religious entities are quite similar. Both expect religious belief to direct public policy.[9]

Hamilton claims that one can reject the claim that a liberal state must accommodate polygamy for the same reason that one can reject the claim that a liberal state must prohibit same-sex marriage.

Hamilton is right to claim that religious belief cannot be the basis for law in a liberal state. Norms of public reason require of citizens that when they support policies that call upon the powers of government they should present a justification that can be shared by other citizens many of whom will not share religious convictions. Public reason is in this sense strictly secular and non-sectarian. However, there is something very misleading about Hamilton's characterization of why those who argue in favor of accommodating polygamy violate norms of public reason. Hamilton seems to imply that were a citizen to advocate polygamy for religious reasons alone it follows that this is sufficient to disqualify polygamy as a candidate for inclusion in the liberal conception of permissible marriage arrangements. This can't be right. The liberal conception of public reason is restrictive, but not this restrictive. To see why, consider the religious convictions invoked by abolitionists and civil rights activists. Arguably, these are the best counter examples to a conception of public reason that rules out policies simply because those who support them have religious reasons for doing so.[10] Since abolitionists and civil rights activists advocated policies that in principle satisfy the norms of public reason, the mere fact that some abolitionists and some civil rights activists were motivated by religious conviction is beside the point. In fact, the liberal conception of public reason should be construed in a way that shows that even if every abolitionist and every civil rights activist was motivated by religious conviction, the policies they defended satisfy public reason.

Norms of public reason require only that reasons for law and public policy *can* be advanced on secular grounds; it does not require that citizens' actual reasons cannot be religiously motivated.[11] There are familiar reasons for qualifying the liberal conception of public reason in this manner. The example just mentioned regarding abolitionists and civil rights activists illustrates that the liberal conception of public reason does not reject policies simply because they are supported by citizens with religious convictions. The principled test for whether a policy is compatible with public reason is *counterfactual: we ask, can the policy be supported by non-sectarian reasons that all reasonable persons can accept?* In practice this entails that norms of public reason have both lateral and vertical reach; they impose demands on the kinds of reasons that citizens can reasonably expect other citizens to endorse; and they impose demands on the kinds of reasons that government can invoke in the name of its coercive authority. Norms of public reason bind both citizens and public officials.

If my formulation of the liberal conception of public reason is sound, then it follows that Hamilton's claim that polygamous marriage ought not to be accommodated because its proponents invoke religious convictions is false. Of course, it doesn't follow from this that polygamy should be accommodated, but at this point I am claiming only that, from the standpoint of the liberal conception of public reason, Hamilton misconstrues the perspective from which liberals should evaluate polygamous marriage. The argument from public reason would support the conclusion that a liberal state should prohibit polygamy if the following two claims could be established. First, only religious reasons can be invoked in support of accommodating polygamy. Second, non-sectarian reasons can be invoked to prohibit accommodating polygamy. Since it is false, the first does not support the conclusion that polygamy is a practice which violates norms of public reason; and establishing the second requires showing that polygamy is in principle incompatible with a liberal conception of justice.

IV. The Argument from Democracy

Hamilton proposes a procedural test which she claims is a fair measure for deciding which practices to accommodate and which to prohibit:

> [there are] three necessary conditions for legitimate religious accommodation. [policies must be] (1) duly enacted by a legislature, not decreed by a court; (2) debated under the harsh glare of public scrutiny; and (3) consistent with the public good.[12]

Since this procedural test rests upon a conception of democracy, I will term the anti-polygamy argument which rests upon it *the argument from democracy.*

Hamilton's proposal is that a majoritarian procedural test should be the means by which a democratic society seeks to adjudicate claims by religious and cultural minorities which demand that public policy accommodate distinct ways of life. This proposal does not necessarily qualify as a conception of pure procedural justice because principle 3) implies that the public good is a constraint on both legislators and citizens. Nevertheless, it is clear that in Hamilton's view, the public good is a matter to be defined by the legislature, not the courts.

To support her argument, Hamilton focuses on recent developments in U.S. law relevant to the issue of cultural and religious pluralism. *Wisconsin V. Yoder* is a well-known example.[13] In this decision the Supreme Court granted a religious exemption to what Hamilton regards as a legitimate and democratically enacted state education statute. The Court treated an argument motivated by religious conviction as sufficient to exempt parents of the Old Order Amish community from a state education law that required parents to provide an education for their children at least up to the age of sixteen. According to Hamilton, by granting the Old Order Amish an exemption that permits parents to end their children's education at fourteen, the will of the people, expressed through the Wisconsin state legislature, was annulled by the Supreme Court in an undemocratic act of judicial review.

The relevance of *Yoder* for polygamy is clear. Were one to advocate Hamilton's procedural test, then state laws prohibiting polygamy are sound policy just so long as such laws are a product of the legislative process. At the same time, as Hamilton herself concedes, the pro-polygamy argument might persuade enough legislators to rethink state anti-polygamy statutes. In her words,

> All of this is proper fodder for legislative consideration, including the experiences of those in the United States who have lived within the institution [of polygamy and], the views of those who have left it. . . . There may be those polygamous situations which do not entail the severe civil rights abuses apparent in the religiously motivated polygamy that has been at the forefront of the debate. Those individuals should be encouraged to make their case to their legislators. But in the end, it is the obligation of the legislators to determine what is in the best interests of all people—men, women, children, and society as a whole. And that debate belongs in the legislature, not the courts.[14]

Were one to accept Hamilton's procedural test, there is every reason to believe that anti-polygamy statues will not be challenged by legislators anytime soon. Yet liberals should reject this procedural test for reasons that are independent of the debate on *Yoder* and polygamy.

The main problem with Hamilton's test is that it leaves the status of claims on behalf of rights *that are not already recognized* subject to their popularity. This imposes a significant burden on minority groups that claim their equal standing is not affirmed. This is among the reasons many liberals reject majoritarian conceptions of democracy. Anytime the state coercively distributes resources to some but not others, the burden of justification should be on the state and on those who enjoy access to such resources; the state and its beneficiaries must show why those denied access have no grounds for complaint. Liberalism is not a doctrine of the status quo; instead, it is a doctrine for the unjustly denied and excluded.[15] Hamilton's procedural test puts liberal ideals into the hands of the powers and thus where they don't belong.

To highlight this problem with Hamilton's argument from democracy we can consider two ways of construing the debate on same-sex marriage. Were the issue of same-sex marriage left to the legislature or to popular referenda, demands for equal access to resources on the grounds of equal treatment will succeed only so far as a minority group can persuade the majority to favor a more inclusive conception of marriage. By contrast, were the issue of same sex marriage construed as an issue of equal treatment understood as a constraint on legislation, then defenders of same-sex marriage are required only to show that as a matter of principle current marriage law is in violation of due process and other fundamental principles of political morality which animate constitutional law in the U.S.

One thing to note is that the difference between these ways of construing the same sex marriage debate does not reflect a choice between democratic and non-democratic forms of governance. Rather, each reflects differing conceptions of democracy: the first is majoritarian, and the second is egalitarian. To be sure, some critics of judicial review claim that a majoritarian procedure for deciding disputes about religious and cultural toleration is the only option compatible with democracy. Yet anyone who holds this view has to reject the thesis that justice—understood to be inclusive of liberty and equality—is the first virtue of political institutions.[16] In Dworkin's words, "the institution of rights . . . represents the majority's promise to minorities that their dignity and equality will be respected."[17] There are well-known and compelling arguments which show that a majoritarian conception of democracy fails to take rights and moral equality seriously and Hamilton's argument from democracy all but ignores them.

Although her procedural test is clearly majoritarian, considered in light of what Hamilton argues in other parts of her book it is arguable that her conception of democracy is ambiguous between a majoritarian and an egalitarian conception of democracy. For instance, Hamilton does not believe that the majority should be allowed to impose its religious or cultural conceptions of the good on minorities. The most important point here, however, is that the egalitarian conception of democracy is clearly superior once the decision is made to favor institutions whose design ensures the protection of unpopular minorities from illiberal treatment by the majority. The conviction that a truly democratic society must profess a willingness to protect its most unpopular members from being denied access to resources which the more popular and powerful enjoy cannot be reconciled with a majoritarian conception of democracy.

The policy implications of the egalitarian conception of democracy differ from Hamilton's position in the following ways. On the topic of same-sex marriage and polygamy, the debate should not be left to the legislature and popular referenda. Rather, insofar as the state already sponsors and subsidizes heterosexual monogamous marriage, equality before the law and equal access to resources that are coercively allotted by the state should be understood as substantive constraints on the legislature and popular referenda; and it is the judiciary's job to enforce these substantive constraints. Moreover, an egalitarian conception of democracy can serve as the basis for a critique of *Yoder* which differs from Hamilton's critique. Since *Yoder* has the effect of undermining some citizens' fair equality of opportunity, it was a problematic decision. In contrast to a majoritarian conception of democracy, however, this objection does not rest its case on an appeal to a public policy with popular support. This is important because if Hamilton defends a majoritarian conception of democracy, then had Congress and the Wisconsin legislature granted Old Order Amish an exemption from education law, her view would have to be that such a policy is legitimate. By contrast, those committed to an egalitarian conception of democracy will claim that no policy is legitimate, no matter how popular the policy, if it violates a substantive conception of equality.

I acknowledge that these are complicated issues and that this is merely a sketch of a longstanding debate over competing conceptions of democracy. A complete account of the arguments for and against each requires a systematic evaluation of such contested issues as judicial review, the nature of political equality, and individual rights. I raise these issues here in order to make the following point: if one holds the view that there are principled constraints on legislation (including 'due process' and 'equality before the law' for example) and that one of the functions of a just government is that it enforce these principles by means of law, then one must reject the claim that debates about the kinds of marriage the state should sponsor should be left up to the will of the people.

Moreover, it does not follow from the egalitarian conception of democracy that polygamy should be accommodated. One could argue, as some have, that only monogamous marriage can be realized in a non-exploitative form. If true, this would show that the egalitarian conception of democracy favored by egalitarian liberalism can rebut the claim that polygamy should be accommodated on the grounds that polygamy is not compatible with equal treatment and fair equality of opportunity. To show that an egalitarian liberal should favor the accommodation of polygamy one must offer more than an argument which purports to show that polygamy can be accommodated without compromising values such as 'equal treatment before the law.' One must also show that polygamy is a form of marriage which can be realized in a non-exploitative form. I now consider Hamilton's argument that the exploitative nature of polygamy is a sufficient reason for a liberal state to prohibit polygamous marriage.

V. The Argument from Exploitation

Hamilton's strongest argument against polygamous marriage appeals to empirical facts that support the claim that polygamy is exploitative. Much of this evidence is drawn from recent cases studies of polygamy in the U.S. and Canada. For example,

> In the last decade in the United States there has been a growing rumble from formerly polygamous wives, who criticize the notion that polygamy is a victimless crime. Tapestry Against Polygamy was founded by a group of formerly polygamous wives who decided to fight polygamy. . . . Former polygamous wives argue that the typical religious polygamy community elevates certain men over all others, and that women and children are nothing more than property.[18]

These facts must be taken seriously; they provide a compelling reason to reject proposals to accommodate some forms of polygamy. Additional support for Hamilton's claim comes from an examination of nineteenth-century polygamy as practiced by the Mormon Church, which under the leadership of Joseph Smith was especially exploitative. The disingenuous appeals to specious concepts such as "spiritual wifery"[19] were no doubt a ruse to justify the sexual and personal domination of women by men.

It is beyond dispute that there is a lot of empirical evidence showing that polygamy in contemporary North America is morally problematic and often exploitative. However, it does not follow that polygamy is necessarily exploitative; nor does it follow that polygamy cannot in principle be realized in a manner compatible with liberal principles of justice. None of the examples cited by Hamilton support an inference to the claim that polygamy is necessarily exploitative wherever it is practiced and whoever practices it. Of course, the burden remains on defenders of polygamous marriage to show that polygamy can be realized in a non-exploitative form.

In order to address these considerations, an assessment of polygamy must evaluate social, economic, and anthropological facts about marriage. Such an empirical investigation could establish one of three claims: 1) polygamy is necessarily exploitative; 2) polygamy is exploitative because of background conditions extrinsic to polygamous arrangements; or 3) polygamy is not exploitative. In spite of claims by those currently in polygamous relationships,[20] 3) is unlikely to withstand even a superficial investigation of polygamy as practiced today—at least in the U.S.—and I will proceed on the assumption that it is false. My own view is that liberals must be open to the possibility that either 1) or 2) might turn out to be true in light of economic, anthropological and social facts about polygamy. From the standpoint of political theory, unless there is an anti-polygamy argument establishing that even in a society that has realized just background conditions polygamy cannot be realized in a non-exploitative form, then 2) is a live option.

Hamilton focuses on those instances of polygamy which are involuntary or in some other way constituted by terms that are incompatible with the liberal conception of justice. This is evidence in favor of the claim that in some cases polygamy is exploitative and ought to be prohibited. Moreover, it also illustrates that empirical facts about marriage are essential to any attempt to assess claims about the forms of marriage which ought to be accommodated. For example, the facts assembled by Mary Wollstonecraft in *Vindication of the Rights of Women* provide empirical evidence for the claim that monogamous marriage in eighteenth-century Europe was unjust and made to be unjust by law and public policy.[21] However, granted that there is indisputable evidence that polygamy in some contexts is exploitative, does this evidence entail that liberals should as a matter of principle be opposed to accommodating polygamy? Or does it establish something analogous to what Wollstonecraft thought she was able to establish about monogamous marriage in the eighteenth century (i.e., that the institution of marriage must be transformed in order to enable egalitarian relations among men, women, and children)?

The empirical evidence marshaled by Hamilton shows that polygamy as it is illegally practiced in certain parts of the U.S. and Canada is morally problematic and ought to be both outlawed and proactively eliminated. But suppose questions about whether polygamy is intrinsically exploitative are put more abstractly, as they ought to be from the standpoint of political theory. Is polygamous marriage inevitably exploitative? Or might current forms of polygamy be exploitative as a result of factors extrinsic to the nature of polygamous relations? Answers to these questions require careful examination of both empirical evidence and principles of justice. Moreover, answers to empirical questions about human relations might not track universal features but instead may track culture-specific and historically contingent features of human relations.

Claims about which forms of marriage can be accommodated by liberal principles are difficult to generalize.[22] Sorting contingent and non-contingent features of interpersonal relations is an exercise far beyond the ambitions of this paper but my point here is that there are good reasons to be skeptical of the way in which Hamilton evaluates empirical claims about marriage. In his well-known account of why and how the family is subject to the principles of justice that are to regulate the design and practice of the basic structure of society, Rawls argues that the forms of marriage compatible with a liberal society are limited to those consistent with fair equality of opportunity and equal liberty for all. Here is a representative passage reflecting Rawls's final statement on the topic:

> political principles do not apply directly to its internal life but they do impose essential constraints on the family as an institution and guarantee the basic rights and liberties and fair opportunities of all its members. They do [so] by specifying the basic claims of equal citizens who are members of a family. The family as part of the basic structure cannot violate these freedoms.[23]

Rawls also claims that "no particular form of the family (monogamous, heterosexual, or otherwise) is . . . required by a political conception of justice . . . so long as it does not run afoul of other liberal virtues."[24]

What does the Rawlsian position imply regarding polygamy? The short answer is that it depends. It depends on whether in a context of just background conditions polygamy could be practiced in a manner consistent with principles of justice. One issue that makes this question so difficult to answer—even if one affirms the Rawlsian conception of justice—is that just background conditions do not exist and thus it is difficult to marshal empirical evidence which can settle the debate on polygamy. Of course it is easy to marshal empirical evidence which shows that under current conditions, polygamy is morally problematic; but then so too are all forms of marriage. From the standpoint of ideal theory—that is, theory engaged from a point of view of a society whose systematic injustices are removed—questions about marriage have potentially different answers than do the same questions posed in real societies. It is arguable that monogamous marriage—same-sex and heterosexual—is permissible because it can be engaged without violating the charter principles which constitute a just society. What about polygamy? My suggestion here is that, lacking a justification for the prohibition against polygamy in all contexts, liberals should be open to accommodating it provided other facts about society do not conspire to undermine the possibility that polygamous marriage can be realized in ways compatible with principles of justice.

None of what I am arguing for is intended to deny that there are serious moral concerns about polygamy. Liberals should take exploitation seriously. A liberal state should regulate marriage in ways that protect agents from circumstances which will diminish the worth of their liberty and their access to resources essential to opting out of their intimate personal relations. However, since no state which fails to secure these background conditions for its members is just, no states are just; and this complicates any discussion of the liberal position on marriage in all of its forms.

VI. Conclusion

Hamilton offers three kinds of arguments for why polygamy is not compatible with liberalism: 1) polygamy should be rejected because its proponents offer religious rather than secular reasons for accommodating polygamy; 2) polygamy should be rejected because arguments for it fail a reasonable test for deciding which practices should be tolerated and which should be prohibited; and 3) polygamy should be rejected because it is exploitative. The first argument fails because it rests upon a conception of public reason that is too restrictive. Both the duty of civility and liberal norms of judicial review require only that a policy be one for which there *could be secular reasons* consistent with liberal principles. The second argument fails because Hamilton's procedural test for balancing rights against the common good rests upon a flawed conception of rights. The third argument deserves careful consideration because if true, then liberals should be opposed to accommodating polygamous marriage (and for that matter, polygamous cohabitation too). However, this is an empirical claim about an institutional arrangement's incompatibility with liberal principles of justice, and I have tried to show that Hamilton provides no justification for why polygamy is in principle necessarily incompatible with a liberal conception of justice.

In a just society, no persons would find the option of marriage more appealing than non-marriage due to a lack of meaningful alternatives. I concede—as those who defend a liberal conception of justice should—that when just background institutions and fair access to resources are lacking, then polygamy or *any other form of marriage* must be examined in light of empirical facts about social relations and the ways in which institutions affect such relations. My own view is that given just background conditions it would not be regrettable in the least if marriage, as Marx predicted of the state, withered away as persons found alternative means by which to arrange their intimate and familial relationships. Since just background conditions do not exist such that all citizens can be truly said to enjoy meaningful alternatives to marriage, any argument on polygamy must be made in a qualified way. Yet marriage as a social institution legally protected and subsidized by the state does exist and will continue to exist. This is why liberals should have something to contribute to debates about marriage. In this paper I have tried to show that the debate on polygamous marriage requires an open-minded position regarding which forms of marriage can be realized in ways consistent with liberal justice. On this point, Rawls's account of the basic structure and the family is a good guide; polygamy can be accommodated if it can be realized in ways compatible with sound principles of justice. Familiar anti-polygamy arguments of the sort advanced by Hamilton have not established that polygamous relations cannot be realized in ways compatible with liberal justice. Therefore, the polygamy question is an open one for liberals.

Jon Mahoney, Kansas State University

Notes

1. Marci Hamilton, *God vs. the Gavel: Religion and the Rule of Law* (New York: Cambridge University Press, 2005), 6.

2. As Deborah Satz notes, some contractarian feminists favor the abolition of state-defined marriage and support the claim that various kinds of contract-based marriage ought to be permitted, including plural marriage. "Feminist Perspectives on Reproduction and the Family," *Stanford Encyclopedia of Philosophy* (2004), 6-7. For good accounts of some classical

liberal positions on polygamy and marriage, see Bruce Baum, "Feminism, Liberalism and Cultural Pluralism: J. S. Mill on Mormon Polygyny," *The Journal of Political Philosophy* 5:3, (1997): 230-253; and Donald Wilson, "Kant and the Marriage Right," *Pacific Philosophical Quarterly* 85, (2004): 102-123.

3. See Richard S. Van Wagoner, *Mormon Polygamy: A History*. 2nd ed. (Salt Lake City: UT, Signature Books, 1989).

4. *Reynolds v. United States* (1879), quoted in Hamilton, 67.

5. See for instance John Rawls, *Justice as Fairness: A Restatement* (Cambridge, MA: Harvard University Press, 2001), 163.

6. In this paper I endorse Rawls's conception of the *ideal of public reason*. See, John Rawls, "The Idea of Public Reason Revisted" in *The Law of Peoples* (Cambridge, MA: Harvard University Press, 1999), 131-180.

7. Utah's anti-polygamy statute prohibits polygamous cohabitation and thus is something many liberals will oppose. Moreover, in *Lawrence v. Texas* (U.S. 558: 2003) the Court recently struck down an anti-sodomy law in part on grounds that the government has no compelling interest in regulating the consensual intimate relations among adults. Arguably, should Utah's anti-polygamy statute be challenged, *Lawrence* could be invoked to support overturning it.

8. Hamilton, 50.

9. Ibid., 65.

10. These examples are considered by Rawls in "The Idea of Public Reason Revisited."

11. Of course when citizens fail to recognize that religiously motivated reasons can't serve as the basis for law and public policy they may be more likely to affirm policies which do run afoul of public reason.

12. Hamilton, 275.

13. *Wisconsin v. Yoder* (U.S. 205: 1972).

14. Hamilton, 76.

15. For more on this see Ronald Dworkin's critique of the majoritarian conception of democracy in *Freedom's Law: The Moral Reading of the American Constitution* (Cambridge, MA: Harvard University Press, 1996), 1-38.

16. John Rawls, *A Theory of Justice*, revised ed. (Cambridge, MA: Harvard University Press, 1999).

17. Ronald Dworkin, "Taking Rights Seriously," in his *Taking Rights Seriously* (Cambridge, MA: Harvard University Press, 1977), 205.

18. Hamilton, 73.

19. Van Wagoner.

20. See for example Elizabeth Joseph's op-ed piece "Polygamy is Good Feminism," *The New York Times*, May 1991, A31.

21. Mary Wollsonecraft, *Vindication of the Rights of Women* (Penguin Classics: Reissue Edition, 1993).

22. This issue becomes even more difficult in the context of non-liberal societies. For example, the marriage practices in Domoni in the Comoro islands off the eastern coast of Africa involve a complex social and economic network in which husbands have multiple wives. The marriage unit consists of wives who continue to live with their parents and who participate in farming and other business ventures and thus contribute economically to the marriage unit in ways that reflect something more akin to an extended family in western societies. Is it inevitable that such an arrangement is exploitative? Perhaps anthropological evidence will show that "Marriage in Domoni contradicts the conclusion that a marriage system with both polygyny and matrilocal residence is impossible, and challenges the assumptions about human relationships that lead to this declaration of impossibility." Martin Ottenheimer, *Marriage in Domoni: Husbands and Wives in an Indian Ocean Community* (Prospect Heights, IL: Wavleand Press, 1985), 16.

23. Rawls, *Justice as Fairness: A Restatement*, 164.

24. Ibid., 163.

Can Liberalism Account for Women's "Adaptive Preferences"?

Lisa H. Schwartzman

Abstract: Feminist philosophers have questioned whether liberal theory can account for the phenomenon of adaptive preferences, specifically women's preferences that are formed under conditions of sexist oppression. In this paper, I examine the argument of one feminist who addresses the problem of women's "deformed desires" by relying on a liberal framework. Assessing her argument, I conclude that liberalism provides inadequate resources for responding to this issue since it errs in understanding adaptive preferences as exceptional, provides little explanation of how changes in individual preferences are motivated, and often fails to identify the adaptive nature of such preferences. I illustrate my arguments through a brief discussion of women's choices around motherhood and sexuality, and I conclude by offering several suggestions of how an alternative theory might better address the problems raised by preference adaptation in the context of oppression.

I. Introduction

Feminist philosophers and social theorists have raised a variety of questions about the meaning and value of the concept of "choice," noting that an emphasis on choice can be liberatory and yet also problematic for women. While liberal feminists typically embrace "choice" as central to women's freedom, radical feminists contend that despite its importance in legal and political discourse, the concept of choice can function ideologically to justify sexist oppression. For instance, Catharine MacKinnon and Carole Pateman argue that in debates about issues such as abortion, pornography, prostitution, and rape, a narrow focus on questions of individual choice can obscure deep-seated oppression. Radical feminists also object to liberal justifications of state power based on the abstract ideal of agreement among rational, independent, self-interested individuals. Working from a somewhat different framework, relational feminists and feminist care ethicists contend that liberalism pays inadequate attention to community, context, and connection. Both radical and relational feminists object to the individualism and abstract nature of liberalism's focus on choice.

Rather than delve into the details of these important debates, my focus here is more specific: I consider feminist questions about the role of choice in liberal theory through examining recent feminist work on a particular type of choice—those based on what have been called "adaptive preferences." Several feminist philosophers recently have addressed this issue: Martha Nussbaum offers her perspective in a lengthy chapter, "Adaptive Preferences and Women's Options," in her book *Woman and Human Development: The Capabilities Approach*; questions about adaptive preferences arise in discussions of autonomy in recent essays by Uma Narayan and Marilyn Friedman; and the relationship between adaptive preferences, liberalism, and women's oppression is explicitly addressed in writings by Ann Levey, Anita Superson, and Ann Cudd.[1]

After a brief definition of adaptive preferences, I consider various problems that arise when feminists employ a choice-based liberalism in analyzing situations in which oppression's effects are manifested in individuals' preferences. I suggest that choice-based liberalism may prove to be an inadequate tool for identifying and challenging certain forms of sexism. Because it focuses on individual choice, it can obscure larger social structures and call attention away from power relations that influence preference formation. Moreover, I contend that while liberals who have taken feminism seriously may be able to acknowledge that some choices made under oppressive conditions are coerced and therefore not authentic, liberal theory itself does not aid in either the identification or eradication of such preferences. Instead, it often works to make them harder to detect and to alter. To illustrate the problems with a feminist reliance on choice-based liberalism, I briefly discuss two contemporary issues: (a) women's choices regarding motherhood and paid employment; and (b) young women's desires around sexuality. Ultimately, I conclude that the problem of women's adaptive preferences is best addressed with a theory that focuses attention on social power relations, not on the isolated choices and preferences of individuals.

II. Adaptive Preferences and Feminist Liberalism

In *Sour Grapes: Studies in the Subversion of Rationality*, Jon Elster discusses various ways that a person's preferences may be influenced by what is available to her. Adaptive preference formation (otherwise known as the "sour grapes" phenomenon) is "the adjustment of wants to possibilities."[2] In other words, if certain options are not possible, or come to no longer be possible, a person may adapt her preferences to her circumstances so that she is satisfied with what she already has.[3] Although Elster states that his aim is to highlight a problem arising within utilitarianism,[4] adaptive preferences also pose a problem for other forms of liberalism. My concern in this paper is with liberal theorists who emphasize the central value of individual choice, especially those liberals who define justice in terms of state neutrality between individually-devised theories of "the good" (such as Ronald Dworkin and Will Kymlicka). On this view, one's life goes best if it is lived "from the inside," according to one's own conception of value.[5] As liberal feminist Ann Cudd explains, liberalism "holds the human individual to be the pre-eminent moral concern" and thus the state must ensure that each person has a zone of privacy, which is a "domain of free choice . . . in which persons may choose according to their preferences, whatever those preferences turn out to be."[6] In cases of internalized oppression, however, such a theory can lead to problems. As Cudd herself acknowledges, the oppressed may adapt to their limited options and develop desires that reinforce the status quo, thereby entrenching their own subordination. Examples of this phenomenon include cases as severe as a battered woman desiring to stay with her abuser[7] and as seemingly trivial as a young woman giving up her desire to pursue a career in science upon learning of the sexist barriers to women's success. Given the importance of individually-made choices within liberalism, feminist liberals appear to face a problem. If women do in fact make choices that reinforce their own oppression, then it seems that women are choosing to be oppressed, and that they are therefore responsible for their own oppression.[8]

While several feminists address this issue, I focus on a recent essay by Anita Superson that lays out the problem and proposes a liberal solution. Using the term "deformed desires" as interchangeable with "adaptive preferences" and citing a variety of feminist authors, Superson identifies the following problems with desires that have been deformed by the patriarchy: (1) They have their source in unjust social conditions, which often involve indoctrination, manipulation, and the denial of women's autonomy; (2) Deformed desires "benefit not their bearers, but the privileged and patriarchy itself";[9] (3) Women often hold the false belief that they benefit from their deformed desires; (4) Deformed desires "often conflict with the person's *own* desire to promote her own welfare";[10] and (5) "deformed desires at base involve a person's not having appropriate regard for herself as an intrinsically valuable human being."[11]

After explaining these problems, Superson considers various "informed desire" tests that appeal to the perspective of an "ideal observer" to exclude any irrational desires that an agent might possess.[12] While these tests aim to protect the agent's autonomy and promote her good, Superson concludes that because they neither mention deformed desires nor consider cases where the agent does not recognize her/his own moral worth, such tests fail to exclude deformed desires. To exclude such desires, Superson adds to these tests a "Kantian-inspired addendum" which would require the woman to be "visionary" and see herself as having equal worth and dignity:

> The visionary woman will see herself as having equal worth to men She will see her opportunities and choices in a new light, and see herself as part of the moral community and as an individual deserving of respect. . . . For example, the abused woman

> will not just imagine that she doesn't want to stay with her abuser, but will envision herself as having equal worth, as not deserving abuse, as not having principles that endorse women's servility to men, and as asserting her right to act on desires she has that will promote her own welfare.[13]

Illustrating an application of her test, Superson considers and rejects an argument by Uma Narayan. In "Minds of Their Own: Choices, Autonomy, Cultural Practices, and Other Women," Narayan examines women's attitudes towards veiling in the conservative Muslim community of Sufi Pirzada in Old Delhi. Narayan contends that Muslim women who decide to veil after carefully assessing their realistic alternatives—after "bargaining with the patriarchy"—have in fact made their desires to wear the veil "their own." According to Superson, although a woman in such conditions makes a choice, if her decision is based even partly on "patriarchal reasons," then it does not reflect a commitment to her equal worth and thus cannot truly be her own: "The veiling woman does not make deformed desires her own by bargaining about them; instead, she needs to rid herself of them to assert her individualism and moral worth."[14]

III. Limitations of Liberal Responses to Adaptive Preferences

No Practical Solution Provided

In this section, I contend that Superson fails to address the problem underlying adaptive preferences, and I suggest that her work illustrates several general limitations of feminist liberalism. First, although Superson recommends that women give up their adaptive preferences and assert their individualism, it is unclear how this is to be accomplished. In many cases, significant changes in the social context may need to occur before it would be advantageous or even possible for an individual to rid herself of these preferences. A woman who is unable to leave the house without being ostracized or beaten may find her desire to wear the veil makes sense, at least strategically. Similarly, given that the likelihood of murder increases when women attempt to escape abusive partners, a battered woman's desire to stay may also be understandable. At least in some cases, it might be that the circumstances of women's lives, as well as the larger socio-cultural context, would need to change before their deformed desires could be eradicated.

Second, even desires that hold little advantage to an oppressed person might be impossible to eradicate by the force of sheer will. As feminist discussions of internalized oppression demonstrate, just because one learns a particular principle or understands a concept, one does not necessarily forgo all desires that conflict with that principle or concept.[15] For instance, a woman may come to believe that she is oppressed by the beauty industry and by the grooming practices she has learned were appropriate for women—including spending hours a day and a great deal of money on cosmetics, hair products, and clothing. And yet her desire to continue spending her time and money in these ways might remain.[16] Thus, a woman's simply learning that she has self-worth, or envisioning herself in an ideal state where she was appropriately valued, is unlikely to eliminate her deformed desires.

Third, Superson fails to offer another approach to the problem. Once the woman's "deformed desires" are eliminated, what will replace them? If the social context is oppressive in a way that encourages a woman to develop these preferences, an abstract and idealized knowledge of her individual self-worth likely will be insufficient to provide her with an alternative source of values, interests, and desires.

Difficulty Identifying the Existence of Adaptive Preferences

In addition to failing to offer a workable solution to the problem of preference adaptation, liberal theory provides inadequate resources for identifying the existence of such preferences. Although liberalism may be able to address sexist oppression once it has been identified, its methodology of focusing on the individual and appealing to what would be chosen in an abstract ideal can conceal the power of social forces and the existence of group-based domination. In describing how group membership affects women's preferences, Superson, Cudd, Nussbaum, and other feminist liberals often rely on the work of feminists that either goes beyond or falls outside a liberal individualist framework; for instance, Superson draws heavily on Sandra Bartky's analysis of repressive satisfactions, "false needs," indoctrination, and psychological manipulation, and Cudd offers a definition of oppression that very closely resembles that of Marilyn Frye.[17] In contrast to Frye's radical feminism and Bartky's Marxian-inspired phenomenological approach, liberal theory does not highlight the effects that social structures have on the development of individual preferences and desires. Focusing primarily on individuals and their choices, liberal approaches may obscure and even reinforce the effects of structural oppression.

Interestingly, some feminist liberals write about the problem of preference adaptation and desire "deformation" as if these occur only in rare circumstances. One example of this tendency can be seen in cases where feminist liberals discuss this phenomenon by invoking the lives and choices of Third World Women rather than women in their own countries. Nussbaum's discussion of adaptive preferences centers on Indian women, as does Superson's example cited above. Taking the problem of adaptive preferences seriously would mean acknowledging the myriad ways that power, oppression, and social hierarchy shape and mold all of us. Yet when Western feminists move so quickly to discussing the preferences of women in cultures that are different and allegedly less developed, they suggest that it is only these "Other women" who are deeply affected by oppression and possess desires that are not truly their own. This distorts Western women's own understanding of ourselves, obscures the depth of patriarchy's influence on us all, and sets in place a potentially racist and ethnocentric understanding of women's cultural differences. Although such problems do not *necessarily* follow from liberalism, because liberal theory pays less attention to the myriad ways that power shapes and molds personal desires and choices, relying primarily on a choice-based liberalism may be a poor strategy for feminists aiming to expose and challenge deep-seated sexist oppression.

Focus on Government Respect for Individual Choices

Finally, in addition to these specific problems, liberal discussions of adaptive preferences often assume a frame of inquiry that is too narrowly focused on the individual. Typically, questions about adaptive preferences arise when considering whether the state must respect the choices of individuals; liberals generally hold that the state is not obligated to respect choices that are in some sense unfree (for example, due to the coercion or non-autonomy involved in adaptive preference formation). In other words, if we can show that a woman's desire to stay with her abuser or to wear the veil is based on deformed desires, then the state need not respect this choice—or at least it need not give it the same consideration it would receive were it formed in a noncoercive environment. But there are several problems with this position. As Narayan argues, Western feminists discussing the choices of non-Western women often fail to grasp the meanings of various practices in the lives of the women affected by them, and they may overlook the effects of other interlocking systems of power, including race relations, colonialism, and various forms of religious discrimination. This can lead to a skewed and incomplete understanding of the ways that preferences have been "deformed." Secondly, why must discussions of adaptive preference formation center on the question of state respect for individual choice? As noted above, the idea that the state must respect the choices of individuals is central to many liberal conceptions of justice. As some feminist critics of liberalism have argued, however, justice cannot be understood without careful attention to social groups, as one's social position in various hierarchies of power affects one's options and the preferences one develops.[18] While liberalism as a theory does not in principle preclude the recognition that desires can be affected by various forms of oppression, my argument suggests that a choice-based liberalism may be ineffective in identifying and addressing this problem. Thus, feminists might be better off turning to a theory that has a different understanding of social power and domination, one that does not define justice in such individualistic terms. Such a shift would allow for a deeper analysis of the causes, consequences, and processes of desire formation, and thus would be better able to address the issues that lie at the root of women's adaptive preferences.

IV. Social Development of Desires in the Context of Sexism

To illustrate the importance of moving away from a narrowly focused liberal analysis of women's preferences, I briefly consider two issues that have gotten quite a lot of attention in both the mainstream press and in theoretical feminist discussions: (A) women's preferences regarding children and paid employment and (B) young women's sexual desires.

Women's Preferences Regarding Family/Career

In a 2003 *New York Times Magazine* cover story, Lisa Belkin declared that "while the absence of women in positions of power was once chiefly a result of sexism, the fact that women still don't rule the world is now increasingly a result of deliberate choice."[19] Clearly, there are a number of problems with this analysis: Belkin's unstated focus was on white, upper-middle class women, and she provides little evidence to demonstrate a causal relationship between men's workplace dominance and women's choice to stay home. But what concerns me here is the narrow focus on women's choices—as if what women prefer and desire is the appropriate beginning and end point for such a discussion. Liberal feminists aim to improve women's available options and thus advocate increased state funding for childcare, more flexible jobs, and fewer penalties for maternity leave. While such changes surely would benefit women, understanding the problem as being about women's "choices" is far too simplistic. Deeper questions about the formation of women's and men's "preferences" underlying these choices must also be asked. If we acknowledge (as many feminists do) that preferences develop in a social context, and that our social context is sexist and patriarchal, we need to look at the structures of power that encourage women to think that they must make more sacrifices than men if they want children. While women who are not economically advantaged rarely have the privilege of "choosing" to forgo paid employment, they are still held responsible for the double burden of paid work and childcare, often being told that having children was their "choice" and so they must find a way to make it work. In such cases, the discourse of choice and individual preference may actually call attention away from larger social patterns and problems. Social norms encourage women to care for children and to prioritize men's careers; individual women who prefer this arrangement did not develop this preference in a vacuum. While we could conceptualize women's preferences to be primary caretakers of children as "deformed desires" since they may well have arisen because of patriarchal norms, focusing on liberating individual women from such desires seems not to be the most effective way to address the underlying problems. What must change is the cultural norms and expectations that socialize both men and women to have particular preferences, as well as the socio-economic forces that structure the workplace and the economy on the assumption of a traditional male-dominated household.

Young Women's Sexual Desires

The second issue that I will briefly address concerns the sexual desires of adolescent girls and young women. I draw on the work of Lynn Phillips and Deborah Tolman, feminist researchers who conducted extensive interviews with college women and adolescent girls respectively. Although both studied the desires, passions, and feelings of the individual girls and women, their interviews reveal a great deal about gendered social norms and about the complex and often conflicting cultural pressures young women must negotiate—pressures from family, friends, peers, and their communities.

In *Flirting With Danger: Young Women's Reflections on Sexuality and Domination*, Lynn Phillips interviewed college-aged women and found that while questions about rape and sexual assault typically center on whether sexual activity was chosen, the discourse and ideology around choice can work to occlude power relations. Phillips discovered that although most of the women she interviewed were "quite willing to use words like 'rape,' 'battering,' 'victimization,' and 'abuse' to describe *other* women's experiences," when analyzing their own, they tended to blame themselves for having "chosen" to take part in some aspect of the encounter.[20] For instance, in the following quotation one young woman describes an experience that turned out to be painful and humiliating. And yet because she had chosen to have intercourse, she did not feel that she was really a victim. She explains,

> I don't think of it as abuse or victimization or anything, because even though it may have looked that way with his hand over my mouth and his hurting me and all, I just don't think I could ever call myself a victim, because I like to think I have it too much together to ever let myself be victimized like that. I went into the whole thing willingly, and even though I got hurt, I figured, well, I wanted to be a grown-up, so this just comes with the territory I guess.[21]

This quotation is revealing in a number of ways—it illustrates the stigma attributed to victimhood and the association drawn between sexual intercourse and maturity—but my interest here is in the connection between victimization and choice. Numerous young women in Phillips' study suggested that because they made various choices (to engage in some kind of intimate contact, to be alone with a man, or to go out to a club dressed in a certain way), whatever follows from their choice is their own responsibility, thus precluding their being victims. Phillips connects this attitude to the conflicting pressures on young women to control both their own and men's sexual desires and to be sexually available and responsive to male desire. Because women do actively negotiate these complex cultural pressures, they are always making choices of some sort and thus don't experience themselves as pure victims without agency. Phillips' work suggests that rather than focusing on the seemingly simple question of whether or not a woman "consented" and "chose" to engage in a particular activity, greater critical attention must be paid to the social processes that shape both cultural norms and individual desire. Insofar as liberal theory focuses on the preferences, desires, and choices of individuals, it provides inadequate resources for such analysis.

A related problem concerns the very existence and substance of women's desire itself. As I noted above, the liberal model begins from the idea that individuals have strong preferences and clear desires on which they are inclined to act. Yet the work of Phillips and Tolman reveals the many ways in which society denies and ignores the sexual desires of young women and adolescent girls. While girls are increasingly sexualized and warned of the threats of pregnancy, disease, and rape, little attention is paid to their actual passions and embodied sexual feelings; this stands in sharp contrast to the prevailing view that boys have strong sexual desires that are often uncontrollable. What Tolman found in her extensive interviews with adolescent girls was that many had learned to pay close attention to male sexual desire and to distrust and fear their own. She explains,

> Girls' *lack* of desire serves as the necessary linchpin in how adolescent sexuality is organized and managed. To the extent that we believe that adolescent sexuality is under control, it is adolescent girls whom we hold responsible, because we do not believe boys can or will be. We are left with a circuitous argument that fails to include the reality or importance of female adolescents' own sexuality: Boys will be boys ergo sexuality is dangerous for girls.[22]

This sexist double standard reveals a troubling ideology in which girls are blamed and held responsible for boys' actions and yet are denied their own sexual agency. Moreover, Tolman argues that uncertainty about their own sexual feelings and desires can make girls more vulnerable to sexual exploitation, and it can also affect their overall agency, leading to a diminished sense of what it is that they really want.[23] Without a culture that teaches girls that they are entitled to their desires, girls and women can be disadvantaged by the liberal focus on individual choice. Appealing to the abstract value of individual self-respect and dignity (as Superson's liberal model advocates) will be insufficient without deeper changes in sexuality, gender relations, and patterns of socialization.[24]

V. Conclusion: Toward an Alternative Approach

Having explained and illustrated some of the problems with using a choice-based liberal theory to analyze women's adaptive preferences, in this final section I offer some suggestions toward constructing an alternative. First, as I argued earlier, feminists should not begin with the liberal assumption that the deformation of desires due to oppression is unusual, abnormal, or exotic—something that happens in "Other Cultures" but not in our own lives and communities. By acknowledging that preferences frequently are shaped, molded, and even created by people's circumstances, and by noting that we live in a society where there are various systems of oppression, we can become more aware of the impact that social structures have on individual desires. Second, rather than the individualistic focus that characterizes liberalism, feminists must—and often do—call attention to the ways that power affects persons as members of social groups. As a method for political theorizing, liberalism tends to privilege the individual, whereas understanding the effects of oppression requires a critical analysis of social groups. Finally, rather than responding to adaptive preferences by simply trying to do away with them and assert the individuality of the oppressed person, a more radical approach would emphasize changing the social structure that gave rise to the deformed desires in the first place.[25] Although the discovery that a person's preferences are "deformed" by oppression *does* reveal a problem with the specific individual, it must also be understood as an indication that deeper and more widespread social changes are needed. Although liberals can of course support such reforms, my work here suggests that the analysis motivating these changes reaches beyond the confines of liberal individualism and requires a more radical social critique.

Lisa H. Schwartzman, Michigan State University

Notes

1. See Martha Nussbaum, *Woman and Human Development: The Capabilities Approach* (New York: Cambridge University Press, 2000), 111–66; Uma Narayan, "Minds of Their Own: Choices, Autonomy, Cultural Practices, and Other Women," in *A Mind of One's Own: Feminist Essays on Reason and Objectivity*, 2nd edition, ed. Louise M. Antony and Charlotte E. Witt (Boulder, CO: Westview Press, 2002), 418–32; Marilyn Friedman, "Autonomy and Male Dominance," in *Autonomy and the Challenges to Liberalism: New Essays*, ed. John Christman and Joel Anderson (New York: Cambridge University Press, 2005), 150–73; Ann Levey "Liberalism, Adaptive Preferences, and Gender Equality," *Hypatia* 20, no. 4 (Fall 2005), 127–43; Anita Superson, "Deformed Desires and Informed Desire Tests," *Hypatia* 20, no. 4 (Fall 2005), 109–26; Ann E. Cudd, "Oppression by Choice," *Journal of Social Philosophy* 25 (1994), 22–44; and Ann E. Cudd, *Analyzing Oppression* (New York, Oxford University Press, 2006).

2. Jon Elster, *Sour Grapes: Studies in the Subversion of Rationality* (New York: Cambridge University Press, 1983), 25.

3. Elster contrasts this "purely causal process of adaptation," which takes place behind the back of the person concerned, with the related but distinct phenomenon of "character planning," which he finds less problematic. Character planning also involves adjusting preferences in response to circumstances, but unlike the sour grapes phenomenon, it is a process that the individual herself controls by intentionally engineering the adaptation of her preferences to her possibilities (Ibid., 110).

4. Ibid., 109.

5. Will Kymlicka explains this central tenet of liberalism: "[N]o life goes better by being led from the outside according to values the person doesn't endorse. My life only goes better if I'm leading it from the inside, according to my beliefs about value" [Will Kymlicka, *Liberalism, Community and Culture* (New York: Clarendon Press, 1989), 12].

6. Ann E. Cudd, "The Paradox of Liberal Feminism: Preference, Rationality, and Oppression," in *Varieties of Feminist Liberalism*, ed. Amy R. Baehr (Lanham, MD: Roman and Littlefield, 2004), 38.

7. I do not mean to suggest that "desiring" to stay with an abuser is the most common reason women remain in abusive relationships; other factors typically affect this decision, such as economic dependence on the man (where moving out could mean homelessness), fear of increased violence (which often follows a woman's attempt to leave), worries that the man may attempt to take away her children, etc. Nonetheless, in a situation where the woman loves the man and her desire to remain is not due to these other factors, her preference to stay with him might be described as "adaptive."

8. Calling this the "paradox of liberal feminism," Ann Cudd offers the definition of liberalism cited above and then continues: "Feminism claims that women are oppressed materially and psychologically. Under conditions of psychological oppression, preferences tend to be molded by oppressive forces in a direction counter to the good of the oppressed. . . . Women's choices, then, may tend to reinforce their oppression. Hence, some feminists have argued that under conditions of gender oppression, liberalism is inimical to feminism; while liberalism purports to offer justice, it can only deliver injustice to women against the background of women's oppression" (Cudd, "The Paradox of Liberal Feminism," 38).

9. Superson, 110.

10. Ibid, 11.

11. Ibid.

12. For instance, Superson briefly discusses tests for the "rationality" of desire proposed by Bernard Williams, Richard Brandt, and Peter Railton (among others).

13. Ibid., 120.

14. Ibid., 116.

15. For a detailed and very personal description of some examples, see Sandra Lee Bartky's *Femininity and Domination: Studies in the Phenomenology of Oppression* (New York: Routledge, 1990).

16. In teaching introductory-level feminism classes, I often hear students say that although they are now troubled by some of their habits and practices, their conflicted desire to continue them persists.

17. For instance, see Cudd's definition in *Analyzing Oppression* (New York: Oxford University Press, 2006), 23–6. She offers four conditions that are necessary and sufficient for oppression: 1) the harm condition; 2) the social group condition; 3) the privilege condition; and 4) the coercion condition. She states explicitly that this definition "resembles Marilyn Frye's" except that the fourth condition is "left implicit in her analysis" and is not spelled out like the other three. Cudd's work is interesting insofar as she spends a great deal of energy articulating an account of oppression that she suggests is a liberal one. However, insofar as she relies on a more radical understanding of social groups, I would argue that her

definition transcends liberalism. Moreover, I am unconvinced that the methods of rational choice theory are beneficial to feminists (as Cudd contends), though I do not have the space to make that argument here. For Cudd's views on this matter, see "Rational Choice and the Lessons of Feminism," in *A Mind of One's Own: Feminist Essays on Reason and Objectivity*, 2nd edition, ed. Louise M. Antony and Charlotte E. Witt (Boulder, CO: Westview Press, 2002), 398–417; and Elizabeth Anderson's reply, "Should Feminists Reject Rational Choice Theory?," in Antony and Witt, 369–97.

18. See Iris Marion Young, "Equality of Whom? Social Groups and Judgments of Injustice," *The Journal of Political Philosophy* 9, no. 1 (2001), 1–18.

19. Lisa Belkin, "The Opt-Out Revolution," *New York Times Magazine* (October 26, 2003). This quotation is taken from the summary of the article on p. 10.

20. Lynn Phillips, *Flirting with Danger: Young Women's Reflections on Sexuality and Domination* (New York: New York University Press, 2000), 7.

21. Ibid., 96, quoting "Cynthia."

22. Deborah L. Tolman, *Dilemmas of Desire: Teenage Girls Talk About Sexuality* (Cambridge, MA: Harvard University Press, 2002), 15.

23. On this point, Tolman cites the following quotation: "The psyche cannot cut off one kind of desire without affecting another. When sexual desire is truncated, all desire is compromised—including girls' power to love themselves and to know what they really want" [E. Debold, M. Wilson, and I. Malave, *Mother Daughter Revolution: From Betrayal to Power* (Reading, MA: Addison-Wesley, 1993), 211; cited in Tolman, 21]. In a chapter on the girls who were least in touch with their desire, Tolman explains: "[G]irls who are not able to sense the presence or absence of their own sexual desire risk becoming dissociated from their own experience and from reality, thereby impairing their psychological integrity and their understanding of what is happening in the world around them. Such dissociation makes it difficult for these girls to know and name sexual exploitation" (Tolman, 78).

24. Noting that abstract discussions of self-respect can be problematic if not accompanied by more significant changes in the messages girls receive, Tolman warns: "without the message that girls are entitled to sexual desire, self-respect usually translates into a girl's resistance to giving in to a boy's desire; the self in question should not by definition have her own desire. And boys who respect a girl do not engage her on sexual terms" (Tolman, 176).

25. This would ultimately result in transformations in the desires of both the oppressed and the oppressor group, whose preferences are also shaped by powerful social forces.

Part III:
Terrorism and Torture

Female Terrorists: What Difference Does Gender Make?

MARILYN FRIEDMAN

Abstract: Should women's terrorist acts be understood differently than similar acts carried out by men? Does the gender identity of a terrorist make a difference to the meaning of a terrorist's acts? Commentators who explain women's involvement in terrorism often offer explanations other than political commitment. They often refer instead to factors in the women's personal relationships, thereby drawing on gender stereotypes and diminishing the women's political commitments. I suggest instead that terrorism by a woman involves symbolic political "testimony." It amounts to saying that someone who is a typically nonviolent sort of person has engaged in violence on behalf of a political cause. Because of this significance, women's terrorism merits a more serious consideration as testimony than similar acts by men.

I. Introduction

In her book, *The Demon Lover: On the Sexuality of Terrorism*, feminist Robin Morgan writes:

> The majority of terrorists . . . are men. The majority of women, caught in the middle, want no more of this newly intensified form of the old battle to the death between fathers and sons. . . . Even when we collaborate—and we do, either in traditional roles of support or as tougher-than-thou token militants—we do so out of a disbelief, a suspended knowledge, a longing for acceptance, a tortured love we bear for the men we have birthed and sustain.[1]

Morgan considers numerous female terrorists[2] and, in each case, argues that the woman in question did not act out of a direct commitment to using violence on behalf of the cause. In Morgan's view, women are peace-, love-, and life-oriented. She portrays each female terrorist as engaging in terrorism because of attachment to some man or men who somehow got her involved. Morgan even dismisses in this way the commitments of women who are widely regarded as having been terrorist *leaders*, women such as Ulrike Meinhof and Gudrun Enslinn of the Baader-Meinhof Group/Red Army Faction that was active in Germany from 1968 to 1972.[3]

Morgan is not the only commentator who doubts that female terrorists are ever directly committed to terrorism. Yet, women as terrorists have killed and maimed with the same deadly force and accuracy as men; women have blown themselves up as suicide bombers and taken other lives with them. Did these women really have some other aim in mind for doing what they did?

Should the terrorism that women carry out be understood differently than similar acts carried out by men? Does the gender identity of a terrorist make a difference to the meaning, motivation, or justification of a terrorist's acts? There are certainly some cases in which aspects of identity matters to moral assessment. The existence of special words, for example, for the acts of killing one's own parents, matricide and patricide, mark the idea that killing is, on the face of it, a greater wrong if one is a child of the person one kills. Also, the *gender* identity of an agent clearly matters to the *public* assessment of behavior in at least some cases. A *female* parent, a *mother*, who kills her child will be more harshly condemned than a *male* parent, a *father*, who kills his child.[4]

I ask: does the gender of a *terrorist* make a moral difference to understanding or justifying that person's acts of *terrorism*?

II. Some Ways in which Gender Matters to Terrorism

Gender makes *some* difference to terrorism. Women may be more *effective* as terrorists than men. This can happen in several ways. First, if women become terrorists, the sheer number of *potential* terrorists in a population increases. If both women and men in a population group are potential recruits who might fight for a cause, then there could be as many as *twice* the number of potential recruits as there would be if only men participated.

Second, women can be more effective at *carrying out* terrorist acts than men. This is due largely to the different ways in which women and men are stereotyped and perceived. There are more male than female terrorists overall, so the "typical," or paradigm, terrorist is assumed to be male. In dangerous situations, men are therefore scrutinized much more carefully than women for signs of suspicious activity. As a result, female terrorists may have an easier time than their male counterparts in gaining access to sites of potential terrorist action. As well, in Muslim societies with strict modesty requirements, the police or military forces that would search suspicious men for weapons may refrain from searching women in order to avoid antagonizing the local population. Women would then have more leeway to hide concealed weapons and explosives in their clothing. Wearing a burkha gives an obvious advantage to a terrorist.

Third, female terrorists may be more effective than male terrorists in promoting *publicity* for the terrorist cause. This is because women seem to gain more media coverage than men for the same sorts of terrorist actions, such as suicide bombing.[5]

Why this might be so is an intriguing question. Social theorist Rhiannon Talbot writes that there is something disturbing in "the thought of those who bring forth life actually destroying it."[6] Theorist Melanie Reid claims that, "Women who kill are hot news."[7] A woman who kills may prompt a public audience to take notice of what she has done, out of both revulsion and fascination. A female killer may even be considered more ruthless than men who kill if she regards her cause as a "surrogate child;"[8] maternal self-sacrifice is a well-known phenomenon. These various attitudes may not be mutually consistent, but ambivalence and inconsistency do not necessarily diminish public fascination.

Fourth, terrorists are, on the face of it, agents who act in ways that require fearlessness, determination, and self-discipline. They are often viewed as heroic by those who sympathize with their cause. If a woman can become a terrorist within and for her culture, this constitutes evidence that the culture in question allows women to attain high levels of culturally valued achievement and status. Depending on the audience, this odd sort of "equal opportunity" might enhance the global reputation of a culture that is otherwise stereotyped by many outsiders as traditional or backward in its treatment of women. This sort of enhanced reputation might indirectly win sympathy for a terrorist cause that defends such a culture.[9]

Because women can enhance the effectiveness of terrorism in these ways, more and more terrorist groups are coming around to employing women as terrorists. Even groups regarded as conservative in their treatment of women have recently been relenting. On 27 January 2002, Yasser Arafat gave his "army of roses" speech in which he urged Palestinian women to fight as equals with Palestinian men against Israel. In his speech, Arafat coined a new word, "shaheeda," as a feminine form of "shaheed," the Arabic word for martyr. That very afternoon, Wafa Idris became the first woman to commit a suicide bombing for the Palestinian cause.[10] Other women have followed her. In May 2003, Hiba Da'arma became the first woman to commit suicide bombing for Palestinian Islamic Jihad. The first woman to carry out a suicide bombing on behalf of Hamas was Reem Raiyshi in January 2004.[11] A December 2005 article in *Newsweek* magazine reported that *Al Qaeda*, long considered a hold-out on this issue because of its fundamentalist norms that denied women a place in public life, has recently used several female suicide bombers in Iraq.[12]

III. Explanations Given for Female Participation in Terrorism

These conditions explain why terrorist groups might want to use women as terrorists; they do not explain why women might want to become terrorists. Yet, there is an ample supply of those explanations as well. However, the scholars and other commentators who analyze terrorism tend, on the whole, to portray and explain women's terrorist acts somewhat differently than those carried out by men. Some of the differences lie in what are supposed to be the terrorist's own motivations or reasons for engaging in terrorism while other differences pertain to conditions and circumstances postulated as *causing* women to become terrorists.

Three types of reasons or motivations for terrorism that seem to be attributed more frequently to women than to men are these:

1. to avenge the death of a husband, brother, or other close male person who was killed by the enemy forces;[13] although men who commit suicide bombings are often also avenging the death of a relative or close friend, this relational motivation seems to be emphasized more heavily when the terrorist is female;[14]
2. because she was lured, pressured, or coerced into participating by a husband or lover;[15] again a personal relationship is emphasized over and above the cause to which the woman might be committed and the relationship is romantic or sexual and therefore fits into patterns of what is considered appropriate or expected feminine behavior;
3. to overcome some dishonor she suffered in her community, which may have marginalized her socially and shamed her family; this dishonor may have been due to her own behavior or to some behavior inflicted on her, such as a rape; it is sometimes part of this explanation that some terrorist organization *perpetrated* the initial sexual dishonor on the woman by, for example, arranging to *have* her raped and then persuading her that her only hope of restoring her honor was to sacrifice herself for her people.[16]

Aside from the reasons or motivations attributed to female terrorists, there are also certain distinctive *causal* factors that are cited to explain women's involvement in terrorism, for example:

1. a tendency toward masculine personality and physical attributes, even including excess body hair,[17] on the parts of women who engage in violent crimes of all sorts (this sort of explanation has thankfully fallen out of favor in recent years);
2. the absence of traditional *feminine* traits such as maternal instincts; Rhiannon Talbot challenges this explanation on the grounds that some female terrorists do have children, many express maternal feelings, and many envisage their terrorist activities as a kind of maternal self-sacrifice;[18]
3. the influence of *feminism* in recent decades, either through training or encouragement that feminist organizations provide for anti-social behavior or in virtue of feminism's general tendency to reduce the power of traditional gender roles and norms;[19] granted, feminism does aim to reduce the power of traditional gender norms; however, the idea that feminism trains women for anti-social behavior is a bit far-fetched if anti-social behavior means terrorist attacks on innocent noncombatants; granted, one feminist group did encourage violent action many years ago in the U.S., namely, SCUM, the Society for Cutting Up Men, founded and led by Valerie Solanas, the woman who shot

Andy Warhol; however, feminist training for terrorism seems frankly atypical; even SCUM engaged more in propaganda than in actual terrorism.[20]

What is common to all these explanations and portrayals is that women's participation in terrorism is characterized as something *other* than whole-hearted dedication to the terrorist cause itself. Women's participation in terrorism is, furthermore, often depicted as subordinate to the activities carried out by the men of the organization.[21] This is not an explanatory factor but rather a reinterpretation of women's terrorist activities that downplays its importance. This reinterpretation coincides with the pattern of explanations listed above, however, which also diminishes the significance of women's terrorist acts compared to those of men.

This widespread pattern of downplaying women's direct commitment to terrorist causes calls for explanation. Some feminist theorists have attributed this tendency to the power of female gender stereotypes.[22] Female gender is understood in terms of an "essential" nature that is non-violent[23] or peaceful.[24] On this view, female terrorists are conceptualized, or "constructed," according to the same gender norms and stereotypes that are applied to females in most or all social contexts. Thus, one feminist argument is that the female gender stereotype by itself drives the tendency to downplay women's participation in terrorism. Women's agency is simply being discounted in yet another realm in which women do in fact act.

This explanation, however, does not seem to me to be sufficient. There is another factor at work, I suggest, one that is specific to the context of terrorism. Denying women's agency *per se* is not the *primary* aim of the tendency to downplay women's participation in terrorism. Instead, something important about women's agency *as terrorists* seems particularly threatening to some observers and this is what they try especially hard to downplay. To best understand this alternative account, we need to take a detour through the concept of terrorism and the question of its justification.

IV. Definition and Presumptive Wrongness of Terrorism

Definitions of terrorism abound. Perhaps over a hundred definitions of it have been proposed.[25] For this discussion, I shall borrow and slightly modify David Rodin's definition: "terrorism is the deliberate, negligent, or reckless use of force against noncombatants, by state or nonstate actors for ideological ends and in the absence of a substantively just legal process."[26] The concept of ideological ends is used broadly here to cover any "systematic scheme of ideas, usually relating to politics or society, or to the conduct of a class or group, and regarded as justifying actions."[27] In this broad sense, religion falls under the concept of "ideological ends" and may provide the "systematic scheme of ideas" that justifies acts of terrorism as legitimate forms of killing or martyrdom for the sake of a religiously sanctioned cause.

On the face of it, terrorism is a wrong, an evil. Noam Zohar argues that "The special evil of terrorism lies in its very nature as indiscriminate killing, that is to say, in its purposeful slaying of the innocent."[28] Michael Walzer considers the special evil in terrorism to extend to the wider impact of such killing: "it is infinitely threatening to whole peoples, whose individual members are systematically exposed to violent death at any and every moment in the course of their (largely innocuous) lives."[29] Bat-Ami Bar On construes this wider impact as the cruelty of *terrorizing* people and thereby diminishing them psychologically and morally.[30] Even when people do not feel terrorized,[31] terrorism still involves the evil of targeting violence indiscriminately against noncombatants or the innocent, and this feature remains at the core of what is wrong with terrorism.

However, saying that terrorism is wrong because it indiscriminately targets noncombatants or innocent persons does not by itself indicate whether such acts are wrong *all things* considered. I argue that the wrongness of terrorism should be construed as presumptive and defeasible. Moral reasons of sufficient weight *might* justify particular terrorist acts and the causes for which they are undertaken and thereby override the presumptive wrongness of the acts themselves. Whole peoples, for example, may suffer long-standing oppression in which their own innocent civilians or noncombatants are targeted indiscriminately for violent political repression or torture, and terrorism may be their only means of resistance.

However, we should never forget that terrorism, as defined here, targets noncombatants deliberately with the use of force. The burden of proof is on those who would *defend* particular terrorist acts. Even when terrorism is justified, it remains a wrong in itself; its wrongness does not disappear in those cases but is merely overridden as the lesser evil. What matters for this discussion, however, is that the justification of terrorism is not out of the question. Some terrorist acts may be justifiable even given their *prima facie* wrongness.

Public deliberation is a crucial forum in which to debate terrorism. It is important that such deliberation be informed, informative, and reliable. People with various perspectives should be included. One important sort of component of any public deliberation is testimony.[32] In the newly emerging field of social epistemology, which seeks an account of the social nature of knowledge, testimony has been recognized as an important source for the social production and acquisition of knowledge.[33] Testimony can involve declaring a viewpoint or bearing witness to experiences that are relevant to the topic of deliberation. Sometimes testimony can take the form of an act with symbolic value, an act that makes a statement about a public issue. An act of terrorism is, in part, a symbolic act. Terrorism has been described as part politics and part theatre.[34] A terrorist claims by her action, "See how much this matters to me. I am willing to kill and perhaps die for my cause." The terrorist act asserts, either explicitly or implicitly, that the cause on behalf of which it is carried out is so morally momentous as to outweigh the *prima facie* wrongness of killing innocent civilians. The terrorist declares symbolically that she fights against an evil that is so bad it justifies committing terrorist acts as a "lesser evil" to bring the greater evil to an end.

Suicide terrorists are especially noteworthy in their symbolic acts because they make the ultimate sacrifice for their cause and they stand to gain nothing earthly for themselves personally. Although they may believe devoutly that their suicides will earn them an afterlife in paradise, still many people believe in an afterlife yet would shrink from committing suicide to hasten its arrival. Those who take the suicidal step testify to the intensity of their reasons for doing so.

Of course, that someone declares or implies a belief that his or her terrorist act is justified does not *make* it justified. It does, however, make a claim for consideration on the parts of others. Because of the horrific nature of what might be involved in the terrorism *or the conditions that the terrorist fights against*, such claims should not be lightly dismissed. Matters of enormous moral importance weigh in the balance. Although anyone's testimony about terrorism has an equal claim to be taken seriously, the terrorist's identity affects the *degree* to which his or her testimony should be taken seriously. The testifier's identity can be a kind of "credential" that enhances the claim on others to take her testimony seriously.

National, ethnic, or racial identity can obviously be important to testimony about terrorism. My main point here is that *gender* identity is also important. Both women's and men's terrorist acts make the symbolic claim that the cause for which they fight is morally weighty enough to justify violence against innocent civilians. The fact that a terrorist is female, and thus a type of person who does not tend to act violently for public purposes, adds weight to the public recognition that her testimony deserves. It matters that women are conceptualized as non-violent and that empirical evidence shows that women participate in extreme physical violence far less than do men. Ideas of female "nature" may constitute this gender difference as a social construct; the causal origin of the empirical data is not important here. What matters is that because women generally are, and are conceptualized to be, non-violent, women's symbolic claims of justified violence deserve even more serious consideration than similar acts or claims by men.

V. Women's Testimony on Behalf of Terrorism

Women's stereotypic non-violence is crucial to my argument. Women are believed to behave less violently than men in general and empirical evidence upholds this belief.[35] Women are far more often than men associated with peaceful and non-violent modes of human interaction, including the whole range of mothering, nurturing, and caring activity. Caring and nurturing are frequently considered to be part of women's "nature."[36] The concept of a female "nature" is widely disputed, yet it seems empirically undeniable that women enact far less physical violence than men, especially in public settings.[37] When a woman does resort to violence to deal with a social problem, this adds additional weight to her demand that others take seriously the claim implicit in her terrorist act that it is justifiable. A violent woman, on the face of it, bears a kind of enhanced witness to the thought that her violent behavior might be justified.

Male terrorism does not derive any extra credibility from male gender identity, especially from an unmarried male in his late teens or twenties—the "typical" terrorist.[38] Critics who wish to discredit the actions of male terrorists have a relatively easy task since violence by young unmarried men does not bear any *special* witness to the legitimacy of their causes. Being more violence-prone in general than other age or gender groups, young unmarried men, for all we know, might fight for any cause that comes along—or for no cause at all.[39] A female terrorist, on the other hand, defies expectations; the sort of being she is widely presumed to be, with empirical support, strengthens her claim to be taken seriously when she bears witness to the importance of the cause for which she perpetrates terrorist action.

That is, unless it can be shown that the woman acted as she did for some reason other than for the sake of the terrorist cause. Explaining a woman's terrorist acts as the result of pressure from her husband, grief at the death of a brother, an attempt to overcome dishonor, or the influence of nasty feminism seems to show that she did *not act* out of direct commitment to the terrorist cause. An alternative motivation on her part reduces, and may discredit altogether, the extra force of her testimony on behalf of the cause. Thus, the opponents of her terrorist movement may be highly motivated to show that women's involvement in it has reasons *other than* the cause itself. Hence the various *alternative* explanations I listed earlier that are given to explain women's terrorism.

The fact that a woman engages in violence on behalf of a cause is certainly not a *full-fledged epistemic warrant* to believe that her cause is legitimate. It is evidence about the woman's strength of conviction. It is not *per se* a reason for anyone else to conclude that her cause is justified. Rather, it adds a degree of strength to the claim that others take seriously the testimony implicit her terrorist act. This extra degree of strength warrants others in taking a female terrorist's testimony more seriously than the testimony of a male terrorist.

The added weight of a female terrorist's testimony is, like the *prima facie* wrongness of terrorism, presumptive only and therefore defeasible; it is open to counterargument. Perhaps the cause for which she fights is *not* worth the loss of innocent life on the opposing side. We should not downplay the wrongs of terrorism. Nor should we forget that even if terrorism is sometimes justifiable, it is hardly always so. In the United States, for example, terrorism is sometimes used by the Ku Klux Klan, the Christian Identity movement, Skinheads, and neo-Nazis on behalf of racist and anti-Semitic causes.[40] Women can be found in these rightwing terrorist groups as well as in leftwing groups. Granted, female terrorists participate much less often in rightwing terrorist causes than in leftwing causes,[41] and this difference may serve as a kind of collective female testimony as to which causes are more justified overall. Nevertheless, some women do participate in rightwing terrorist groups. Women's participation across the terrorist political spectrum thus serves as a reminder that women's moral testimony about terrorism does not settle the issue. It simply makes an extra claim for recognition as testimony in the public debate over the causes for which women are willing to take up arms and sacrifice their lives.[42]

I return in the end to Robin Morgan. Morgan was right to grasp the importance of the idea that women are far more non-violent than men and that this is crucial to understanding the nature of women's participation in terrorism. Morgan, however, thought this meant that women participate in terrorism only because of pressure or coercion from men. While this explanation may be true in some cases, there is extensive evidence that it is far from true in all cases and that many female terrorists are dedicated directly to the causes for which they act. And women's gender identity as non-violent amplifies their claim to be taken seriously and given uptake when they testify through their actions that terrorism on behalf of these causes is justifiable.

Marilyn Friedman, Washington University

Notes

1. Robin Morgan, *The Demon Lover: On the Sexuality of Terrorism* (New York: W.W. Norton, 1989), 24.

2. *The Demon Lover*, chap. 6.

3. *The Demon Lover*, 207–8.

4. I do not endorse all the norms according to which gender makes a difference to moral assessment. For example, I reject all double gender standards that pertain to sexual behavior. My point here is not that such norms are always to be trusted but rather simply to illustrate that the concept is familiar and available for use in case it can be made plausible in particular contexts. I argue later in this paper that a double gender standard is plausible in the assessment of violent behavior such as terrorism.

5. Debra Zedalis, "Female Suicide Bombers," (Carlisle, PA: Strategic Studies Institute, U.S. Army War College, 2004, available online at http://www.carlisle.army.mil/ssi/pdffiles/00373.pdf., 9; accessed 3 May 2006.

6. Rhiannon Talbot, "Myths in the Representation of Women Terrorists," *Eire-Ireland* (Fall 2001), available online at http://www..dushkin.com/text-data/articles/31680/body.pdf, 6; accessed on 10 October 2006. Of course, the terrorist does not kill the same life she might have brought forth. The idea of "givers of life" may often be romanticized as a general female identity.

7. Melanie Reid, "Myth that Women Are the Most Deadly Killers of All," *Glasgow Herald*, 29 January 02, sec. A, 14.; cited in Zedalis, "Female Suicide Bombers," 9.

8. E. MacDonald, *Shoot the Women First* (London: Fourth Estate, Ltd., 1991), 237.

9. See Itamar Marcus, "Encouraging Women Terrorists," Special Report #39: Palestinian Culture and Society (Study #6–March 12, 2002), 1–5; available online at http://www.pmw.org.il/specrep-39.html; accessed on 3 May 2006; Itamar Marcus, "Promoting Women Terrorists," (PMW-Palestinian Media Watch), October 12, 2003; available online at http://www.unitedjerusalem.org/index2.asp?id=357924; accessed on 3 May 2006.

10. Terri Toles Patkin, "Explosive Baggage: Female Palestinian Suicide Bombers and the Rhetoric of Emotion," *Women and Language*, 27:2 (Fall, 2004): 82; Barbara Victor, *Army of Roses* (© Barbara Victor, printed by Rodale, distributed by St. Martin's Press, 2003), 19–20.

11. Clara Beyles, "Female Suicide Bombers: An Update," 2–3; available online at http://www.ict.org.il/articles/articledet.cfm?articleid=508, accessed on 14 May 2006.

12. Christopher Dickey, "Women of Al Qaeda," *Newsweek*, 12 December 2005, 27.

13. See, for example, Kevin Toolis, "Why Women Turn to Suicide Bombing," *The Observer*, 12 October 2003, available online at http://www.countercurrents.org/pa-toolis121003.htm; accessed on 3 May 2006.

14. Boaz Ganor, "The First Iraqi Suicide Bombing: A Hint of Things to Come?" March 30, 2003, online at http://www.ict.org.il/articles/articledet.cfm?articleid-477.

15. Talbot discusses this explanation, "Myths in the Representation of Women Terrorists," 4.

16. Israeli Ministry of Foreign Affairs,"Blackmailing Young Women into Suicide Terrorism," Jerusalem, 12 February 2002, 3 pp, available online at http://www.mfa.gov.il/MFA/Government/Communiques/2003/Blackmailing%20Young%20Women%20into%20Suicide%20Terrorism%20 ; accessed on 9 Oct 2006.

17. This explanation is discussed by Daniel Georges-Abeyie, "Women as Terrorists," *Terrorism: An International Journal* 1:1 (1977): 77–81; Georges-Abeyie does not entirely dismiss the masculine explanation.

18. Talbot, "Myths in the Representation of Women Terrorists"; see also Luisella de Cataldo Neuberger and Tiziana Valentin, *Women and Terrorism*, trans. Leo Michael Hughes (New York: St. Martin's Press, 1992, 1996), 76–8.

19. Georges-Abeyie, "Women as Terrorists." Mike Benson, Mariah Evans, and Rita Simon conclude that women's participation in terrorism is not a side-effect of the feminist movement, "Women as Political Terrorists," *Research in Law, Deviance and Social Control* 4 (1982): 128.

20. Talbot, "Myths in the Representation of Women Terrorists," 9, n. 23.

21. Patkin, "Myths in the Representation of Women Terrorists," 81–2. Patkin, however, reports that female terrorists seem to be moving away from support roles.

22. Talbot, "Myths in the Representation of Women Terrorists"; Patkin, "Myths in the Representation of Women Terrorists"; and Inger Skjelsbæk, "Is Femininity Inherently Peaceful?"

in *Gender, Peace, and Conflict*, eds, Inger Skjelsbæk and Dan Smith (Thousand Oaks, CA: Sage, 2001), 47–67.

23. Talbot, "Myths in the Representation of Women Terrorists," 1.

24. Skjelsbæk, "Is Femininity Inherently Peaceful?" 48–50.

25. C. A. J. Coady, "Terrorism, Morality, and Supreme Emergency," *Ethics*, 114:4 (July 2004): 772.

26. David Rodin, "Terrorism without Intention," *Ethics*, 114:4 (July 2004): 755. In my discussion, I will use the terms "noncombatant" and "innocent person" interchangeably. Nothing in this discussion turns on the distinction between those two terms.

27. Rodin takes this quotation from the definition of "ideological" in the *Oxford English Dictionary*, 2nd ed.; Rodin, "Terrorism without Intention," 756.

28. Noam Zohar, "Innocence and Complex Threats: Upholding the War Ethic and the Condemnation of Terrorism," *Ethics*, 114: 4 (July 2004): 735.

29. Michael Walzer, *Just and Unjust Wars* (New York: Basic Books, 1977), 200.

30. Bat-Ami Bar On, "Why Terrorism is Morally Problematic," in *Feminist Ethics*, ed. Claudia Card (Lawrence, Kansas: University of Kansas Press, 1991), 107–25.

31. Rodin argues that Walzer exaggerates the affect of terrorism "considerably," that a whole population experiences "terror or panic" only during extreme emergencies, and that individuals experience it only when personally affected. Otherwise, he argues, populations tend to return to their daily lives; 760–1.

32. For a discussion of how to assess and improve the quality of the available expert testimony through institutional means, see Allen Buchanan, "Political Liberalism and Social Epistemology," *Philosophy and Public Affairs*, 32:2 (Spring 2004): 95–130.

33. See Alvin Goldman, "Social Epistemology," *Stanford Encyclopedia of Philosophy*, available online at http://plato.stanford.edu/entries/epistemology-social/, accessed on 18 May 2006.

34. This idea is attributed to Brian Michael Jenkins by Don Mullan and James Mullin, "Terrorism Defined and Exemplified," *The Blanket: A Journal of Protest and Dissent* (14 March 2004), available online at http://www.phoblacht.net/phprint.php , 1; accessed on 10 October 2006.

35. V. Spike Peterson and Anne Sisson Runyan, *Global Gender Issues* (Boulder, CO: Westview, 1993), esp. chap. 4, "Gendered Divisions of Violence, Labor, and Resources."

36. These popular generalizations could be the reflection of "essentialist" assumptions about women's nature. However, the issue of essentialism is beside the point. The social constructionist hypothesis does not actually undermine essentialist assumptions. If women's "nature" or attributes are genuinely the products of social construction, and if processes of social construction are effective and successful in constituting women's "nature" as consisting of certain essential attributes, then it follows that women *are essentially* what they have been socially constructed *essentially to be*.

37. Whether women use violence in private, or domestic, settings less than men is an issue I can ignore for the purposes of this paper.

38. Zedalis writes that the U.S. Department of Homeland Security portrays the "typical terrorist" as male; "Female Suicide Bombers," 1. Jessica Stern characterizes the typical Palestinian suicide bomber as young, male, and unmarried; Jessica Stern, *Terror in the Name of God* (New York: Harper Collins, 2003), 51.

39. This is a rhetorically enhanced statement of the relevant gender stereotype.

40. See Kathleen M. Blee, "Women and Organized Racial Terrorism in the United States," *Studies in Conflict & Terrorism*, 28 (2005): 421–33.

41. Talbot, "Myths in the Representation of Women Terrorists," 2.

42. The credibility of women's testimony on behalf of terrorism is enhanced by some of the studies and commentaries that explore female terrorism sympathetically. For example, Rhiannon Talbot reports that Astrid Proll describes female terrorists as "social workers with guns" (Talbot, "Myths in the Representation of Women Terrorists," 6), an image that suggests tough love but not unjustifiable homicide. Some researchers assess female terrorists as being more emotionally driven than their male counterparts and more deeply committed to changing society for the better. (See V. Spike Peterson and Anne Sisson Runyan, *Global Gender Issues* [Boulder, Colorado: Westview, 1993].) Luisella de Cataldo Neuberger and Tiziana Valentini, who studied female Italian terrorists of groups such as the Red Brigades and Prima Linea, found that captured female terrorists were far *less* likely than male terrorists to take advantage of an Italian law that allowed them to win a reduced sentence in exchange for becoming a "penitent." A "penitent," in this context, is someone who expresses repentance for her terrorist acts and helps the authorities to apprehend her collaborators (Neuberger and Valentini, *Women and Terrorism*, 3, 78, and *passim*).

The Ticking Time Bomb Case for Torture

Bernard G. Prusak

Abstract: I make two arguments in this paper. First, I argue briefly that the ticking time bomb case is unrealistic and as such is liable to mislead us badly on the ground. Second, after conceding that the conditions of the ticking time bomb case might someday be realized, I argue that it may in fact be morally permissible to torture a terrorist in this case on the grounds of self-defense. My reason for making this argument is that rejecting torture in even the ticking time bomb case risks discrediting objections to torture in other, more realistic cases. Yet the principle established by the ticking time bomb case is of extremely limited application. Given the extreme improbability that the conditions of this case could ever be realized, public authorities who sanction torturing someone should have to bear a heavy burden of proof that this decision was justified on the grounds of self-defense.

There is a standard philosopher's example," the moral philosopher Henry Shue wrote nearly thirty years ago, "which someone always invokes [in discussions of torture]: suppose a fanatic, perfectly willing to die rather than collaborate in the thwarting of his own scheme, has set a hidden nuclear device to explode in the heart of Paris. . . ."[1] In the recent controversy in the United States over the McCain Amendment prohibiting torture of persons "in the custody or under the physical control of the United States Government," only the city has changed. "Let's take the textbook case," the political commentator Charles Krauthammer wrote in the magazine *The Weekly Standard*. "Ethics 101: A terrorist has planted a nuclear bomb in New York City. It will go off in one hour. A million people will die. You capture the terrorist. He knows where it is. He's not talking."[2] Shue concludes, "I can see no way to deny the permissibility of torture in a case *just like this*." According to Krauthammer, "the conclusion—yes, in this case even torture is permissible—is telling because it establishes the principle: Torture is not always impermissible."

Krauthammer's article shows that this so-called "philosopher's example" has sprung the bounds of Ethics 101. The Bush administration, too, has invoked this case. After signing the McCain Amendment into law, President Bush issued a statement that the executive branch would interpret the amendment "in a manner consistent with the constitutional authority of the President" as Commander in Chief responsible for "protecting the American people from further terrorist attacks." A senior administration official explained that the purpose of this statement was to reserve to the President all necessary powers in the case of a ticking time bomb.[3]

I make two arguments in this paper. First, I argue briefly that the ticking time bomb case is unrealistic and as such is liable to mislead us badly on the ground. (By 'us' I mean the public authorities who act in a democratic people's name.) Here I follow Shue. After reluctantly allowing that he could "see no way to deny the permissibility of torture" in the ticking time bomb case, Shue immediately questioned the relevance of this case for thinking about the ethical and legal permissibility of torture. In his words, "there is a saying in jurisprudence that hard cases make bad law, and there might well be one in philosophy that artificial cases make bad ethics."[4] I give reasons for agreeing with him. My second argument is much different. Here I begin by conceding that the conditions of the ticking time bomb case might someday be realized. Then I argue that it may in fact be morally permissible to torture the terrorist in this case, in particular on the grounds of self-defense. But I also argue that the principle established by this case—to quote Krauthammer again, "Torture is not always impermissible"—is of extremely limited application. Similarly, homicide is not always wrong—it is not always wrong in self-defense—but certainly it is normally wrong.

I. What Is Misleading About the Ticking Time Bomb Case

To reiterate, then, my first argument is that "artificial cases make bad ethics" and that the ticking time bomb case is artificial in this bad way. What is artificial about it is not that it is unlikely that there will ever be a ticking time bomb. What is artificial about it is that by its terms we *know*, not merely *suspect*, that the person we have captured knows what we need to know. As Elaine Scarry has observed, "in a world where knowledge is ordinarily so imperfect, we are suddenly granted the omniscience to know that the person in front of us holds this crucial information about the bomb's whereabouts." She then asks, "Why not just grant us the omniscience to know where the bomb is?"[5]

On the ground, it is quite unlikely that soldiers or even intelligence operatives will know, without reasonable doubt, that the person they have captured knows where the bomb is. Instead, they will have to work with probabilities or hunches. Scarry also observes that, "[i]n the two and a half years [after] September 11, 2001, five thousand foreign nationals suspected of being terrorists [were] detained" by the United States. Only three of these were ever eventually charged with terrorism-related acts, and two of these three were acquitted.[6] The probability that we will know that we have captured the ticking time bomb terrorist himself is then extremely low.

The ticking time bomb case makes for bad ethics by making the case for torture seem much less problematic than it realistically is. We should not forget, too, that in interrogational torture "the victim has no convincing way of demonstrating that he or she cannot comply" with the torturer's demands.[7] If you believe that I'm the terrorist, but I'm not, how can I make you think otherwise? My refusing to tell you where the bomb is, or crying that I don't know where it is, will most likely lead you, the torturer, to think that you need to do more in order to break me. Accordingly, "only the committed and the innocent are likely to be severely tortured"[8]—which means that torture will often be pointless, and all too often both pointless and horrifically unjust.

II. Utilitarianism and Absolutism

That's the first argument; now on to the second. Here is how former Assistant Attorney General Jay Bybee argued for the permissibility of torture in the so-called "Torture Memo" prepared for the White House in 2002:

> [A]l Qaeda plans apparently include efforts to develop and deploy chemical, biological and nuclear weapons of mass destruction. Under these circumstances, a detainee may possess information that could enable the United States to prevent attacks that potentially could equal or surpass the September 11 [2001] attacks in . . . magnitude. Clearly, any harm that might occur during an interrogation would pale to insignificance compared to the harm avoided by preventing such an attack, which could take hundreds or thousands of lives.[9]

Bybee's argument is framed in simple, utilitarian terms. Moreover, he appears to be proposing a rule for action in such "circumstances." Let us consider possible grounds for this argument.

One way to defend Bybee's conclusion in the ticking time bomb case is to say that sometimes it is *necessary* to do a lesser evil to prevent a greater one.[10] But this principle—that torture may be justified on the grounds that it is *necessary* in order to prevent a greater evil—has implications that should make us uneasy. After the United States captured Khalid Sheikh Mohammed in Pakistan—the organizer of the 9/11 attacks—it also took into custody his two young children.[11] Ethics 101: Let's say Khalid Sheikh Mohammed has planted a nuclear bomb in New York City. It will go off in one hour. A million people will die. You capture him. He knows where it is. He's not talking. But he will if you torture his children, or perhaps slowly torture and kill one and then threaten to do the same to the other. On a simple utilitarian calculus, it is necessary to torture and perhaps kill the children. I find this conclusion morally repugnant. Here, so to speak, my spade turns up. Human life should not be protected at the price of the inhuman.

The defense of torture on grounds of "necessity" should then be rejected. But, as I indicated earlier, there is another defense of torture that can be made on the grounds of self-defense. This defense is consistent with what is sometimes called absolutism, the tradition of moral thought that prohibits the doing of some deeds no matter what may happen. I should say that I am not happy to be presenting an argument for the permissibility of torture, but I think that an argument needs to be made that belongs to the absolutist tradition. Rejecting torture in even the ticking time bomb case (unrealistic as it is) will strike many as the position of a moral fanatic and make a simple, if not coarse, utilitarianism more attractive than it ought to appear.[12] A further risk here is that objecting to torture in this case might discredit objections to torture in other, more realistic cases.

It is useful to begin by considering absolutist restrictions in warfare. Thomas Nagel has observed that these restrictions "appear to be of two types: restrictions on the class of persons at whom aggression or violence may be directed and restrictions on the manner of attack." Hostility toward a person "must be justified in terms of something *about that person* which makes the treatment appropriate." Accordingly, "it should be directed at the person or persons who provoke it and . . . it should aim more specifically at what is provocative about [these persons]."[13] These restrictions would not generally rule out killing an armed enemy in battle, but they do rule out killing an enemy who has been taken into custody and disarmed. There is no longer anything "provocative" about this person that could justify killing him. To attack him in battle is to attack him as a soldier attacking you; to attack him in custody is to attack him as a person presenting no danger to you.[14]

Now it might be thought that torture too should be prohibited for the absolutist, since after all we can only torture somebody in custody. Shue has written that

> torture is . . . not analogous to the killing in battle of a healthy and well-armed foe; it is a cruel assault upon the defenseless. In combat the other person one kills is still a threat when killed and is killed in part for the sake of one's own survival. The torturer inflicts pain and damage upon another person who, by virtue of now being within his or her power, is no longer a threat and is entirely at the torturer's mercy.[15]

It is certainly true that the victim "is entirely at the torturer's mercy." But, in the ticking time bomb case, it is not quite true that the terrorist "is no longer a threat." In this case, as Alan Donagan observed some years ago, the terrorist "is, at the very least, deliberately allowing innocent persons to be killed and mutilated by withholding his knowledge; and if he had a hand in placing the bombs, he is allowing the consummation of murders and mutilations he himself has set in train."[16] We are threatened by an ongoing event for which he bears responsibility. So torture here may in fact be analogous to killing an enemy in battle if the torture is in fact the *only* means—an important qualification—that we have of defending ourselves against an attack on our lives.

This argument needs both elaboration and further qualification.[17] For present purposes, however, I want to note that it justifies torturing only the terrorist, and emphatically *not* his children or any other innocents. There is something about the terrorist that may make torture appropriate, namely, his hand in placing the bomb or his withholding his knowledge. There is nothing about his children that is "provocative." We could never justify our torturing the children *to the children*: imagine telling them that, though they are innocent, they must suffer and die for the good of others. And so, for the absolutist tradition, for which justifications must be addressed to and receivable by the persons in question,[18] torturing the children could never be justified.

It might be thought further that, "in a world where knowledge is ordinarily so imperfect," very little torture could in fact be justified, if not next to none. Yet an important legal philosopher, Michael S. Moore—important in this context because his work is cited by Bybee at a critical point in the "Torture Memo"—has claimed that torture may be justified on the grounds of self-defense not only in the ticking time bomb case but in several others that seem much more realistic. According to Moore, torture by public authorities may be justified on the grounds of self-defense "if the terrorist knows [1] the location of the hidden bombs, or [2] of buried hostages, or [3] of caches of arms, or if he knows [4] of future terrorist acts to be executed by others that he has aided."[19] I turn to his argument to close.

Moore writes that "we may gain some insight into the moral basis for self-defense" by "attend[ing] to our sense of fittingness when an aggressor trying to kill someone is instead killed himself":

> Notice that the aggressor creates a situation in which someone must be killed, either he or his intended victim. He has wrongfully created a threat of harm that his intended victim can only redirect but not eliminate. Since he is the one creating such a threat, he in all fairness is the one to be selected when someone has to bear the harm threatened.

The application of this account to the case of a captured terrorist is simple: If the terrorist "has culpably caused [a] situation where someone must get hurt," and "[i]f hurting [the terrorist] is the only means to prevent the death or injury of others put at risk by his actions," then it is fair to hurt him in order to prevent others' getting hurt.[20]

I am willing to agree with Moore that such a terrorist may be hurt if further we know or at the very least have very good reason to believe, not merely suspect, that he knows what we need to know. Yet Moore's second, third, and fourth cases—in which the captured terrorist knows (2) "of buried hostages," or (3) "of caches of arms," or (4) "of future terrorist acts to be executed by others that he has aided"—seem much more questionable.

The second case is the most ambiguous. If the terrorist had a hand in taking the hostages, his action may be considered "over" in a sense—the hostages have been taken—but obviously the effects of this action persist: the hostages remain taken. Even if the terrorist did not himself take hostage the persons in question, his withholding his knowledge of the hostages' whereabouts makes him culpable.

But do we have here "a situation where someone *must* get hurt"? I presume for the sake of the argument that we believe the hostages to be in danger of grave injury or death (I also assume that by "buried" Moore means hidden). But do we *know* that they will be harmed? There might be some cases in which we have very strong reason to think so; and then perhaps—but only then—it would be morally permissible to torture the terrorist "[i]f hurting him is the only means to prevent the death or injury of others put at risk." This argument, however, seems practically to invite abuse.

In the third case, all that the terrorists or would-be terrorists have done is to procure arms. Moore does not stipulate that the arms have been used culpably, or even that they were obtained illegally. In the fourth case, all that the terrorists have done is to have planned future attacks. Such a conspiracy is certainly culpable, but it is a stretch to claim that we have in either of these cases "a situation where someone *must* get hurt," thus warranting our hurting the terrorist before he hurts us. The terrorist in the ticking time bomb case had set in train a course of events with established causal consequences; in the third and fourth cases, no such course of events has been initiated. We do not know whether the arms will be used to harm innocents; we do not know whether the plan will be carried out. And we also certainly don't know that "hurting [the terrorist] is the *only* means to prevent the death or injury of others put at risk" (my italics).

The rejoinder to these objections is predictable: be realistic! Certainly we *do* know that a terrorist organization will at least try to use its arms culpably; certainly we *do* know that terrorist organizations like al Qaeda will strive to execute plans to strike us. Bybee's "Torture Memo" was prepared in this context. Bybee explicitly draws from Moore in claiming that, "even though a detained enemy combatant may not be the exact attacker . . . he may still be harmed in self-defense if he has knowledge of *future* attacks" (my italics).[21]

I think that the answer to self-styled realists about torture is to be more realistic than they are about the consequences of instituting the use of torture as a policy. The lesson that Hannah Arendt drew from the trial of Adolf Eichmann in Jerusalem is that evil does not need profoundly demonic people in order to "overgrow and lay waste."[22] In extraordinary circumstances, the most ordinary will all too often do. The torture exposed at Abu Ghraib and elsewhere exemplifies Arendt's thesis. It was done by ordinary people who were sometimes ordered, sometimes subtly encouraged to "use 'enhancements' . . . that qualify as torture even under the most nonchalant readings of international law."[23] These "enhancements"—dogs and hypothermia—quickly escalated. The guards got very much carried away. Torture tempts because we are afraid of the evil that terrorists might do to us. But if we became afraid of what Arendt called the "banality of evil," which is to say how it infects ordinary people and institutions, I think we would be much warier of arguments like Bybee's and Moore's that open the way to brutalization of others and ourselves.

Given the extreme improbability that the conditions of the ticking time bomb case could ever be realized, I conclude that torture should then be illegal, as in fact it is under international and U.S. law.[24] Public authorities who sanction torturing someone should have to bear a heavy burden of proof that this decision was justified on the grounds of self-defense.[25]

Bernard G. Prusak, Villanova University

Notes

1. Henry Shue, "Torture," *Philosophy and Public Affairs* 7 (1978): 141. The ticking time bomb case is often associated with Michael Walzer; see his "Political Action: The Problem of Dirty Hands," *Philosophy and Public Affairs* 2 (1973): 166–7. But it can also be found two centuries ago in Bentham's manuscripts.

2. Charles Krauthammer, "The Truth about Torture," *The Weekly Standard*, December 5, 2005, www.weeklystandard.com/Content/Public/Articles/000/000/006/400rhqav.asp.

3. Charlie Savage, "Bush Could Bypass New Law," *Boston Globe*, 4 January 2006, sec. A.

4. Shue, 141.

5. Elaine Scarry, "Five Errors in the Reasoning of Alan Dershowitz," in *Torture: A Collection*, ed. Sanford Levinson (New York: Oxford University Press, 2004), 284.

6. Ibid., 284.

7. Shue, 135.

8. Ibid., 140.

9. Jay S. Bybee, "Memorandum for Albert R. Gonzales Counsel to the President, RE: Standards of Conduct for Interrogation under U.S.C. §§2340–2340A," in *The Torture Papers: The Road to Abu Ghraib*, ed. Karen J. Greenberg and Joshua L. Dratel (Cambridge: Cambridge University Press, 2005), 208–9. Bybee's memorandum has since been "supersed[ed] in its entirety" by another memorandum prepared by then-Acting Assistant Attorney General Daniel Levin, dated December 30, 2004, and entitled "Legal Standards Applicable under 18 U.S.C. §§2340–2340A." See www.usdoj.gov/olc/18usc23402340a2.htm.

10. To be fair to Bybee, it should be noted that he need not be read as committing himself to the principle that it is necessary to do a lesser evil to prevent a greater one. In the text quoted, he says only that it is permissible to torture a terrorist with the information needed to prevent an attack.

11. Alan Dershowitz, "Tortured Reasoning," in *Torture*, ed. Levinson, 270, citing Jess Bravin and Gary Fields, "How Do Interrogators Make Terrorists Talk?" *Wall Street Journal*, 4 March 2003, sec. B.

12. A utilitarian argument against *instituting* torture can be framed taking R. M. Hare's argument against slavery as a model; see Hare, "Wrong Is Wrong with Slavery," *Philosophy and Public Affairs* 8 (1979): 103–21. Hare's argument turns in the end "on general

beliefs about human nature, and in particular upon the belief that people in the power of other people will be exploited" (119); the belief that the exploiters themselves will become brutalized (120); and the belief that, "[b]y being subjected to the threat of legal and other punishment, but at the same time deprived of legal defences against its abuse . . . , the slave becomes, or is likely to become if his master is an ordinary human, the most miserable of all creatures," terrified of what the future holds (121). I believe that instituting torture would have much the same consequences. But I nonetheless hold that an argument needs to be made against torture that belongs to the absolutist tradition, and for two reasons. First, it seems that even Hare's sophisticated utilitarianism would warrant torture of the innocent in some circumstances. See here his parenthetical remark on Hiroshima in his "Rules of War and Moral Reasoning," *Philosophy and Public Affairs* 1 (1973): 181. Second, I believe that sophisticated utilitarianism gives rise to coarse utilitarianism. In other words, Hare's second-level utilitarianism corrupts first-level morals—a claim that admittedly needs elaboration. See, for a beginning, Hare's own reflections in "Rules of War and Moral Reasoning," 177–8.

13. Thomas Nagel, "War and Massacre," *Philosophy and Public Affairs* 1 (1973): 133, 135.

14. It is worth noting that not every way of attacking the enemy is permitted: there is reason to oppose, for example, "weapons designed to maim or disfigure or torture [the enemy] rather than merely to stop him." These attack persons as such, not persons as soldiers. See Nagel, 141. See also G.E.M. Anscombe, "War and Murder," in vol. 3 of her collected papers, *Ethics, Religion and Politics* (Minneapolis: University of Minnesota Press, 1981), 53.

15. Shue, 130.

16. Alan Donagan, *The Theory of Morality* (Chicago: The University of Chicago Press, 1977), 188. Compare, more recently, David Sussman, "What's Wrong with Torture?" *Philosophy and Public Affairs* 33 (2005): 16–8.

17. For example, it may not be quite accurate to say that torture here may be justified on the grounds of *self-defense*. After all, if public authorities in Washington authorize the torture of a terrorist in order to save people in New York City, the authorities are strictly speaking defending these people, not themselves. Donagan justifies the torture as observing the precept, "Thou shalt not stand idly by the blood of thy neighbor" (Leviticus 19:16), derived from what he calls the principle of beneficence.

18. Anscombe puts the absolutist position: "If [a man] could justly say 'Why have you done this to me? I have not deserved it,' then the state would be acting with injustice." See "Mr. Truman's Degree," in *Ethics, Religion and Politics*, 68. Absolutism is what Nagel calls "agent-relative": the reasons that the absolutist tradition recognizes as justifications "include an essential reference," in Nagel's language, to the point of view of the agent in his relations with others. Deontological constraints "are not impersonal claims derived from the interests of others, but personal demands governing one's relation with others." As he succinctly puts it, these constraints "operate through that relation." See Nagel, *The View from Nowhere* (Oxford: Oxford University Press, 1986), 153, 176, 184.

19. Michael S. Moore, "Torture and the Balance of Evils," *Israel Law Review* 23 (1989): 323.

20. Ibid., 321–2, 323. Donagan gives a more traditional account of the moral basis for self-defense than Moore's. According to Donagan, "the immunity to violence to which

everybody . . . has a moral right [as a rational being] is obviously conditional; and perhaps its most obvious condition is that one not further one's own ends by resorting to violence or threatening it." One forfeits one's immunity by violating that of others and so may be forcibly resisted. See Donagan, 84–5. Compare Aquinas, *Summa theologiae* II–II, q. 64, a. 2, ad 3.

21. Bybee, 212.

22. See Arendt's July 24, 1963 letter to Gershom Scholem in "'Eichmann in Jerusalem': An Exchange of Letters between Gershom Scholem and Hannah Arendt," *Encounter* 22 (1964): 56.

23. See Anthony Lagouranis, "Tortured Logic," *New York Times*, 28 February 2006, sec. A.

24. The definition of torture is another, critically important matter.

25. I thank Margaret Kowalsky, Lydia Moland, two anonymous reviewers, and my audience in Victoria for criticizing drafts of this paper.

Tortured Ethics

Matthew R. Silliman and David Kenneth Johnson

Abstract: This dialogue discusses a proposal for the legalization of torture under specific circumstances and contrasts it with arguments for a total ban on torture. We consider three types of objection: first, that the difficulty of having adequate knowledge renders the stock "ticking bomb" scenario such a low-probability hypothetical as to present no realistic threat to a policy banning all torture; second, that empirically the information gleaned from torture is so unlikely to be reliable that it could not justify the moral risk; and third, that sanctioning torture, even if only under the most extreme circumstances, would generate a 'culture of torture,' hence undermining fragile advances in international human rights rooted in unwavering commitment to human dignity. Compelling as these arguments appear, not all the conversants are wholly convinced by them; to this extent the dialogue ends aporetically.

The Characters: *Erica Wolfe is a professor of political philosophy at a major state university; Clarence Riggs is a prominent attorney who has publicly advocated the legalization of torture in special circumstances; and Aaron Langston is a building contractor recently discharged as an officer in the National Guard. The three meet in a public-access television studio that airs unscripted discussions of controversial topics.*

Erica: I'm glad finally to meet you, Attorney Riggs. I thought your editorial in last week's *Times* was misguided in extremely interesting ways.

Clarence: I accept that as a compliment, Professor Wolfe; and please call me Clarence. Have you met Lt. Aaron Langston?

Aaron: No more military titles for me, thank you; I am recently, and happily, retired from the National Guard. What do you mean, Professor Wolfe?

Erica: We can all dispense with formalities, Aaron; just Erica. [*to camera operator in back of room*]: Is the tape rolling?

Aaron: Fine, Erica. Why do you say that Clarence's editorial is misguided?

Erica: Well, it strikes me as clever and superficially persuasive, but ultimately confused and, I think, very dangerous.

Clarence: I accept most of that as complimentary, too, Erica. Dangerous times sometimes call for harsh measures—and harsh measures are in fact being meted out on all sides. With my proposal for judicially authorized torture *under very specific and limited circumstances*, with oversight and accountability, I am in fact hoping to control, not heighten this grave moral and legal danger. Clearly torture is taking place worldwide; shall we smugly condemn it, or would it be better to engage the logic of its justification and hold it to account?

Erica: I am far from convinced that your proposal would not simply normalize torture as an institutional procedure, eroding natural and proper repugnance for the practice, and making it more readily defensible, as you say, on all sides.

Aaron: I still haven't made up my mind about this one. Like any decent person, I am in principle against the routine use of torture, but I can imagine times when it might be necessary. Clarence, could you please explain what you call the "logic of its justification"?

Clarence: It's an old argument, famously known as the "ticking bomb" case. Say a major city is threatened by a hidden time bomb; the police know that they have the person who planted it and are convinced that only the use of extremely coercive measures will force the bomber to talk in time to prevent certain catastrophe. As morally ugly as this necessity may be, we arguably have a moral obligation to torture the perpetrator. It seems to me, therefore, that in cases such as this, the law ought to grant a legal warrant for torture, through a transparent, accountable process.[1]

Aaron: Are you suggesting that torture in such cases would not merely be morally permissible, but an actual *duty*?

Clarence: In such an extreme case, I think we must weigh our duties to protect the innocent against our duty to respect the autonomy and personal integrity of a known terrorist. I think we might well have an unwelcome duty to do something quite drastic. At a minimum, the law ought to make room for whatever morality may require of us.

Aaron: That sounds pretty reasonable to me. My experience in Iraq tells me that there will inevitably be a need for coercive interrogation during times of extreme conflict; and when the stakes are as high as in Clarence's example, full-on torture could indeed become necessary. So, Erica, why *not* change the law to reflect these few legitimate uses of torture?

Erica: The philosopher Henry Shue many years ago addressed this problem in a way that I think is still compelling. He concedes that torture might indeed be morally permissible (or even obligatory) in cases *exactly like this one*, but he doubts that such cases are a meaningful guide to the morality of torture, since they are wildly unrealistic. Clarence will surely agree that, as the saying goes, hard cases make bad law, and I would add the corollary that fantastic hypotheticals make equally bad moral philosophy.[2]

Clarence: Ticking bomb cases might once have seemed imaginary to Shue, but we're living in an age of terrorism, where events previously relegated to science fiction sometimes come true. What about the Al Qaeda operative Jamel Beghal, for example? After (alleged) mistreatment and some weeks in captivity, he gave interrogators information that almost certainly prevented a planned bombing of the U.S. Embassy in Paris. It seems positively immoral *not* to use any methods necessary to get such information.

Aaron: Clarence does have a point there, Erica. These are evil times, and there do seem to be people who are without scruples, highly intelligent, and very well-funded, plotting mass murder. Can we really afford to be gentle with them?

Erica: Not gentle, perhaps, but always respectful of their autonomy as persons, since we never know with certainty everything the ticking bomb case presumes we know. I suspect the core of Shue's rejection of the example is epistemological—concerning barriers to what we can know in practice. The dilemma we face, we can all agree, is that we need information; that is why we are tempted to torture a prisoner. But given that by hypothesis our present knowledge is severely limited, it is highly likely that we don't know these two crucial things: (1) that the people we torture actually have the information we need; and (2) that torture can produce useful information in a timely fashion.[3]

Clarence: With all due respect, Erica, that looks to me like a cheap lawyer's trick. If you demand perfect, absolute knowledge to justify any action, you are doomed to paralysis, since you are asking for something that neither morality, nor law, nor science can ever provide.

Erica: You're no cheap lawyer yourself, Clarence, so you know I did not ask for absolute knowledge, which of course is beyond the reach of everyone (except perhaps logicians). I simply expressed reasonable doubt that our *degree* of knowledge of these two desiderata for the justification of torture is ever, in practice, *sufficient*. We can agree that all meaningful knowledge comes in degrees and is never beyond all question. What we would need is some basis for assurance that we can ever have *enough* of the requisite information.

Aaron: I understand the difficulty well enough; in the field we were always acting on fragmentary evidence. It's all we've got most of the time. But we do have to act!

Erica: Agreed. We must act, but I would contend that we must not torture even in extreme cases, since as a practical matter the knowledge we have will always be insufficient to justify such horrific means of seeking information we can only *hope* the torture will yield.

Clarence: A tidy formula, Erica; but one that demands a more robust defense than you've given it so far. Take the first of your two 'epistemological' questions as it applies to the Jamel Beghal case: We have very good reason to believe he was well-enough placed in Al Qaeda to have given us detailed advance information about the Trade Center and Pentagon attacks.

Erica: Your example makes my point exactly: It was only *after* those attacks that anyone knew enough to ask him about them. Even granting that he *could* have told his captors about the attacks in advance, and that he *might* have done so under torture, officials were in no position beforehand to understand the magnitude of what he might know. Besides, if his co-conspirators knew he had been captured, surely we have every reason to suspect that they would have altered their plans.

Aaron: I don't see why that matters—surely the point of torturing him is to discover what he *does* know.

Erica: Yes, but since you don't know what that is, you can't know when to stop. If he gives no pertinent information, it may be because he is stubborn or it may be because he has none. The innocent torture victim's only option is to protest his ignorance, which will look to the torturer *exactly like* guilty resistance.[4]

Clarence: But Beghal certainly *did* know about the 9/11 plot. That his interrogators did not get the information from him might just have been incompetence, or it might have been misplaced scruples about coercing information, even from such a dangerous person. In our post-9/11 world, that should not be allowed to happen again.

Erica: It *might* have been scruples or incompetence, counselor, but we don't know that even now, do we? Even hindsight is less than 20-20 about what Beghal might have known or intended at any point in time. Besides, even if you could answer the first question in some rare instances, the second one is harder.

Aaron: You mean the question of whether torture produces meaningful information?

Erica: I do. It is in part an empirical matter, though it is probably impossible to settle it scientifically, for how would you devise a controlled test of the information gleaned through torture? But, since there are serious grounds for doubt that such information is reliable, the burden of proof surely rests on those who say it can be. For the purpose of meeting this burden, I will even grant Clarence the lighter standard of 'preponderance of evidence' rather than 'reasonable doubt'.

Aaron: Wait a minute. Why exactly should the advocate of torture have to prove its efficacy?

Erica: You yourself noted a moment ago, and correctly, that any decent person is opposed to torture on principle. By deliberately savaging the autonomy of the suspect and tapping into the ugliest vein in the torturer's own character, torture threatens to undermine any possible basis of civilized, moral conduct.[5] At the very least, if you propose to step over that edge you had better be able to demonstrate that it will reliably *work*!

Aaron: And what is the basis of your doubt that torture is effective? I thought successful resistance to torture was just Hollywood heroism.

Erica: I have no doubt that it is, and that's the problem. Torture victims are likely to say anything they think their torturers want to hear, whether it's true or not. Disoriented by fear and pain, they will say and do anything they think might make it stop.

Clarence: That's hardly fair as a general claim; surely torture sometimes produces useful information. I can think of at least one documented case of a terrorist plot foiled thanks to information obtained through torture.

Erica: I have heard of such an alleged case as well. There are also many, many well-documented examples of brutally coerced criminal confessions, domestically and internationally, that later proved groundless. Where does the preponderance of your evidence lie here?

Aaron: Maybe ordinary domestic crimes and international terrorism are distinct sorts of cases, and maybe it is more likely to work in the case of terrorism than other crimes . . . ?

Erica: Or perhaps it's the other way around, as international terrorists are often motivated by ideologies deeper than personal gain, and commit their crimes cold sober. It seems we can at best *speculate* on its efficacy, while the moral justification of torture demands of us a rather firm basis of *knowledge*, which in practice is always less than sufficient.

Aaron: But surely those barriers to knowledge can be overcome. Didn't Governor Romney of Massachusetts recently propose a death penalty statute which would require a stricter standard than "beyond reasonable doubt"?[6]

Erica: And what would that standard be?

Aaron: I think the phrase was "no doubt."

Erica: No doubt it was! But taken at face value that is an impossible standard of proof; it breaks the knowledge barrier that separates us mortals from absolute certainty. Early Modern European judges, we should recall, employed torture itself specifically as a means of establishing objective certainty of guilt. They rapidly abolished the practice when "lesser" punishments such as imprisonment came under their purview, which they could impose on the basis of persuasive evidence rather than objective certainty.[7] Does Governor Romney also plan to bring back torture in hopes of establishing absolute truth?

Aaron: Wait a minute. Torture was believed to be a source of objective certainty?

Erica: Confession, under torture if necessary, was the only criterion, absent two unimpeachable eyewitnesses to the crime, by which early modern European courts could legally execute a prisoner. The defendant had to repeat the confession in open court while not being tortured, and the torturers took pains to elicit information they thought only the guilty could know. The idea was that since life and death belong in the hands of God, the courts could execute only if there was, as Romney puts it, "no doubt." I suspect the presumption that confession, even elicited under torture, had such a magical power of indubitability stemmed from an analogy with the spiritual confession of sins, bolstered by the dubious reasoning that false confession to a capital crime was irrational.

Clarence: I won't quibble with your judicial history, Erica, but I think you are being unfair to Romney's proposal. The bill called for mandatory DNA evidence in capital cases, as well as much more support for state-appointed attorneys for indigent defendants. The governor acknowledged that the procedure "would not absolutely rule out wrongful convictions" but merely aimed to make them vastly less probable. And he certainly was not advocating torture.

Erica: DNA evidence, like all evidence, can be mishandled; however, if they make verdicts more reliable, such judicial safeguards ought to be in place for all serious criminal trials. It is telling, though, that torture was *not* a part of this proposal. If we really believed, as did European judges in the seventeenth century, that it could produce better information and more just convictions, I suspect torture would have more supporters than it does.

Aaron: So Erica, I take it you hold that, for at least these knowledge-based reasons, ticking-bomb cases are a misleading measure of the need for torture.

Erica: Deeply misleading. If I am right that such hypothetical fantasies have no bearing on moral or legal analysis of real-world situations, any effort to construct procedural safeguards based on them will simply be window-dressing for a culture of torture. Such a culture will not be so easy to regulate as Clarence supposes. In practice, for example, search warrants often lead to *less* rather than more oversight or public scrutiny of official conduct by lending them a fig leaf opaque to further inquiry.[8] I don't question Clarence's motives, but I think his reasoning has nowhere to rest its head.

Clarence: It won't perhaps surprise you that I remain unconvinced. Despite robust proscriptions in the Geneva Conventions and the International Covenant on Civil and Political Rights, people are being tortured all over the world, often by interrogators who believe they must do so. You are correct about my motives, Erica; I would like to eliminate almost all of this by making the reasonably defensible instances (if any) accountable to the rule of law. Your absolutist objection is unhelpful.

Erica: It is not my view but yours that would grant absolute power to the state to determine whose fundamental rights are negotiable.

Aaron: Wait, slow down, you two. I mentioned before that it seems some degree of coercion is inevitable in interrogation under crisis conditions. What if, as my comment implied, torture is simply a higher degree of such coercion, and moreover, what if even relatively mild coercion might be equivalent to torture, when it threatens to escalate?[9] After all, I expect both of you would agree that the distinction between "cruel and inhuman treatment" and torture is an unsustainable distinction–a government lawyers' dodge.[10]

Clarence: I do agree that there is no such clear distinction. This sort of scalar analysis would support my position, since torture (or its component parts) understood as part of this continuum could not in principle be absolutely banned, and consequently ought to be regulated by law, independently of the efficacy of archetypal ticking-bomb arguments.

Erica: I will take that as a concession, Clarence, that ticking bombs probably won't get you where you wanted to go. But let's examine Aaron's suggestion that torture is just more of the coercion inherent in any high-stakes interrogation. A suspect under interrogation is of course in an inherently coerced situation

Aaron: My point exactly. Powerless, deprived of liberty, not knowing how long he or she will be held, badgered with hostile questions while unable to trust the questioner, largely cut off from outside news, and so forth—such things are in themselves harsh treatment.

Erica: Of course they are, Aaron. I hope I don't sound tendentious in pointing out that this is *precisely* why criminal suspects are traditionally accorded due-process protections against self-incrimination, confidential access to counsel, *habeas corpus* protection against unlimited detention without charge, and so forth. Even prisoners of war have clearly defined rights and protections. Such safeguards are designed, among other purposes, to prevent a naturally coercive situation from sliding into abuse and torture.

Aaron: I sense a "but" in your tone.

Erica: Rightly so. I will grant you and Clarence that coercion and brutality are related notions, and in one sense represent different points on a single scale, but it does not follow that we can't distinguish them. Permit me this analogy: In a visible light spectrum, the manipulation and verbal bullying of a powerless suspect might correspond to blue, where crossing some ill-defined boundaries of lengthening waves would land you in the deep red of excessive force or brutality. But torture is in the infrared range—nominally on the same scale, yet qualitatively very different.

Clarence: I rather like your rainbow image; it is precisely my hope in calling for officially sanctioned torture (when circumstances demand it) to render it *visible*, hence accountably governable, thereby reining in its extrajudicial occurrence.

Erica: My first concern about that revolutionary suggestion is whether it would in fact be governable in an institutional context, or whether it would instead substantively destroy any democratic institution it touched. The idea that torture is beyond the pale is not an historical accident; it may in fact be a critical feature of our legal system's progressive (though incomplete) repudiation of brutality over the past three centuries. That is, the gravitational weight of an absolute prohibition on torture may be what enables us to critique everyday brutality and distinguish it clearly from the necessary exercise of state or legal force.[11]

Clarence: I fail to see what is so "revolutionary" about my modest suggestion.

Erica: It's about as modest as Swift's proposal to raise Irish babies for food! Your proposal is revolutionary in at least the Kuhnian sense that it, like the more covert 'torture memos' of the Bush Justice Department, constitutes a radically new moral and legal paradigm. Without the legal and social gravitational pull of a widely understood and institutionalized rejection of torture, the hope of becoming a society that is less, rather than more, prone to brutality and cruelty becomes vastly more remote.[12]

Aaron: Are you suggesting that we ought to resist the temptation to torture even if we encounter actual cases approximating the ticking bomb example?

Erica: I really believe it's a moot point since, as I said earlier, we are never likely to know enough to have a robust example of such a case. For the reasons I have given, I think making institutional provision for such cases would seriously compromise our collective humanity, so if you insist, I choose to bite the bullet and forbid torture even in cases where we were fairly certain there was a ticking bomb.

Clarence: . . . And see large numbers of innocent noncombatants maimed and killed in a gesture of respect for the autonomy of one fanatical terrorist murderer!? That's quite a human sacrifice for an abstract principle, and strikes me as hollowly moralistic in the most blinkered and absolutist sense.

Erica: I will accept that as a backhanded compliment from you, Clarence. Your own tidy moral formula neglects our wider responsibility to humanity as such. I should clarify that I do not think the evil of torture is a universal moral absolute in any theological sense, but I do think it functions as a "practical moral absolute" for any decent human community.[13] The real world provides no clear cases of justifiable torture—or at least none worthy of the abandonment of our deepest commitments to dignity.

Clarence: We're looking at the same world and seeing very different things. It is clear as day to me that in some extreme situations, torture is not only justified but absolutely required. If we refuse to deal openly with the ugly realities of the world as it is, you may not have a human community left to live in.

Aaron: I still don't know what to think. While we all seem to agree that torture is very serious business, I'm worried that Clarence's proposal might have the effect of normalizing or institutionalizing some illegitimate instances of torture. On the other hand, I'm equally worried that Erica's "practical absolute" prohibition on torture, which sounds good in theory, might be unrealistic given the problems we face in the world today.

Clarence: So whose side are you on?

Aaron: It's not clear to me yet that I need to choose between your two positions. Maybe there's a third way: Admit at least the theoretical possibility that some acts of torture are morally justifiable, but resist any temptation to legalize or condone those acts.

Erica: We will need to clarify what you are saying. Your position might be very close to mine, though slightly more willing to concede the abstract possibility of a real-world ticking bomb case. On the other hand, you might be proposing that we give the authorities the discretion to disobey, which I think would be even more dangerous than what Clarence proposes. As they say in utilitarian circles, "the act accuses, the outcome excuses"!

Clarence: There's no call to side with those misguided few who claim that the ends might justify the means, if the means themselves—the rare, legitimate uses of torture—are in fact justified.

Aaron: I didn't mean to suggest that we should risk immoral actions to achieve our ends. Rather, it seems to me that Clarence is right to find some acts of torture morally just while Erica is right to demand an institutional ban on all forms of torture. Perhaps the law shouldn't track morality in this case, as in some others. So, in actual, ticking bomb scenarios, what the authorities are morally permitted—or obliged—to do and what the law allows them to do will be very different.

Erica: That is often the case, of course; law must remain an incomplete map of morality. You seem to suggest a civil disobedience principle—torture remains *prima facie* illegal and is understood to be immoral in almost all cases, but we expect those who believe circumstances compel them to torture a suspect to do so, and then subject themselves to judgment.[14] Is this what you have in mind?

Aaron: Something like that might make sense, I think.

Erica: It might, if we could rely on authorities to fall on their swords after making such a horrific choice, but outside of novels, moral courage like that is rare, especially among politicians.[15]

Aaron: But couldn't we simply treat cases like self-defense killings in which the defendant simply has to show that under the circumstances he reasonably believed he had to kill to protect his own life?

Erica: Perhaps, but that would make torture a procedurally normalized part of jurisprudence, which would accomplish through the back door something very like what Clarence has proposed, and as I pointed out before, torture hardly resembles self-defense.

Clarence: I still think your proposal has merit, Aaron. Unlike Erica's it honestly acknowledges the frightful possibilities of our times. However, necessity is the most lawless of legal defenses, proclaiming in effect the incapacity of the law.[16] I think it would be far more consistent and accountable for the law to acknowledge in advance the possible need for torture.

Erica: Despite the concerns I have expressed, Aaron, I do prefer your suggestion to Clarence's. If we change the law to reflect the very remote possibility of a morally legitimate act of torture, we step onto a very slippery slope.

Clarence: This slope is not so slippery as you say; it is made secure, in my view, by the rarity of circumstances that will justify the use of torture.

Erica: I see this as terribly sandy ground on which to build an institutional culture committed to human dignity and limited state power. Once torture is understood to be acceptable, even under a few circumstances, we have abandoned a clear and potent argument for respecting the most fundamental rights of persons.

Aaron: Both of you insist on the rarity of justifiable torture, yet your practical recommendations are still miles apart, which I find disconcerting given the gravity of the issue. Could we perhaps revisit our differences another time, and try to resolve them?

[*Camera operator at the back of the room shouts*: "So, are you guys ready to start taping now?"]

Matthew R. Silliman and David Kenneth Johnson, Massachusetts College of Liberal Arts

Notes

1. Alan Dershowitz argues at length in favor of some form of official legal process for warranted torture in *Why Terrorism Works: Understanding the Threat, Responding to the Challenge* (New Haven: Yale University Press, 2003).

2. Henry Shue, "Torture," in *Torture; A Collection*, ed. Sanford Levinson (New York: Oxford University Press, 2004), 47–60.

3. The epistemological concern articulated here is a version of one of Elaine Scarry's several challenges to Dershowitz; see: "Five Errors in the Reasoning of Alan Dershowitz," in *Torture; A Collection*, ed. Sanford Levinson (New York: Oxford University Press, 2004), 281–90. In the same vein, David Luban argues: "in a world of uncertainty and imperfect knowledge, the ticking time-bomb scenario should not form the point of reference. . . . The real debate is not between one guilty man's pain and hundreds of innocent lives. It is the debate between the certainty of anguish and the mere possibility of learning something vital and saving lives." See "Liberalism, Torture, and the Ticking Bomb," in *The Torture Debate in America*, ed. Karen J. Greenburg (New York: Cambridge University Press, 2006), 35–83.

4. See John T. Parry, "Escalation and Necessity: Defining Torture at Home and Abroad" in *Torture; A Collection*, ed. Sanford Levinson (New York: Oxford University Press, 2004), 145–64.

5. Defending his call for an absolute ban on torture, Christopher W. Tindale writes: "Torture relaxes the constraints that reinforce civilized behavior. The deliberate infliction of pain upon a helpless human being challenges the moral authority of the society which allows it and the principles which justify that society." "Tragic Choices: Reaffirming Absolutes in the Torture Debate," *International Journal of Applied Philosophy*, 19:2 (2006): 218.

6. Raphael Lewis, "Romney Files Death Penalty Bill," *The Boston Globe*, 4/29/05.

7. John H. Langbein, "The Legal History of Torture" in *Torture; A Collection*, ed. Sanford Levinson (New York: Oxford University Press, 2004), 93–104.

8. Scarry, 286–7.

9. See John T. Parry, "Escalation and Necessity: Defining Torture at Home and Abroad" in *Torture; A Collection*, ed. Sanford Levinson (New York: Oxford University Press, 2004), 145–64.

10. See David Luban's analysis of the tortured legal reasoning of memoranda composed by the Bush administration's Office of Legal Counsel, specifically the Loo/Bybee memos, in "Liberalism, Torture, and the Ticking Bomb," in *The Torture Debate in America*, ed. Karen J. Greenburg (New York: Cambridge University Press, 2006), 35-83.

11. This is an elaboration of Jeremy Waldron's detailed argument that the prohibition on torture constitutes an important "legal archetype;" see his "Torture and Positive Law: Jurisprudence for the White House," *Columbia Law Review* 106.5 (October 2005).

12. The "gravitational" image is Waldron's.

13. Michael David, "The Moral Justifiability of Torture and Other Cruel, Inhuman, or Degrading Treatment." *International Journal of Applied Philosophy* 19:2 (Fall 2005): 170.

14. Henry Shue, among others, have proposed a "civil disobedience" model to accommodate perceived instances of necessary torture. See, e.g., "Torture," in *Torture; A Collection*, ed. Sanford Levinson (New York: Oxford University Press, 2004), 47–60.

15. In Eugene Burdick and Harvey Wheeler's 1963 cold-war novel *Fail-Safe* (New York: Dell, 1963), for example, the U.S. president bombs New York to prevent a global nuclear conflagration after an accidental bombing of Moscow, accepting that it is the last act of his

political career, and perhaps his life. The trusted friend and aide who carries out the bombing commits suicide.

16. Alan Dershowitz, "Tortured Reasoning," in *Torture; A Collection*, ed. Sanford Levinson (New York: Oxford University Press, 2004), 257–80.

Part IV:
NASSP Book Award

Reflections on Larry May's *Crimes Against Humanity*

Marilyn Fischer

My reflections here are not so much a critique, as a request for a new eyeglass prescription. Like many of you, I have astigmatism. That means that my two eyes can't bring objects into focus. Pop on my glasses, and the world becomes clear. When I read May's book (which, as you know, I greatly admire), and then think about late twentieth-century history, I can't quite bring the book into focus with that history. The principal elements in May's analysis that I will set next to this history are his working hypothesis that the world is a collection of sovereign states, his decision to focus the book on international crimes committed by "strong states" and not on those committed in weak or failed states, and the way he defines "groups" both among victims and among perpetrators, in his explication of the international harm principle. In thinking through these elements, I will refer to three historical examples of human rights atrocities: Cambodia under the Khmer Rouge in the 1970s; Saddam's attacks on the Kurds in the 1980s; and Nigeria under Abacha in the 1990s. I will explain what is out of focus between the book and this history, and ask May for a diagnosis and a new prescription.

I. Sovereignty and Groups of Perpetrators

Conceptual astigmatism sets in when I juxtapose the political and legal map of the world as a collection of sovereign states, which May assumes, next to history's more ambiguous account. (Remember Faulkner's quip: "The past isn't dead; it isn't even past.") In the historical narrative the nation-state evolved as a relatively recent European creature, with colonial empire building as an integral part of its evolution. This colonial project's growth curve spurted upwards between 1870–1914, thanks in large measure to the telegraph, the maxim gun, quinine, and a weird mix of Social Darwinism with the white man's burden to Christianize and civilize the world. European colonial powers imposed state grid-lines on much of Africa and Asia in 1885 and 1919 that answered to their own interests, particularly for raw materials. Since decolonization, many of these new, artificially drawn states have not been sovereign in any lived sense of the word. During the Cold War, the United States didn't dare let non-aligned countries be strong enough to insist on sovereignty, and if they tried, they were apt to be visited by a CIA-backed coup.[1] Think of Iran in 1953 and Chile in 1973. Throughout the Cold War and since, elites in some of these states have been maintained as virtual clients of multinational corporations.

I take seriously Thomas Pogge's argument that to understand why incompetent, corrupt, rights-abusing regimes persist in the developing world, we need to examine how the international economic order functions. As an example, Pogge identifies the international resource privilege as a mechanism whereby corrupt elites plunder their own countries' natural resources to benefit wealthy nations, multi-national corporations, and themselves, excluding their own citizens from any benefit (334–8).[2] That is, many of these states as a matter of course have violated basic human rights of security and subsistence, the very conditions that, according to May, justify sovereignty (May 64). The question arises: who or what holds sovereignty?

During the 1990s, had there been an International Criminal Court, I would have liked to have seen General Sani Abacha, military dictator of Nigeria, brought before the court for crimes against humanity. In 1996, Freedom House, an international human rights monitoring organization, gave Nigeria its lowest rating and placed it in the company of North Korea and Iraq as a "most repressive state." But would Abacha have stood before the court alone? While Abacha was in power, 80% of Nigeria's federal budget came from Shell Oil revenues. Abacha was happy to lend his death squads to guard Shell's oil pipelines and facilities (Newburry and Gladwin, 523, 528–30). Using May's definition, I would say that the perpetrators of human rights abuses constituted a "group" in that the harms were "systematic, . . . perpetrated in pursuance of a plan by an agent of a State or with active involvement from a State or State-like entity" (May, 89–90). In Abacha's human rights abuses, Shell Oil often functioned as a state-like entity or at least as a fully participating member of the group. Would May place Shell Oil's CEO in the dock, alongside Abacha?

A second concern about sovereignty involves weak or failed states. In Cambodia the Khmer Rouge took control in 1975, after the United States had dropped 540,000 tons of bombs that killed tens of thousands, and after a five-year civil war that killed one million people. During the next 3½ years it is estimated that two of Cambodia's seven million people were either executed or died of starvation (Power 94, 100, 142–3). Where on May's analysis should we place the Cambodian genocide? Do the Khmer Rouge qualify as "a state or a state-like entity?" I hope not. I assume that calling something a state at all entails some measure of legitimacy for which being the strongest thugs in the territory shouldn't quality. Or was Cambodia under the Khmer Rouge one of the "failed" states, regarding which May asserts that prosecution in an international tribunal is "not normally seen as controversial?" (7).

II. Groups of Victims and the International Harm Principle

To clarify what harms constitute international crimes and so are eligible for prosecution before an international tribunal, May carefully differentiates individualized harms from group-based harms. He wants to identify those that "harm humanity," that is, that are "widespread or systematic," and not just directed at discrete individuals (80). Although he leaves room for some exceptions, May states that he is most concerned with those group-characteristics that are "out of that person's control," and according to which a person is treated "as a mere representative of a group that the person has not chosen to join" (87, 85). I suspect that the exceptions are more numerous than May intimates, and that much of the time, group characteristics out of a person's control may be less salient than May implies. In the following examples the victims fit May's criterion in that they "are not treated according to individual differences among fellow humans" (73), yet it feels off-center to stress the victims' group-characteristics more than political and historical contingencies.

During the Iran-Iraq war of the 1980s Saddam Hussein committed genocide against the Kurds, including gas attacks and mass executions against civilian men, women, and children. However, it is not so much false as unbalanced to say he targeted his victims *because* of their group affiliation as Kurds per se. He did not target the large Kurdish populations in Baghdad or in other cities under Arab-Iraqi control. With a long history of Kurdish agitation for self-determination in the background, Saddam targeted those who lived in rural areas and villages along the Iraq-Iranian border and who sided with Iran during the Iraq-Iranian war (Power 174, 179). True, Saddam was ruthless, brutal, genocidal, utterly contemptuous of "individualizing characteristics," but he selected among the Kurds strategically to hold onto his power.

Shell and the Nigerian government officials certainly didn't attend to individual characteristics as they razed villages, rendered agricultural fields unusable, and instructed the Mobile Police Force to shoot protesters. That the victims belonged to various ethnic groups no doubt figured into the equation, but I suspect the best description is that the victims belonged to the group of those whose villages and farms were inconveniently located right where Shell wanted to place its operations.

What I don't see in May's delineation of a group is a large space for a history that includes cold, calculated, opportunistic slaughter, where perpetrators kill because they can, to settle old scores and cement their power. For the past century, most genocides and crimes against humanity, from the Turkish slaughter of Armenians in 1915 to today's disaster in Darfur, have taken place in the context of war.[3] Wars take their course, with strategy and fury, and with little attention to philosophical distinctions. May's repeated emphasis on the victims' group membership does not capture this dimension.

Now May could respond that these cases are covered by his provision regarding the group-like nature of the perpetrators (83). He could be right about this, but we can still ask whether harms to victims based on group-characteristics are better placed at the periphery rather than being a focal point of his argument.

I'd like to suggest a potential diagnosis for my conceptual astigmatism, and ask May what he thinks. He makes the observation, "It is interesting to note that the trials that are most frequently cited as paradigmatic of international criminal law—those concerning crimes against humanity or genocide—turn out the be the hardest to justify. Typically, there is no weak or non-existent State, but rather . . . the problem is often that a State is too strong, perceiving itself to be so strong that it can attack segments of its own population" (81).

Why are *these* trials cited as paradigmatic? Could it be that these trials issue from catastrophes that should not themselves be seen as paradigmatic, given the historical record? My diagnosis is that Nazi Germany's Holocaust has functioned as *the* paradigm case of genocide and crimes against humanity, rather than just one variant. Jews in the 1930s and 40s, unlike the Kurds in the 1980s, were not a political or military threat to the German state, just a convenient scapegoat (Power 191). Hitler came to power, not in a military coup like Saddam and Abacha, but through a constitutional process, and he maintained that power throughout the war. In many cases, as in Cambodia, genocides and crimes against humanity occur opportunistically after war has destroyed the State institutions through which sovereignty is exercised. That is true now in Darfur, and it might become true in Iraq. Noting that the initial UN human rights documents were written in direct response to the horrors of World War II, Ignatieff comments, "Today, however, the chief threat to human rights comes not from tyranny alone, but from civil war and anarchy" (35). Now May might be right that justifying the prosecution of human rights atrocities in weak or failed states is philosophically uncontroversial. However, since these abuses are so prominent historically and politically, I wonder if philosophically interesting things might still be said about them. So my question for May is, to correct my astigmatism, where in the historical and political landscape do I position his excellent and elegant analysis of *Crimes Against Humanity?*

Marilyn Fischer, University of Dayton

Notes

1. This account is standard issue in college-level history of western civilization textbooks. See, for example, Dennis Sherman and Joyce Salisbury, *The West in the World*, 2nd ed. (New York: McGraw-Hill, 680–703). See also E. J. Hobsbawm. *Nations and Nationalism since 1780* (New York: Cambridge University Press, 1990).

2. Pogge discusses the significance of both the international borrowing privilege, i.e., "the power to impose internationally valid legal obligations upon the country at large," and the international resource privilege, i.e., "the legal power to confer globally valid ownership rights in the country's resources" (335, 336). Human rights-abusing dictators use these privileges to augment and secure their power, to the great detriment of their countries' citizens.

3. Much of my information on genocides is drawn from Samantha Power's vivid and exhausting book, *A Problem from Hell: America and the Age of Genocide*. I strongly recommend it.

Works Cited

Ignatieff, Michael. 2001. *Human Rights as Politics and Idolatry*. Princeton, NJ: Princeton University Press.

May, Larry. 2005. *Crimes Against Humanity: A Normative Account*. New York: Cambridge University Press.

Newburry, William E., and Thomas N. Gladwin. 2002. "Shell and Nigerian Oil," in *Ethical Issues in Business*, 7th ed., eds. T. Donaldson, P. H. Werhane, and M. Cording. Englewood Cliffs, NJ: Prentice-Hall, 522–41.

Pogge, Thomas. 2001. "The Influence of the Global Order on the Prospects for Genuine Democracy in the Developing Countries." *Ratio Juris* 14: 326–43.

Power, Samantha. 2002. *A Problem from Hell: America and the Age of Genocide*. New York: Harper Perennial.

Defining and Prosecuting International Crimes: Commentary for Larry May, *Crimes Against Humanity: A Normative Account*

Cheryl Hughes

Larry May's book, exploring the philosophical foundations of international criminal law, is a model of philosophical scholarship on a timely and important topic. May draws insights from some of the earliest philosophical considerations of international law in Grotius, Hobbes, and Hume; he charts the development of the concept of international crime over the last sixty years, from the 1945 Charter of the Nuremberg Military Tribunal to the most recent 1998 Rome Statute establishing a permanent International Criminal Court; and he tests his principles and conceptual claims against particular recent cases. For most of his central arguments, he considers several objections that help to clarify and refine his views and should give rise to further debate and discussion.

In hopes of advancing such discussion, I would like to raise several problems, all of which are in some way related to my sense that awareness of historical context is crucial to our understanding of human rights and the role of international criminal law. First, and most fundamentally, I want to question May's use of Hobbes to outline a moral minimalist position that defines and delimits the scope of international crimes. Hobbesian arguments place too much weight on state sovereignty, which then must be overcome in order to justify international prosecutions of individuals. Reliance on Hobbesian arguments also gives us an inadequate description of the human person who is to be defended as the bearer of human rights. Secondly, with regard to the role of historical context in defining international crimes, I want to suggest that we should place more emphasis on the details of historical narratives rather than less, as May suggests. And finally, I want to challenge May's claim that the use of amnesties and pardons as alternatives to criminal trials requires even a temporary forgetting of atrocities in order to be effective. In short, historical memory seems to me to be a crucial part of any effort to define and properly respond to crimes against humanity.

The problem of sovereignty looms large in the early chapters of this book, both in May's attempts to establish reasonable limits to tolerance and State sovereignty, and in his effort to solve the traditional thorny problem for international law—that where there is no sovereign law-giver, there can be no law. May's appeal to Hobbesian arguments offers one way to define international crime and justify international criminal prosecutions, but I wonder if this isn't taking an unnecessary step back from already established norms of universal human rights and international cooperation. According to May, international law makes sense from a Hobbesian perspective only in a world where sovereign States are motivated by desire for peace to form multilateral agreements to prosecute individuals who violate international laws. When States agree to accept sanctions and enforcement that are reliable and fair, as for example with the Rome Treaty creating the International Criminal Court, then May argues that there may be "enough sovereignty for an international court's opinions to constitute binding international law, at least in the Hobbesian sense that violations of the norm will indeed be sanctioned" (20).

In defining international crimes, May again appeals to arguments from Hobbes to develop a moral minimalism—a minimal standard of basic universally recognized moral rights to security. The familiar arguments from Hobbes start with the hypothetical state of nature and the war of all against all, in which every individual naturally seeks self-preservation and self-defense. The social contract that establishes civil society and gives the sovereign the power to make and enforce laws can only be broken when a sovereign is no longer able to provide security for subjects. Taken one step farther, in May's argument, a State that attacks or fails to provide for the protection and security of its own subjects can lose the sovereign right to prevent international intervention. According to May, "Moral minimalism holds that when States act so as to undermine their subjects' security, a moral minimum of acceptable behavior by States has been violated, and it may not be unjust for international tribunals to take action that would otherwise be unjust violations of a State's sovereignty" (32).

In a world where uncompromising demands for United States sovereignty seem to be the biggest obstacles to progress for international criminal law and the work of the International Criminal Court, it seems to me to be a mistake to provide a liberal political defense of State sovereignty as the starting place for considerations of international crime. We live in the first historical epoch to include consciousness of belonging to a single global civilization and a shared humanity. Especially in the development of scientific knowledge and the diffusion of technology and industry, we have begun to accumulate collective human experience that is not tied to any particular culture or national character. And we are developing new norms, including the UN Universal Declaration of Human Rights, and new international institutions that can guide our efforts to establish a global human community. Re-entrenching state sovereignty by assuming a seventeeth-century norm of violence and hostility does not seem to reflect contemporary norms of peace or the established institutions for international cooperation.

But there is a further problem with May's use of Hobbes, and that is the picture of the sovereign subject, the atomistic individual of liberal political philosophy whose most basic motivation is self-preservation. It is difficult to establish respect for human rights using Hobbes's view of human nature—and this is especially true during any time that civil society is disrupted. Although May admits that a strong defense of human rights is missing from Hobbes's account (17), he nevertheless argues that his own moral minimalism derived from Hobbes can provide a basis for basic human rights to security and subsistence. Since, according to Hobbes, the promise of security is the only reason to obey laws, security and subsistence should be universally recognized as human rights deserving protection by sovereign States and by the international community when the State fails to protect these rights. But individuals thrown back into a state of nature have the unconditional right to use any means to defend themselves, according to Hobbes. Thus there are no human rights that must be respected by individuals under the conditions of a failed state, and yet some of the worst human rights atrocities have occurred during times of civil war.

Hobbes's hypothetical state of nature has been criticized from many sides as an inadequate description of human persons as atomistic individuals reduced to relations of hostility in a world of scarcity and mistrust. The right to self-defense and self-preservation is not a moral right but a materialist fact according to Hobbes—bodies in motion tend to stay in motion. Morality only begins with the first law of nature, discovered by reason, that if you want your body to stay in motion, you should seek peace—a very prudential self-serving reason to form relationships with others. This reduction of the human person to a self-interested, rational calculator whose social ties originate in a contract was perhaps a useful philosophical fiction for resisting various forms of social and political oppression, but it was never an adequate description of the complexity of the human person who is born into a network of relations to other human beings and who develops over time within a context of social and political institutions. We are much more connected to others than a Hobbesian view will admit, and May needs more than a Hobbesian description of the atomistic individual with rights to security and liberty in order to sustain his later appeal to notions of "group ontology" and his efforts to define the "group-based harm" and "collective responsibility" that characterize international crimes against humanity. (See May's discussion of the international harm principle in chapter 5 and his discussion of "Group Ontology and the State" in chapter 8.) Attending to the postmodern reconstructions of subjectivity as social, relational, and historically situated could perhaps offer a viable alternative to liberal individualism, permit a more robust account of the human rights deserving protection, and provide a better starting place for discussions of group membership and collective responsibility.

My other two questions both concern the way that May discounts the importance of historical context and historical memory in his effort to provide a theoretical structure for defining and responding to international crimes. As May points out in his consideration of the existing definitions of international crime, international concern for human rights developed in response to the excesses of the fascists in Italy and the Nazis in Germany, and it did so in shocked response to the horrifying massacres of millions of people in the Second World War. But May resists the idea that this historical context should be retained as part of how we define international crimes, insisting that "if people are still today to be punished for committing these acts, now long after the time has passed during which these acts were first condemned as criminal, then we need a current account of what makes these acts legitimately punishable now . . . and not merely anachronistic manifestations of bygone prejudices" (68).

It seems to me that the historical narrative is the best way, and perhaps the only way, to maintain human connections to victims and a sense of shared responsibility for past acts. Historical narrative provides continuity and context that renews our outrage over past acts as it leads us to condemn current acts of persecution, torture, mass rape, and genocide. Historical narrative also allows us to grow as moral members of the human community, adding human slavery and rape, for example, to our list of crimes against humanity where these were once simply considered the proper spoils of war. We need to recognize our past failures and draw out the continuity between what was condemned in 1945 and what is condemned in 2005.

This leads me to my final problem, perhaps more of a quibble with May's language than his intent. In the final chapter of his book, May considers the benefits of using amnesties and pardons instead of international criminal trials, arguing that "forgiving, and even temporarily forgetting, past harms can be justified in some cases" (236). In his exemplary consideration of objections, he replies to the claim that whereas a trial provides public acknowledgment and condemnation of perpetrators, amnesty or pardon allows perpetrators to forget what they have done and thereby risks repetition of past injustices. According to May, the courts must sometimes "forget" the strict requirements of the law in order to achieve a higher social good of reconciliation and stability. May goes on to argue that "In order to achieve peace and return to democratic rule, it is sometimes necessary that the members of society not only forgive but also, at least temporarily, forget horrible atrocities. One could argue that this is precisely what has not happened in hot spots that continue to experience bloodshed and unrest, such as Palestine, Ireland, Kashmir, and the Balkans. Temporary amnesia is indeed what the people in these regions need if they are ever to experience a lasting peace" (245–6). May admits that such forgetting should not lead to "permanent collective amnesia" that could too easily lead us to repeat past injustices, but he does not spell out how we should achieve the temporary forgetting of atrocities. Does an extra-judicial remedy such as the South African Truth and Reconciliation Commission actually involve forgetting atrocities? The public admission of guilt, often in front of the victim's family, is a way of acknowledging past actions. May is clear that we should not "purchase stability at the cost of repression" (251); and he calls for individual admission of guilt and sincere remorse as well as some form of civil reparation or changes in the social conditions so that "the reconciliation makes things better for those who were the object of harm" (251). None of this seems to require forgetting. It is more properly described as a constructive response to acknowledged and remembered crimes against humanity. It seems to me to be incumbent on the international community not to forget past atrocities, not to neglect the particular context of time and place and ideologies, but to record and retell the historical narratives that partially define us as citizens of a global human community and help us maintain our vigilance and our collective responsibility for crimes against humanity.

Cheryl Hughes, Wabash College

Comment on Larry May's *Crimes Against Humanity*

COLIN M. MACLEOD

It is regrettable that recent human history provides so many atrocities that fit comfortably with the analysis of international crime developed by Larry May in *Crimes Against Humanity: A Normative Account.*[1] Usually, authors are lucky if they have a lot of material with which to work. But I'm sure that in this respect May wishes he were much less lucky. Of course, the depressing litany of human rights violations combined with the relatively modest philosophical literature on the nature and foundations of international criminal law speak to the importance of May's book. The account of the normative foundations of international criminal law developed by May is subtle, sophisticated and informed by reflection on the complexities of real cases and the attendant difficulties of determining just where true justice lies. May is also very good at anticipating and blunting possible objections to his arguments—a skill which renders my assigned task of offering a critical response to his theory all the more difficult. There is, as the book award committee correctly discerned, much more to praise than to critique.

My remarks are very selective. I shall focus exclusively on one of the central theoretical proposals developed in the book, namely on what May calls the 'international harm principle.' But let me try to provide some context for my comments.

May articulates two challenges that a credible theory of international criminal law must address. First, international criminal law theory must suitably acknowledge the moral and political importance of respecting (legitimate) state sovereignty. May argues that special considerations must be invoked in order to justify intrusion into the internal affairs of sovereign states by international bodies. Legitimate prosecutions of human rights violators by international courts must defeat a presumption in favour of respecting a state's sovereignty. We can call this the 'sovereignty challenge.' Second, international criminal law must be attentive not only to the claims of victims but also to the interests of the accused. Since prosecutions jeopardize the liberty of those accused of criminal wrongdoing and since wrongful deprivation of one's liberty is a grave injustice, international prosecutions should be pursued in cases where redress for a significant injustice to the international community is sought. Only particularly egregious kinds of misconduct are appropriately designated 'international crimes' that may be prosecuted by international courts. We need some way of characterizing the distinctive features of crimes that have international import. We can call this the 'moral gravity challenge'. On May's approach, international criminal law needs a principled response to both these challenges. That is, we need a credible moral rationale for determining both when intrusions on sovereignty are warranted and when wrongdoing reaches a threshold of sufficient moral gravity to warrant criminal prosecutions of individuals by international bodies.

Drawing on a Hobbesian inspired 'moral minimalism,' May develops a theory around two core principles—the security principle and the international harm principle. The legitimacy of these principles and of the more specific aspects of international law they underwrite does not lie in their actual endorsement by sovereign states. Rather they have force as jus cogens norms and their acceptance depends on the soundness of expressly moral arguments. The security principle provides May's solution to the sovereignty challenge. It states:

> If a State deprives its subjects of physical security or subsistence, or is unable or unwilling to protect its subjects from harms to security or subsistence
>
> a) then that State has no right to prevent international bodies from "crossing its borders" in order to protect those subjects or remedy their harms
>
> b) and then international bodies may be justified in "crossing the borders" of a sovereign state when genuinely acting to protect those subjects." (68)

The international harm principle provides his solution to the moral gravity challenge. It states:

> Only when there is serious harm to the international community, should international prosecutions against individual perpetrators be conducted where normally this will include a showing of harms to the victims that is based on non-individualized characteristics of the individual, such as the individual's group membership, or is perpetrated by, or involves, a State or other collective entity. (83)

The international harm principle certainly has initial appeal because it seems to nicely fit relevant dimensions of international crime. I think May is right to think that many genuine international crimes pose threats to the international community—e.g., by undermining general peace and security—and that often the crimes involve the targeting of ethnic, racial or cultural groups. However, I am less sure that the conditions emphasized by May correctly track the idea of moral gravity that seems integral to the concept of an international crime. The concept of international crime delineated by the international harm principle has three elements. First, international crime must cause serious harm to humanity itself. (An international crime is an assault on humanity.) Second, harm to humanity typically arises out of group-based harm. Third, the relevant variety of group-based harm is grounded group affiliations that are beyond the control of individuals. I have tentative reservations about each of these elements.

I. Harm to Humanity

First, must humanity be harmed—suffer a significant setback to its interests—by a crime in order for the crime to assume sufficient moral gravity to warrant classification as an international crime? (Is the special moral gravity of international crime a function of serious harm to humanity?) One difficulty here is that it is unclear how we can identify the interests of humanity in a way that satisfactorily distinguishes humanity's distinctive interests from the interests of particular humans. May says that "one interest humanity has is that its members, as members, not be harmed" (82). Perhaps. But this means that humanity is harmed every time an individual is harmed which in turn seems to imply that all serious crimes against individuals are also crimes against humanity. And that's a conclusion May wants to avoid. If the harm to humanity condition is going to be illuminating, we need a fuller account of what makes something a distinct interest of humanity instead of an interest of individual humans or groups of humans. I think this is tricky to do and I'm not sure how precisely May thinks we should go about specifying humanity's interests. Although the phrase 'crimes against humanity' may suggest that humanity can be a victim, the common usage strikes me as more metaphorical than literal. I'm not persuaded that we can develop a clear enough concept of humanity's specific interests in order to say that genocide, ethnic cleansing, torture and the like are of international concern because they victimize humanity. Moreover, I am inclined to think we will mislocate the real victims of these crimes by trying to suggest that what is pertinent from the point of view of international law is humanity being injured by these acts. The bombing of Hiroshima was, as Rawls observes, a 'great evil'[2] but I find it odd to think that its special wickedness consists, even partly, in a claim that all of humanity was victimized. Human beings can have collective concern and responsibility for acknowledging and addressing gross injustices even if we cannot say that humanity was itself harmed. (The same point applies, I think, to crime in the domestic sphere. A community can justifiably condemn and prosecute the murder of one of its citizens without having to demonstrate that the murder harmed the community.)

II. Group-Based Harm

My second reservation concerns the suggestion that group-based harm is typically a defining feature of international crime. According to May, paradigmatic international crime will be group-based in two senses: it will involve a group-based victim such as persons persecuted in virtue of their race or ethnicity and group-based perpetrators such as a state or someone acting on behalf of a state. For the moment, I will discuss the idea of group-based victims. May maintains that the international community has special reason to care about the victimization of individuals in virtue of their group affiliation. From an international law perspective it is putatively a matter of greater legal significance, at least in the standard case, if a person's human rights are violated in virtue of non-individualized characteristics than if they are violated in virtue of individualized features. For example, assassinating a person because of their ethnicity can be an international crime but assassinating the person because she is a dangerous political opponent would not be an international crime since the victim is targeted on the basis of individualized rather than a group characteristic. This strategy seems to provide a way of tracking the special significance attached to crimes such as genocide, ethnic cleansing and apartheid. However, as May admits, the focus on group-based victims fails to capture the international significance of crimes such as torture of political opponents or strategic bombing of civilian populations. In these cases, the victims are not targeted in virtue of their group affiliations but the crimes certainly seem grave enough to warrant international attention. If the focus on group-based victims is clearly insufficiently inclusive as a criterion of international crime why does May give it prominence in his theory? The answer seems to be, at least in part, that he views the focus on group-based victims as a way of developing the idea that humanity is the victim in international crimes: "Humanity is a victim when the intentions of individual perpetrators or the harms of individual victims are based on group characteristics rather than on individual characteristics" (85). This seems plausible in the rather unusual case in which a person is victimized in virtue of their belonging to humanity. But I'm less confident that we can move easily from victimization of a person in virtue of their group affiliation to victimization of humanity. May holds that non-individualized treatment of an individual entails a harm to humanity, but I am not sure that it does. Consider the case of genocide. When the Nazis targeted Jews for elimination, there is a clear enough sense in which Jews as a group and not just individual Jews were victimized. But was humanity also assaulted *qua* humanity? The attribute of Jews that the Nazis despised was arguably not the humanity of Jews but rather their Jewishness. Of course, the Nazis displayed callous disregard for the common humanity of the Jews they murdered and persecuted, but a similar callous disregard for the humanity of persons is often displayed in individual focused murders.

The general puzzle that arises here concerns soundness of the inference from victimization in virtue of one characteristic to victimization in virtue of a different characteristic. If we can infer that humanity has been victimized in virtue of the victimization of subgroups of humans, why can't we infer that humanity has been victimized if the victim is an individual?

III. Unchosen Group Affiliation

My third reservation concerns May's suggestion that group affiliation of the sort that is relevant in the context of international criminal law is non-voluntary or 'beyond autonomous agency.' I do not see how the voluntariness of one's affiliation to a group affects the moral significance of being victimized on the basis of that affiliation. Membership in many religions and political parties is voluntary but that fact does not seem relevant to assessing the moral significance of persecuting an individual in virtue of their group membership. Persecution of individuals who freely joined the communist party seems every bit as repugnant as persecution of an individual in virtue of their unchosen ethnic affiliation. Arguably what matters is not whether one's membership in a group is voluntary but whether discriminatory treatment on the basis of the group characteristic would be morally arbitrary. Whether treatment on the basis on one's group affiliation is arbitrary does not correspond directly with facts about whether the affiliation is voluntary. Finally, there seems to be an asymmetry in the way in which May treats the significance of non-voluntary group affiliation when characterizing the two facets of group-based harm. In his analysis of group-based victims he emphasizes the significance of non-voluntary group affiliation, but no such parallel emphasis seems to apply to his account of group-based perpetrators. In the latter case, it doesn't seem to matter whether a person's affiliation with the state is non-voluntary.

If the foregoing reservations are plausible then it is not clear that the international harm principle provides a fully satisfactory response to the moral gravity challenge. I believe May is right to insist that there should be a principled basis for distinguishing those human rights violations that are sufficiently egregious to qualify as international crimes from those that, though serious and regrettable, should not occasion the interest of an international court. Although I have no alternative to offer, I can report May's analysis illuminates both the reason this problem is so fundamental to international criminal law and why it is so difficult. So even if we have to give up or modify the international harm principle, subsequent attempts to grapple with the challenge should be informed by his arguments.

Colin M. Macleod, University of Victoria

Notes

1. Larry May, *Crimes Against Humanity: A Normative Account* (Cambridge: Cambridge University Press, 2005). Page references to quoted passages from this book appear in parentheses.

2. John Rawls, "50 Years After Hiroshima" in *John Rawls: Collected Papers*, ed. Samuel Freeman (Cambridge, MA: Harvard University Press, 2001), 565–72 at 570.

The Moral Foundations of International Criminal Law: Response to Three Critics

Larry May

I am very grateful that my book, *Crimes Against Humanity: A Normative Account*, received the North American Society for Social Philosophy's best book award this year. The book is the first volume of a projected trilogy that tracks the three crimes that were charged at Nuremberg, surely the most significant international criminal trial. The first volume concerns crimes against humanity, the new category of crimes that were designed to cover the holocaust, that is, an attack on a population that does not necessarily occur in wars and where the crime may be committed by a State against its own people. The second volume, which is now in print, concerns war crimes, that is, the violations of the rules of war by those who are fighting in wars. And the third volume, which I have just finished drafting, concerns crimes against peace, that is, the crime of initiating and waging aggressive war.

In all three books I take a moral minimalist and a defendant-oriented approach to understanding international crime. The moral minimalist methodology is in the liberal tradition of Rawls and Dworkin of non-ideal theory. Dworkin describes the enterprise as follows: one tries to find the best principles already embedded "in the standing political arrangements of his community . . . whether or not he thinks these the best principles from a utopian standpoint."[1] And on my construal of this methodology, one also looks for the least controversial and least far-reaching principles that will nonetheless justify what practices are thought to be intuitively appealing. I have been asked to respond to three critics of my *Crimes Against Humanity* book, which I am happy to do, since these critics have carefully read and thoughtfully criticized my arguments in some detail.

First, I will respond to Marilyn Fischer. She rightly says that I focus on strong rather than weak or failed States. I do this for two reasons. It is strong States, like the United States, China, and Russia, which must be convinced of the legitimacy of international criminal law. The weak States will do what the strong States dictate. In the last ten years we have had ad hoc international prosecutions against leaders from Rwanda, Sierra Leone, Cambodia, East Timor, and the former Yugoslavia.

The ICC is poised to prosecute leaders from Somalia, the Congo, and the Sudan. Notice that all of these are weak or failed States, only one of which is in Europe or the Americas. If there is to be a fair system of international criminal law, we must move past this cherry picking of the weak—it smacks of the old charge of victor's justice. In addition, failed States have no competing system of criminal law and often welcome international tribunals because without them no one will ever be brought to justice for highly divisive atrocities that have further destabilized these States and the surrounding region.

Rather than fall prey to what Professor Fischer calls "conceptual astigmatism" I think my book takes a rather clear-eyed look at the world today. We all might prefer the illusion of living in a cosmopolitan world, but this is indeed a mirage. States, especially very strong States, still dominate in ways that even seventeenth-century thinkers could not have imagined. It is true that some non-State actors, such as al Qaeda and Hezbollah, are also significant actors, just as there were also significant worries about pirates in the seventeenth century. In my other volumes on international criminal law, especially the volume on war crimes, I take up these actors in more detail. Crimes against humanity, though, are still largely perpetrated by States against their own people, just as was true in the case of Nazi Germany, and that is why I continue to focus on States.

Marilyn Fischer also asks whether I would be opposed to possible trials against non-State actors such as Shell Oil. Actually, I'm not opposed to such trials at all. The leaders of Shell Oil could be tried internationally as was true of the leaders of I. G. Farben and the Krupp Works at Nuremberg. Of course, normally corporations are not put in the criminal dock—you need some individual human person. And when this happens, as at Nuremberg, business leaders turn out to be very hard to convict for what their companies did. If Professor Fischer thinks we could put Shell Oil in the dock and get a conviction of it, or that we could easily get convictions of the leadership of Shell Oil, perhaps she does need to get her conceptual astigmatism corrected by considering the Nuremberg cases, our only really good model of such trials—since the I. G. Farben and Krupp leaders were largely acquitted.

Professor Fischer claims that many cases of recent atrocities are not based on group characteristics but rather on political and historical contingencies. I disagree with Marilyn Fischer about how many cases there are of this sort, where as she says atrocities are committed by governments just because they can. But I do agree that my conception, as is true of nearly everyone else's, is that such cases of mass killing of unrelated persons do not count as crimes against humanity. Sheer scale of killing does not necessarily make something an international crime of this sort. We might want to invent a new category of international crime to cover such cases, but I would then want to know what it is about sheer numbers of dead that makes what happened an international as opposed to a domestic crime.

At certain points Marilyn Fischer also asks about things that are not technically crimes against humanity but are war crimes or crimes against peace. During war, State leaders as well as non-State leaders do things because they think that the fog of war blinds people to what they are doing. I address such issues in volume two, which is in part why I do not address them in volume one. But in any event, we need an account of why the international community should be concerned—and I address this by asking what interest the international community has that has been infringed by such acts. I'll say more about this point later. Perhaps the astigmatism will be corrected by what I say in these other volumes, but I am not so blind as to think that all of Marilyn's excellent criticisms will disappear.

Cheryl Hughes is even more insistent that I am on the wrong track from the beginning by proceeding within a liberal Statist framework. She claims that this is a step backward from the "established norms of universal human rights and international cooperation." She says that my approach is at odds with "contemporary norms of peace." I fervently wish that she were right, and that there was universal respect for human rights and wide-spread international cooperation. But as she herself asserts, the United States has continued over the years to make "uncompromising demands" of sovereignty. It is for this reason that I take so seriously the sovereignty issue, trying to provide a reconceptualization of sovereignty that many in the United States would accept, but which also opens the door for international criminal tribunals. Like Marilyn Fischer, Cheryl Hughes is overly optimistic about the likelihood of a cosmopolitan order looming just around the corner. My books are written as non-ideal rather than ideal theory.

Professor Hughes also raises very interesting criticisms of what she calls my atomistic individual liberal political philosophy. I am especially concerned about such criticism since I have spent much of my own career criticizing others for holding just such an atomistic view and for not focusing enough on social groups and institutions. Indeed, I once showed strong sympathy for the post-modern self that Cheryl Hughes champions.[2] But, over the years I've come to see that we don't need to abandon liberalism, which is after all a very big tent. Group-based harm can find a place in certain forms of liberalism. We don't need to choose between a focus on individuals versus a focus on groups.

I am glad that Cheryl Hughes spends some time on the final chapters of my book—I sometimes think that my critics stop reading after the fifth or sixth chapter—perhaps already convinced that I couldn't possibly say anything right-headed in the later chapters after having said so many wrong-headed things early-on. But as Professor Hughes points out, I spend quite a lot of time addressing alternatives to criminal trials as a response to crimes against humanity. And here the tables are turned—since Cheryl Hughes puts on a liberal hat and accuses me of looking past the individual victims. It is true that I suggest that at certain points people need temporarily to forget what their fellow citizens have done to them.

One of the problems with a certain kind of liberal approach is that all harm must get its "comeuppance." Yet, sometimes, when two sides are in a pitched battle of continuing recrimination and retaliation, to break the cycle of violence a temporary amnesia is needed if peace is ever to be achieved. Criminal trials sometimes merely exacerbate the problem—after all these are highly accusatory proceedings that often merely make people more angry with each other, as we have seen in the Balkans. I can't tell if Cheryl Hughes and I disagree a lot or a little about this. She says it is only a quibble to say that I shouldn't call for forgetting of atrocities. But what is clear is that I end the book on this non-standard liberal point and it would be odd to criticize me for being too liberal and also then criticize me for rejecting the kind of standard retributive justice model often thought to be characteristic of liberalism. Nonetheless I am grateful for Cheryl's very perceptive comments.

Colin Macleod focuses on my international harm principle which is meant to indicate both how to circumscribe the domain of human rights abuses that count as crimes against humanity and also to explain why the name of this crime is apt. I'm grateful for Professor Macleod's astute insights here. I should say at the outset that Colin is probably right that this is the part of the book that will be most scrutinized, but it is only one part and I am also grateful to Cheryl and Marilyn for addressing some of the rest of the book. There is a discussion of some of the issues that vex Colin Macleod in a set of responses to a different group of critics I've written in another journal.[3]

Professor Macleod's first point is that I haven't sufficiently indicated how humanity's interests are harmed by certain mass crimes. He says that my view is not that harming any human harms humanity. Rather I said that harming any member of humanity, as a member, harms humanity. By this I meant that harming some human by failing to take seriously what makes that person human harms humanity. Harming one human being by failing to take account of that person's uniqueness is what is key to harming humanity, because of the likelihood that others might similarly be mistreated as well. I am trying to get beyond merely the aggregate claim that when humans are harmed *en masse* humanity is harmed. Indeed, I'm not sure why merely adding more numbers to an atrocity would make it more of a harm to humanity in any event. Rather, it seems to me that harming individuals harms humanity when these individuals are treated in ways that deny them their individuality, which is itself one of the hallmarks of being human. I suppose I am making a claim similar to that made by Martin Luther King that certain harms to individual humans also harm all other humans because they are put at risk of similar harm as well.

The idea is that crimes are different from other legal delicts. Crimes are prosecuted by the State—as in *People v. Smith*. Crimes are not mere legal disputes between individual persons, as in *Jones v. Smith*, because the crime is thought to harm the community. If the Missouri Attorney General prosecutes it is because in some sense Missouri has been harmed by what the individual defendant did, it is not merely a harm to the individual victim. I try to extend this idea into the international domain. If there are going to be prosecutions for international crimes, then it must be shown that in some sense the international community has been harmed by what the defendant did. And this is why I take seriously the idea that crimes against humanity in some sense harm humanity.

Is this some kind of mere metaphorical way of talking? I would resist the "mere" in this question, but admit that much of the talk of harming humanity is indeed metaphor, but importantly so. This is in part because there is no political community that encompasses all humans, and despite the wishes of cosmopolitans there is unlikely to be such a political community in the near future. Yet, there is a sense that humans all have enough in common to talk of a kind of moral community that is more than mere metaphor. Even Macleod admits that there is some sense in which there is literally a community that we can call humanity. What separates us is whether humanity can be harmed in the way that I suggest. But on the question of the status of humanity, our disagreement appears to me to be minor. We differ on how much our talk of humanity is literal and how much is metaphorical, not on whether there is such a thing as humanity as a non-political community of some sort.

The way that the harm is transmitted concerns the second part of Colin Macleod's objection, namely the group-based nature of that harm. Colin rightly says that when Nazis target Jews, they are not targeted as humans. But my claim is that this opens the door for other kinds of group-based targeting to which any of us could be a victim. The harm directed at Jews harms humanity by denying the individuality of the victim, and setting the stage for others to deny the individuality of other victims as well. And it is the denying of individuality that occurs whenever there is group-based harm that, in turn, harms humanity. Hannah Arendt called this a harm to the human status, and while she and I don't mean exactly the same thing I think there are important similarities here.[4]

Professor Macleod then asks why it should matter that certain group affiliations are unchosen, and why it should be worse to treat people on the basis of those affiliations rather than ones that are chosen. In part I take up this challenge in the second volume of the trilogy and in part my answer in the *Crimes Against Humanity* book is by now an old one—it is especially invidious to treat people badly on the basis of things those individuals can't change. If we treat people badly on the basis of things they can change, then it is at least in their power to avoid the bad treatment by changing. But if we discriminate against people on the basis of things they can't change, it is as if we tell them that what they have done and will do as agents makes no difference, and this is another form of denying their humanity. I agree that persecution is a significant wrong whether it is based on characteristics that are chosen or not chosen. But it seems to me that when persecution occurs based on characteristics that are utterly beyond one's control, one denies that a person has agency that matters in the world, and this is an added wrong that is quite significant and that makes the harm stretch beyond the individual to all of humanity.

While various conceptual puzzles remain with the idea of the international community, or humanity, being harmed by what one person does to another, I think this idea can be made plausible. And I agree with Colin Macleod that such an idea is needed because there has not been a good alternative normative proposal that would explain why international tribunals have jurisdiction over certain crimes. Merely to say that when human rights are abused, the International Criminal Court should spring into action is too simple, and in any event one needs then to explain why each and every human rights abuse is a matter grave enough to call for an international response. Nonetheless, I am very grateful for Colin's thought provoking questions

I defend a limited scope for international trials. One of the most important limitations is that we respect the international rule of law and not merely prosecute on the basis of our heartfelt moral outrage in the face of mass atrocities. Some will undoubtedly wish for a wider scope for international criminal law than that which I defend here; still others will think that I have gone too far, and will criticize me for employing the very idea of an international crime. Human rights are indeed important and need to be protected, especially when it is a State that seeks to abridge these rights. I do not think that individuals should be held legally accountable in international proceedings for every human rights abuse. But, if we limit our scope, we will have a better chance of defending trials for the most egregious of human rights abuses.

Larry May, Washington University

Notes

1. Ronald Dworkin, *Law's Empire* (Cambridge, MA: Harvard UP, 1986), 213.
2. See my book, *The Socially Responsive Self* (Chicago: University of Chicago Press, 1996).
3. *Ethics & International Affairs* 20:3 (2006).
4. See Hannah Arendt, *Eichmann in Jerusalem* (New York: Viking Press, 1963).

Printed in Dunstable, United Kingdom

91340607R00147